Protecting the Nation's Health

Protecting the Nation's Health

The Problems of Regulation

Edward J. Burger, Jr., M.D.

Lexington Books
D.C. Heath and Company
Lexington, Massachusetts
Toronto

Library of Congress Cataloging in Publication Data

Burger, Edward J.
  Protecting the nation's health.

  Bibliography: p.
  Includes index.
  1. Public Health laws—United States. 2. Environmental law—
United States. 3. Medical policy—United States. I. Title. [DNLM:
1. Environmental health. 2. Environmental health—Legislation.
WA30 B954p]
KF3775.B87   344'.73'04   76-7163
ISBN 0-669-00657-2

Copyright © 1976 by D.C. Heath and Company

Published simultaneously in Canada

Printed in the United States of America

International Standard Book Number: 0-669-00657-2

Library of Congress Catalog Card Number: 76-7163

Government is a contrivance of human wisdom to provide for human wants. Men have a right that these wants should be provided for by their wisdom.

Edmund Burke

We live under a government of men and morning newspapers.

Wendell Phillips

Contents

List of Figures

List of Tables

Prologue

As this work was being completed, the U.S. Court of Appeals for the District of Columbia ruled that the Environmental Protection Agency had erred in ordering the reduction of tetraethyl lead in gasoline. The court, in this case, declared that EPA had wrongly interpreted the intent of the law and, more important, said flatly that the scientific evidence used by EPA was insufficient and unconvincing. Within weeks of that decision, the EPA administrator, Russell Train, reversed his agency's long-held stand on the reliance upon catalytic exhaust devices to reduce polluting emissions from automobiles. The administrator made this move because the scientific evidence (indicating sulfuric acid mists from the catalytic devices) strongly suggested a new human health hazard associated with the widespread use of the converters. Further, he admitted publicly that he had "made a mistake" in earlier support of this emission control strategy.

Both of these instances illustrate an important point. The information fabric for decision making for the environment and health is exceedingly thin—much thinner than most people realize and much thinner than the importance of the decisions would dictate. Nor do these two reversals stand in isolation. Cyclamates, banned by administrative decision by the FDA in 1969, were raised again in 1974 as an issue. The earlier decision was found to have been made on the basis of less than adequate scientific evidence. In similar fashion, the appeal courts in 1974, reversed a lower court's decision concerning the Reserve Mining Company's disposal of asbestos-containing waste into Lake Superior.

This work was inspired by my experience as a member of the staff of the president's science adviser for the past five-plus years. During this period, the health-related regulatory processes of the federal government figured heavily in the agenda of successive science advisers. The holder of that title had passed in front of him a never-ending series of regulatory decisions representing most of the permutations of three-letter words including DDT, DES, PCB, etc. In each case, he was asked for his counsel as to the quality of the scientific evidence available for each decision as well as the quality of the advocate judgments used by each of the principal parties to the question under consideration. Beginning with the herbicide 2,4,5-T in late 1969, the series began to take on some common characteristics. The scientific evidence concerned with risk or hazard was exceedingly poor in quantity and quality. The remainder of the information concerning economic effect, utility, or benefit, etc., was of no better quality. The arguments used in interagency discussions as well as by private, interested parties were often highly contrived but poorly supported with much rigor or analysis.

There were some surprising aspects that emerged as common threads. As much as my naive wisdom would have led me to think otherwise, I found that there were very few incentives on anyone's part to gird these decisions with better information and better analysis. In fact, there appeared to be some frank disincentives. One was a Congress that read (correctly) a lack of any real public understanding or concern for this neglect. Another was a group of congressional members and senators who found it to their personal advantage to inveigh against "studying" that which they saw simply as a delaying tactic to the important business of regulating. A third was the scientific element of the country (mainly based in universities) that found the issue either too applied or too remote from their concerns. (In some cases the exceptions were loudly proclaiming, pro-environmentalist advocates who actually allied themselves with the advocate arguments, science aside.) Finally the issue of human health in particular loomed ubiquitously as *the* political issue to be seized upon. Health was very often treated as a surrogate for other desired features of the environment.

At this writing, government regulation is under fire increasingly as economic impacts are more and more strongly felt. Regulation done by the FDA or the EPA or the Consumer Product Safety Agency or by the Occupational Safety and Health Administration is pounced upon as the root of all economic evil—antithetical to a sound and competitive nation and the paradigm of unproductive expenditures. The president, in January 1975, called for the establishment of a Regulatory Review Commission. In April he addressed a letter to certain members of Congress in which he volunteered the need for regulatory reforms and pleaded with the legislature to postpone further action on an additional Agency for Consumer Advocacy.

Hence, this work was launched to look into several aspects of regulation, which were intended, as publically declared, to protect or improve human health. A panel of the President's Science Advisory Committee had examined a number of aspects of regulation of chemical substances in 1973. This book refers frequently to that review.

The work was begun because I was impressed with the number of false or at least questionable promises made through regulation. As a physician and as a scientist whose own research was from this very field, I was increasingly anxious over the contrived positions and the enormous uncertainties that were guiding private and public decisions. Further experience and the examination afforded by this review have more than confirmed my fears. All parties to environment and health questions will ultimately be poorly served by poorly informed decisions even though there seem to be short-term "successes" from time to time. It is my prediction (which I believe is now being demonstrated to be correct) that a measurable disaffection from the environmental momentum will occur as a result of the public's progressive realization that environmental decisions are so poorly founded. Such a disaffection will, as well, play against the scientific community, which, albeit perhaps unwittingly, is a party to the issue because of public expectations as to the role of science in regulation.

This review, therefore, examines several aspects of regulation for health with the thought that the system can be improved.

Protecting the Nation's Health

1 Introduction

The federal government is presently engaged in a large spectrum of regulatory activity in the name of protection of human health. The Food and Drug Administration is perhaps the longest lived of the health-related regulatory endeavors and is representative of those institutions termed "independent" regulatory agencies. Another is the Environmental Protection Agency (EPA). This more recent evolution of portions of other government agencies owes its strength to roughly a dozen pieces of environmental regulatory legislation, essentially all of which, in their legislative history, were based on some consideration of human health and its protection. The Atomic Energy Commission (AEC), although it gave up some of its regulatory tasks to EPA at the time of the latter's formation, retained both the roles of promotion or development of uses of atomic energy as well as concerns for health and safety through regulation. A recent addition to the list of independent, health-related regulatory bodies is the new Consumer Product Safety Commission. In addition to these visible and well-known entities, there are a number of instances of health-protective regulatory authority intermixed in other agencies by virtue of various pieces of legislative authority. The Department of Agriculture retains regulatory control over the wholesomeness of meat and certain other foodstuffs. The Department of Commerce is charged with the regulation of potentially flammable materials. If one includes the safety and healthfulness of occupational environment, the departments of Labor and Interior are the agencies mandated by law to be most concerned with standards and enforcement.

In one sense, the health-related regulatory activities are a part of the totality of the government's attempt to exercise policy choices through regulation. Viewed in this manner, they are a part of a larger number of regulatory bodies—some clearly more "independent" than others. In theory, regulatory agencies such as the Interstate Commerce Commission, or the Federal Aviation Agency, or the Food and Drug Administration, are looked upon as the foremost institutionalized advocates of the public's interest. The theory continues by suggesting that independence from the mainstream of the political process is in the net desirable and may even be a requisite for successful accomplishment of regulatory goals. The regulatory activity, in brief, is thought to be a "purer" affair if it is removed from at least some of the influences that drive governments in

1

their reflections of various public desires. Very few, perhaps until recently, have examined the theory. Past history has been filled with criticisms of the practice of regulation, viewing in it much imperfection and deviation from the hoped-for results. Thus, it is common to hear descriptions of how the regulatory agencies (including or perhaps especially the independent ones) have been guilty of clientelism, that is, how they have been "captured" by the very industries or segments of national life they are supposed to regulate.

The questions raised by that admonition are as important as they are iconoclastic. Students of the regulatory scene in other fields have begun to perceive a broadening of the spectrum of questioning toward an honest reappraisal of the goals of regulation and a review of just how well they are met. Insurance regulation, for example, traditionally preoccupied with solvency of the industry, has more recently broadened its concerns to protection of policy holders and claimants from losses due to insolvency [3]. Much of the economically oriented, early regulatory activity of the federal government was focused on items such as rates and their control in the face of oligopolistic or monopolistic industries. With the broadening of the base of the inquiry about regulation has come such uncomfortable questions as, what rates are correct? Or, upon what does one base equity? With the entry of what has been termed "pluralism," reflective of the heterogeneity of interests of a complex democracy, it has become apparent that satisfying or accommodating the public interest in many cases can mean only satisfying a part of the public's interest at a time. While this type of discussion may not make the articulation of goals any easier, it may make the difficulty of this analytic process more explicit.

In the case of the health-related regulatory activities, it has been commonly felt that the goals were easier to visualize. The promise of regulation in this case is prevention of ill health through avoidance of human exposure to noxious agents, unsafe products, dangerous environments, and so forth. As such, these are opportunities seized in the name of preventive medicine.

Since the Pure Food and Drug Act was passed in 1906 (considered the first comprehensive measure of control), there has been a succession of statutory authorities over the years that have extended the breadth of regulation, sometimes its strength, and often its details. Food quality, therapeutic drugs, cosmetics, meat inspection, household products, machines emitting ionizing and nonionizing radiation, have in succession all been added to this list. Successful legislative moves have characteristically been advanced immediately following a perceived crisis. The Food, Drug, and Cosmetic Act of 1938 was passed following the elixir of sulfanilimide disaster of that year. The next increment of this sort was the 1962 drug amendments following on the heels of the Thalidomide tragedy [5].

In parallel with this succession of health-related regulatory legislation has occurred another trend—seemingly complementary to the first. This has been the separation of the government's protection and regulatory activities from its promotion activities. Successively, the nation through its Congress has demanded that an institutional distinction be made between those agencies of the government responsible for encouraging productivity in agriculture or favoring the development of new drugs and those responsible for protection from those products and their by-products. The Food and Drug Administration, which began its life as a part of the Department of Agriculture, was separated from it and made a part of the Federal Security Agency in 1940, and of the Department of Health, Education, and Welfare in 1953.

In 1970 the federal government established the Environmental Protection Agency—a new department conceived of fragments and bureaus from several federal agencies: Interior, Agriculture, HEW, AEC. Again, the legislative intent was clearly to bring about a separation between agencies and institutions that aimed at development and promotion and those that were responsible for human protection from the undesirable or unexpected by-products of these developments.

The rationale behind this insistence on division between protection and promotion was the feeling that the conflict of interest in the case of agencies that combined the two was too strong and that protection through regulation could not be carried out under the shadow of a primary mandate to develop and promote. Regulation was therefore thought to be inevitably compromised if left in the hands of agencies such as the Department of Agriculture or the Department of Interior. The presidential statements accompanying the Reorganization Plan submitted to Congress proposing the establishment of EPA reflected that philosophy [6]. The parallel and related proposals for consumer product legislation over the past few years have all touched more or less strongly on this aspect of independence of regulatory authority. This was true of the Consumer Product Safety Commission [7] and of the proposals for a totally independent Food and Drug Administration [8].

The pages that follow examine a large number of aspects of the health-related regulatory enterprise in the federal government. A common thread throughout this discussion, however, is an appraisal of the consequences of these twin trends of increasing and increasingly sophisticated health-related regulatory legislation and the separation of promotion from protection through the creation of more independent agencies.

On the surface, while protection and preservation of health appear appropriate national goals, they are soon found to be other than simple ones. How safe should safety insure? For which particular groups should safety apply—the most vulnerable, the average, the eldest? Protection of health through regulation costs money and in some cases it is very expensive. It is, perhaps, this almost hackneyed phrase, consideration of costs and benefits, that more than anything else has raised the health-related regulatory affair to its present prominence. If, in fact it is desirable to articulate balanced decisions, the process of balancing, paradoxically, appears unusually difficult to achieve in the setting of an "independent" regulatory agency. Separation from some political aspects of government may not mean independence but simply a new set of dependencies. Administrative isolation brings with it a marked narrowness of constituency. In fact, in some important aspects, the agency may become wholly dependent or responsive to certain elements or institutions of public and private life and, thereby, skewed in its views. Thus, while regulatory agencies have been viewed on occasion as the ". . . foremost institutionalized advocates of the public interest" [1], they may in fact represent only a portion of the public's interest (or the interest of only a part of the public). There is, in brief, very little incentive on the part of regulatory agency administration to derive thoughtful, analytically conceived, balanced decisions. The incentives that flow from the interested constituency are for regulation and for protection— to the exclusion of most else.

In a related manner, there typically has been little incentive for independent regulation to invest in the type and quality of scientific information really needed as a foundation for regulatory decisions and standards. While the supply of good information on risks and benefits is vital to good regulatory decisions, in fact there has been frighteningly little support to insure the availability and the quality of this information. Decision makers have been left more empty handed of information more often than may generally be realized.

One of the strong, underlying currents within the consumer movement in the United States during the past few years has been that it is ". . . time to stop studying and to start regulating." There has been a feeling expressed by some that science is inhibitory to desirable regulation rather than supportive and contributory. Congress, too, has reflected this view in its dealing with regulatory practices and issues [9]. (This phenomenon, as seen below, is reflected in the fact that nearly half of the total federal budget dedicated to research on the health effects of environmental agents is spent on ionizing and nonionizing radiation and most of this is at the initiative of the AEC.)

This lack of a suitable scientific fabric behind standards and regulatory decisions has a number of serious and long-range consequences. Where balanced decisions would be desirable, where risk-benefit analysis has become a household phrase as the guideline for decision making in this area, in fact the doing of risk-benefit analysis is severely limited by a lack of information about both risks and benefits. This, of course, leads to errors in judgment in both directions. It is a cause for lost opportunities to exercise protection in the case of real yet unperceived risks. It also leads to the exercise of faulty judgment in the imposition of restrictions or overly tight standards on the occasion of implied yet poorly understood threats.

Because of the particular incentives that govern regulatory business, and because of the severe shortage of basic scientific data, regulatory agencies are prone to back their decisions with a series of advocate position papers. One of the results in turn has been a high degree of executive frustration from time to time and a strong temptation (contrary to the will of Congress) to lift important regulatory decision making out of the independent agencies to a higher governmental level for review. This, of course, makes the regulatory agencies, at least temporarily, less independent.

An important political and legislative phenomenon observed in the past few years has been that, in the face of a lack of scientific information, Congress and the regulatory agencies tend strongly toward conservatism (i.e., protection of human health). This is seen in all three of tighter environmental standards, more conservative interpretation of the laws and, most important, a trend toward standards mandated directly by Congress. An important and perhaps most controversial feature of the amendments to the Clean Air Act of 1971 was the quantitative limitations for automotive emissions. The administrator of EPA enjoys essentially no discretion in this case, but, rather, is obliged simply to enforce the imposed numerical standards. An additional important example is the amendment to the Food, Drug, and Cosmetic Act relating to suspected carcinogens in food additives and animal feed additives (Delaney amendment).

These are clearly examples of a Congress' lifting the regulatory decision process out of the hands of the executive branch and placing it in its own. A broader pattern of reserving the "social" decision process to Congress while leaving only the technical issues and enforcement to the executive agencies has been advocated by some, yet has had remarkably little national debate. Its protagonists seem to assume that we already know for sure much that, regrettably, is quite uncertain [10].

James Wilson commented that the power of an agency is diminished the greater the degree there is of codification of its policies and rules. Power, he asserts, depends on uncertainty [2]. In addition, however, codification brings with it rigidity. There has been a tendency for the health-related regulatory laws to be rigid and to promise the absolute. What has emerged is a running conflict between the rigidity of the regulatory process and the dynamic character of science. By definition, science is a dynamic affair—continually raising new questions and new concepts and often overturning old ones. It is, in fact, this aspect of old decisions (especially for regulated products) perturbed by new scientific insight that has been at the heart of nearly all of the health-centered regulatory crises of the past four to six years. There has been remarkably little accommodation made in regulatory statutes and practices to this need for flexibility.

Finally, a third undesirable consequence of rigid and mandated standards is that they tend to limit or discourage further research, which is often needed to gain real understanding of the character and seriousness of an implied hazard. Once the preliminary observation was made of bladder tumors in laboratory animals and this was associated with the experimental feeding of cyclamates, there was little incentive to proceed further to understand the meaning of those observations.

Economic considerations have become increasingly prominent in the debate over environmental and "quality of life" decisions. Clearly, there should be no surprises here. These decisions typically implicate large expenditures and these expenditures not infrequently are spread broadly and are felt over long periods. These, of course, are the very externalities that were often ignored prior to the environmental and consumerist era.

Among the costs are those perceived or incurred by those industries that develop and manufacture regulated products. Here, especially in recent times, there have been numerous assertions made concerning the effect of regulatory laws and practices of the regulatory agencies on industrial research and development aimed at new generation and needed products. This debate, perhaps, has been most intense on the subjects of pesticides and therapeutic drugs. It has been argued, for example, that the nation has been deprived (or delayed in its provision) of new and useful therapeutic drugs because of the necessity to accommodate the 1962 amendments to the Food, Drug, and Cosmetic Act, which require proof of efficacy [11,12]. There have been changes in the industries that develop, produce, and market products subject to regulation. There has been investment by them overseas in both R&D and manufacturing capacity. There have been changes with time in the spectrum of products they offer for sale and distribution. However, there are a number of variables operating at any point in time, all of which influence the patterns of business and business investment. What is more difficult than may have been thought is to separate out the particular influence of the regulatory enterprise on the regulated industries. Even more important, perhaps, would be to consider some goals in this area. Is it desirable to have a spectrum of products, some of which may be duplicative? How much assurance of real benefit or utility or efficacy does the consuming public or its surrogate intermediary, the physician, desire? What arguments are there for insuring a variety of sizes of companies in business to produce similar products? (It is said that smaller firms are inevitably giving way to a few larger ones in some of the regulated areas.)

There exists a large series of important issues concerned with how regulation is done. These cut across boundaries of science, political science, and the law. Some of these are ethical in character. (When has enough animal laboratory experimentation been completed to permit clinical testing in human beings?) Some bear particularly heavily on administrative matters. (How much responsibility for decision making should be borne by regulatory agency personnel or administrators and how much should be shared with outsiders?)

Throughout all of these, questions of public insight, information about decisions and decision making, are increasingly seen as important. A protestation not infrequently heard among consumer groups is not necessarily a distrust of the substance of a decision. Rather, it is simply frustration over ignorance about what went into it and how it was made. There is, in brief, a severe problem of credibility and a challenge to reconcile orderly administration with the desires of participatory democracy. This is an extraordinarily tangled maze. The achievement of sound, judicious decisions whose implications are seen reasonably far into the future and that do reflect a balance of competing desires is a laudable goal. That this may, in fact, be far different from simply ratifying bargains struck by competing interest groups [13] is a major point in need of resolution. It is unlikely that classical arrangements of simple delegation of authority through legislation to administrators of programs and agencies will much longer suffice. Neither, however, will a practice of Congress' retrieving some authority for themselves by relieving administrators of discretion in their actions. This pattern, which is seen in standards rigidly mandated in the laws handed to the administrators, is fraught with difficulties. The principal objection one might raise is that it does not square with the flexibility demanded by a dynamic science. There is a need for some new administrative formulation.

Finally, what is perhaps most needed is a perspective. It is time to take stock of the major goals of health-related regulatory activities. It is time to examine public expectations of how much health can be purchased through regulation. Essentially all of the government's regulatory activity is aimed at involuntary exposures to environmental agents. Yet, the impact of these on mortality and on morbidity (as best one can measure it) is overwhelmed by the effects of voluntary exposure to such agents as cigarettes and the combination of alcohol and automobile driving. Again, it is perhaps because regulatory matters are expensive that this question becomes important. At least the nation should be aware of the consequences of its public policy choices and should express them in a well-informed manner.

8

References

1. Leone, R.C., Public Interest Advocacy and the Regulatory Process, *The Annals of the American Academy of Political and Social Science*, 400: 46-58, 1972.
2. Wilson, J.Q., The Dead Hand of Regulation, *The Public Interest*, 25: 39-58, 1971.
3. Stewart, R.E., Insurance Regulation: Current Issues and Problems, *The Annals of the American Academy of Political and Social Science*, 400: 59-68, 1972.
4. Young, J.H., The 1938 Food, Drug and Cosmetic Act, in the Government and the Consumer: Evolution of Food and Drug Laws, *Emory University J. of Public Law*, 13: 197-204, 1964.
5. Janssen, W.F., FDA Since 1938. The Major Trends and Developments in the Government and the Consumer: Evolution of Food and Drug Laws, *Emory University J. of Public Law*, 13: 205-221, 1964.
6. The White House, Fact Sheet on Reorganization Plans 3 and 4, July 9, 1970.
7. National Commission on Product Safety, *Final Report*, Washington, D.C., June 1970.
8. U.S. Senate, Consumer Safety Act of 1972, *Report of the Senate Committee on Commerce on S. 3419*, April 13, 1972.
9. U.S. House of Representatives, *Regulatory Policies of the Food and Drug Administration*, Subcommittee on Intergovernmental Relations of the Committee on Government Operations, June 9, 1970.
10. Turner, J.S., The Delaney Anticancer Clause: A Model Environmental Protection Law, *Vanderbilt Law Review*, 24: 889-902, 1971.
11. Peltzman, S., The Benefits and Costs of New Drug Regulation, Paper prepared to the Conference on Regulation of the Introduction of New Pharmaceuticals, Center for Policy Study, the University of Chicago, Chicago, Ill., December 4-5, 1972.
12. Friedman, M., Frustrating Drug Advancement, *Newsweek*, January 8, 1973.

2 History of the Major Health-related Regulatory Legislation in the United States

Regulation of the production or use of chemical and physical agents in man's environment in the name of human health is performed by several agencies of the federal government by virtue of a number of enabling legal authorities. These have developed by way of an evolutionary process that has reflected changes in patterns of life, shifts in industry, increases in affluence and urbanization, among other things. The development of these legal instruments for regulation also reflects an ever-increasing technical complexity of the issues that serve as the background to regulation. Finally, the evolution has as well (and perhaps most importantly) reflected changing public and governmental philosophies toward the market place and laissez-faire attitudes and toward a number of values espoused by the body politic.

This chapter is not meant to be an exhaustive nor comprehensive treatise on the historical evolution of the food and drug laws. There are already in existence a number of excellent historical reviews of this subject [1, 2, 3, 4, 5, 6]. Neither does it purport to be particularly inclusive of all of the lists of materials regulated. The major aim is rather to point to a number of interesting and important trends. These trends are important as they reflect patterns of national concerns that "drove" the legislative process at various times in the past leading to the present portfolio of environmental and consumer protection legislation. It is precisely because these national concerns did change that the study of the evolution of the regulatory laws is so interesting. This discussion relies most heavily for illustration on a number of laws dealing with chemical environmental agents (e.g., food additives, therapeutic drugs, air pollutants, water pollutants). Again, the list is not purposefully exclusionary for any reason other than sufficiency of examples to make a point. (Also, some of the oldest of the regulatory laws in this country are those dealing with foods and drugs.) Finally, the discussion in this chapter is generally confined in its illustrations to materials found in the environment of the general population. Thus, for the most part, hazards to special groups or in limited settings (such as occupational exposures) are not singled out for concern here.

Food and Drug Laws

The early evolution of the food and drug laws in the United States occurred in a setting where the principal preoccupation was with foods and only secondarily with drugs. The early laws had two major purposes, the safeguarding of the public's health and the prevention of fraud (the safeguarding of the vendor's reputation).

Efforts of the state to prevent food and drug adulteration date back to ancient times. Both Athens and Rome made provisions against the adulteration of wine, and the quality and purity of peppers used as preservatives were closely guarded. With the growth of towns, regulation by governments began to preempt the self-control formerly exercised by guilds. As the United States became increasingly industrialized in the nineteenth century, food was still sufficiently scarce to make adulteration profitable. It was against these abuses of adulteration and fraud in foodstuffs in particular that the original Pure Food and Drug Act of 1906 was directed. Several trends converged during the latter half of the nineteenth century to build public pressure in favor of government regulation.

There were widespread practices of adulteration of foods and of therapeutic remedies as well. As Oscar Anderson noted:

Manufacturers, their ethical standards dulled by the impersonality of their function, debased their goods in the struggle to survive. Some added chicory to coffee, mixed inert matter with ground pepper, or sold a mixture of glucose, flavoring, and hayseed for raspberry jam. Other abuses stemmed less from the necessities of competition and moral insensitivity than from an economy which saw food produced far from the urban centers for which it was destined. Refrigeration was in its infancy; and manufacturers turned to such chemical preservatives as borax, salicylic acid, and formaldehyde [2].

The nation was made increasingly aware of the questions of purity and adulteration by an occasional overt scandal or two and by articles and books for public consumption on the subject. Perhaps the best known of these latter was *The Jungle* by Upton Sinclair in 1906, which was considered as having a key part to play in pushing public opinion over the edge of apathy. As much as anything else, the drive toward regulatory legislation can be laid to the energies of Harvey W. Wiley, a chemist first with the state of Indiana and later chief of the Bureau of Chemistry of the U.S. Department of Agriculture. Wiley arranged to have draft legislation introduced into three successive Congresses starting in 1900. He, too, emerged as the leader of a movement to publicize the hazards of fraud and adulteration.

Economic interests were a powerful force and actually took two forms. On the one hand were those industries that entertained a serious concern for the reputation of the industry as a whole in the face of growing public awareness and anxiety over the quality and purity of food. This concern for public confidence grew steadily during the 1880s as the public's confidence became eroded. A second form of economic interest was the strong business desire to avoid undue competition. It was this type of interest, in particular, that emerged as a strong countervailing force poised against those who favored definitive regulation. A whole mosaic of special interests were involved. These emerged as several powerful and well-organized lobbying efforts. On occasion their effort took the form of special interest legislation reflecting competitive interests among rival industries. In 1886 dairy interests succeeded in obtaining discriminatory legislation against oleomargarine. On a number of other occasions it assumed the form of organized business interest aligned against the government's entry into a regulatory arena seen as threatening to previously unfettered entrepreneural energies. Opposition of cottonseed oil producers, joined by several manufacturers of foods and drugs, was responsible for the defeat in 1892 of a general law in Congress sponsored by Senator Paddock [2]. Alliances of baking powder interests, preservative manufacturers, and others were formed to thwart initial efforts at general legislation. When a bill did pass in 1906, it was strongly colored by the many compromises that had been necessary in the legislative process.

A distinctly secondary but nevertheless important issue leading to the initial piece of federal legislation was a concern for a myriad of therapeutic remedies marketed in a correspondingly large number of ways. The nature of the interests here was similar to that for foods. Adulteration was widespread and there was a double concern for purity—both to avoid fraud and to insure safety. In addition, the growth of nostrums of questionable therapeutic usefulness presented physicians and patients alike with a challenge. This point, while it was relieved of its blatant and pernicious forms by the beginning of the twentieth century was to reappear again in the 1960s under the title of drug efficacy.

Much of the nineteenth century in France had been consumed with attempts to legislate appropriately against adulteration of drugs and against secrecy of ingredients. Success was reached in France in this regard only in 1926 but was clearly aided by the growth of understanding of the sciences of pharmacology and chemistry and by the evolution of better methods of analysis. Also in France, a major debate over drug efficacy had been played out in this period with successful clinical evaluation of *rob Boyveau-Laffecteur* as a cure for syphilis [8].

In Great Britain there was concern, too, for matters of drug purity and drug efficacy and the growth of these concerns paralleled the developments in science and technology that made chemical analysis and detection possible. The British counterpart of Harvey Wiley is Arthur Hill Hassall, who had been particularly responsible for pressing his views on parliament during the second half of the nineteenth century [9].

A final and important influence were the views of the several professions whose practicing members were particularly interested in therapeutic drugs—particularly the medical profession. Physicians saw with alarm the rising tide of nostrums and patent medicine of questionable therapeutic value (or worse) and generally agreed that these products were both a threat to the well-being of their patients and to their own reputation. Yet, the idea of government control and regulation was viewed with abhorrence. Accordingly, there developed a strong and increasing tide of professional sentiment in favor of leaving this bit of policing to the profession itself. Interestingly, the notion of government regulation as a type of interference with the practice of medicine is an idea that has colored the entirety of this short history of drug regulation.

As Anderson reported, the cry arose in the 1890s with each successive attempt at introduction and passage of a food and drug law in the Congress, ". . . if the Federal Government should regulate interstate traffic in drugs on the basis of their therapeutic value, why not regulate the traffic in theology, by excluding from transportation all the theological books which Dr. Wiley and his assistants . . . should find to be misleading in any particular. . . ?" [2] Again, these attitudes in the United States were paralleled by similar expressions and fears in France [7] and in Great Britain [8]. Armand Trousseau, a famous French clinician, had gone so far in his disputations as to attempt to discredit the contributions that chemistry in particular had made to the understanding of pharmacology [10, 11]. It was against the combined view of therapeutic nihilism, yet fear of encroachment on professional judgment, that the fledgling American Medical Association proceeded to establish a Council on Pharmacy in 1905. A year later, the AMA added a Chemical Laboratory—thus effectively proceeding to fill a vacuum of standards of analysis and of regulation by government [12].

Finally, there was the growth of science and technology. One of the products of this scientific evolution, of course, was an increasing list of pharmacologic possibilities. The other, equally important, was a growing ability to analyze commercial products for their ingredients, to determine the presence of impurities and adulterants and to ascertain the strength or concentration of key ingredients. This scientific evolution coincided with public disclosures of fraud and of dangers of worthless or harmful remedies. Edward Bok published a series of editorials in the *Ladies Home Journal* in 1904 about the hazards associated with many of the popular therapeutic preparations available, and Samuel Hopkins Adams stirred the public with a series of articles on patent medicines in 1905 [2]. Thus, the public debate was intensified at the very time that Congress was considering pure food and drug legislation.

The 1906 Pure Food and Drugs Act was the culmination of a prolonged period of heated and intense debate among those who felt strongly about fraud and purity and safety and those who feared economic disaster from any perturbation of the traditional laissez-faire economy. Hence, as are most laws, it was a compromise. The act regulated the interstate commerce of misbranded and adulterated foods and drugs. It was focused particularly at the use of certain food preservatives and dyes, and at claims made for certain nostrums and patent medicines. The Meat Inspection Act was passed the same day—prompted by the disclosure of unsanitary conditions in meat packing plants.

A number of weaknesses were perceived in the early food and drug law. Both the Pure Foods and Drugs Act and the Meat Inspection Act were administered by the Department of Agriculture. This began what others have viewed as a conflict of interest between protection and promotion. This conflict was not to be settled until 1940 when what became known as the Food and Drug Administration was separated from the Department of Agriculture and placed in the Federal Security Administration. There were severe and notable compromises made in the legislation during its legislative history. There was a lack of specificity and guidelines. Cosmetics, originally a part of the bill, were deleted during the course of debate. Further, sections of the bill that authorized the secretary of agriculture to set standards for food products were dropped. As Wilson pointed out, perhaps the most important and fundamental feature of the early food and drug legislation was the presumption that people were unable to protect themselves against misrepresentation and adulteration [1]. As he also quite properly recognized, in spite of the fundamental health goals of the legislation, it also represented a form of commodity control and economic versus health issues have remained the axis of debate throughout the history of consumer and environmental legislation.

A notable characteristic of the first piece of food and drug regulation was that the onus of proof of wrongdoing of fraud or adulteration lay with the government. Manufacturers and vendors were not explicitly required to demonstrate matters of safety and therapeutic efficacy before beginning to market their products. In fact, the law, as it was interpreted by the Supreme Court in the next few years after its passage, seemed to lose some of the few regulatory teeth it was thought to have had at the outset. The Court ruled in 1911 that the law was not meant to apply to false and misleading therapeutic claims [13]. Congress in 1912 passed the "Shirley amendment," which banned therapeutic claims that were both false and fraudulent. By 1922 the term fraudulent proved to be a serious stumbling block as the Court ruled that if drugmakers or purveyors believed in the utility of a drug, they could not be charged with fraudulent intent [14].

Deficiencies in the 1906 law were recognized from the outset. (Harvey Wiley, it is reported, saw no defects in the law and insisted that apparent flaws were simply laid to faulty administration and faulty enforcement

[2].) However, a spirit favoring reform was not strong until around the time of the Depression.

Again, the major preoccupation of the Bureau of Chemistry of the Department of Agriculture was with foods and only secondarily with drugs. It is interesting that into the governmental vacuum stepped the American Medical Association. This organization maintained itself stoutly on the side of the critics of proprietary medicines of questionable value. Lacking a federal facility for drug evaluation, the AMA established the Council on Pharmacy and, in 1912, the Committee on Therapeutic Research, which supported research into the ". . . activity, stability and physiologic action of commonly used non-proprietary drugs. . . ."[15]. This was the same era in which John D. Rockefeller was persuaded to finance a new research institution in order to improve and increase the number of therapeutic drugs capable of truly curative action.

This period, too, was marked by a high degree of cooperation between the regulatory institutions and the industries regulated. This spirit seems to have been fostered by a certain faith of the era in voluntary cooperation and of sparseness of the resources of the government agency. All of this appears to have come to a striking halt with the advent of the Great Depression. Economic forces led to an increasing number of compromised business ethics and a rise in the public demand for reform. Where it had been the pattern for the government to advise the industry informally before it took regulatory action, this pattern was reversed after 1933.

The mood of the country changed and reform became not only palatable but even popular. Relations between the government regulators and industry became more distant and more formal [14]. President Roosevelt sensed this changed mood and encouraged a revision of the Pure Food and Drug Act, a form of which finally emerged as a law five years later. The popular press again played a part—this time not allied with the food and drug regulators but critical of them. The climax was ultimately reached with a visible, tragic incident, the death of over a hundred persons who had fallen victims of Elixir of Sulfanilamide in October 1937. The solvent for this preparation, diethylene glycol, had been examined for appearance and flavor but not for safety.

The new law, again a product of a long process of bargaining and revisions, provided for stricter controls over foods. The law also enabled the establishment of standards of identity for foods. The major and most far-reaching provision was one that gave the Food and Drug Administration the responsibility to insure the safety of new drugs introduced into interstate commerce. Thus, the burden of proof was shifted. No longer did the government have to seek the evidence for and prove misbranding and fraud (the spirit of the prior, Shirley amendment). The manufacturer now was obliged to demonstrate to the government that his product was safe before marketing. Although not entirely a new idea (the Meat Inspection Act of 1907 also had included the provision), this concept was clearly established for drugs in the 1938 statute and became as one observer put it, "one of the most important social concepts of our times" [4]. The law turned from being a punitive instrument to one of prevention. (The law avoided actual licensing or certification of new drugs by simply declaring New Drug Applications "effective" if they satisfied the regulatory agency). The manufacturer was responsible for performing the research and testing and for supplying the results of investigations to the government, which sat in judgment and passed on the quality and the merits of the evidence and data submitted to it.

The 1938 act also established a procedure for the batch testing and certification of coloring substances used in foods, drugs, and cosmetics. Manufacturers underwrote the costs of maintaining and operating a government laboratory dedicated to this batch certification procedure. This same type of control was extended in 1941 to the standardization and testing of insulin and, within the next 17 years, to penicillin and all other antibiotic substances.[a]

During the ensuing years after 1938, a number of statutory provisions were added that had the effect of extending the scope of regulation and of extending the list of items over which regulation was applied. The Federal Insecticide, Fungicide and Rodenticide Act of 1947 established the main legal instrument for registration of pest control chemicals and for controlling the pesticide chemical residues left on food crops after spraying. This was supplemented by the Pesticide Chemicals Act of 1954.

The Food Additives Amendment (to the Food, Drug and Cosmetic Act), introduced by Congressman James Delaney of New York and passed in 1958, did for food additives what had previously been done for drugs. It established the responsibility of manufacturers to establish the safe character of their products prior to use. An important provision (subsequently known as the Delaney Clause) prohibited the use of food additives found to produce cancer in man or in experimental animals.

In 1960 the Color Additives Amendment was added to the list. This law extended the controls formerly applied only to coal-tar color food additives to all colors used in foods, drugs, and cosmetics, and established safe limits for their use.

In the field of therapeutic drugs, certain marked trends were emerging—urged on by those who recognized a need for regulation yet tem-

---

[a] This procedure points up the *capital asset value* of government regulatory and certification procedures. That is, the value of products is *enhanced* through the process of FDA scrutiny and approval for marketing.

pered by others who feared controls. The 1938 version of the Food, Drug and Cosmetic Act had expressly singled out a class of drugs recognized as dispensed by physician prescription. The 1938 act required the labelling of drugs generally but *exempted* prescription drugs when labelling was thought to be unnecessary. In 1951 the Humphrey-Durham Drug Prescription Act clearly separated self-medication drugs from prescription drugs.

A second issue that evolved during this period was that of drug efficacy. Recall that the question of efficacy in the face of ineffective or questionably effective nostrums and patent medicines had been one of the early factors that had provoked governmental concern. This issue was to emerge again during the debate on the Humphrey-Durham amendments where it was proposed that efficacy be a consideration for classification of drugs. This notion was abandoned, however, in the face of opposition from the medical profession, which feared governmental interference in the practice of medicine. The issue was most clearly highlighted, however, in the 1962 amendments to the Food, Drug and Cosmetic Act. Passage of these amendments followed a long series of hearings—mainly on the topic of drug prices and costs sponsored by Senator Estes Kefauver.

Passage of the Kefauver-Harris amendments was at least aided by the thalidomide disasters. The most significant provision of the 1962 law was the explicit obligation of demonstration of efficacy as well as safety by drug manufacturers. The legislative system had finally come full circle in recognition of the relative lack of information concerning effectiveness in the case of a great many drugs on the market. The National Academy of Sciences was engaged in 1966 to review all of the available prescription drugs for documented and experimentally derived evidence of effectiveness and the massive task was completed in 1969 [16]. At the present writing, the Food and Drug Administration is also completing a review of the efficacy of nonprescription or over-the-counter drugs.

Thus, food and drug laws began as punitive statutes—aimed at prosecution of parties who were found to engage in adulteration or false labelling. They evolved, however, into preventive measures—placing the burden of proof on the private sector to "prove" safety and, in the case of drugs, efficacy. At the same time, the scope of regulation was extended with time to an increasingly broad group of chemical substances. As David Cavers has pointed out, the pace of these trends has been the net result of public clamor for reform and control—made periodically more enthusiastic by the news media and reports of specific, serious accidents, of congressional interests and energies, of various interests of practicing medicine, of industrial interests, and of the success of regulatory behavior of the administrative agencies [17].

Consumer Protection

It is interesting at this point to consider a related but somewhat different line of federal legislative development—that encompassing consumer-product safety regulation. A discussion of this subject is inserted at this point partly because it was a logical and expected extension of the established trend of increasing regulation of consumed products (such as foods and drugs). Most important, however, its short evolution illustrated the growing and continuing trend toward more and more independence of health-related regulatory activities.

In 1966 Senators Warren Magnuson and Norris Cotton proposed a national commission to survey product safety. (The term *product* was strictly defined as household products and limited to substances not already covered by existing laws. Hence, food additives, drugs, pesticides, and many other products were explicitly excluded.) The commission, authorized two years later by a Joint Resolution and appointed by President Johnson in March 1968, reported its findings in June 1970 [18]. Among the findings was the conclusion that a significant number of the 20 million Americans who are injured and the 30,000 who are killed in incidents related to consumer products could be spared ". . . if more attention had been paid to hazard reduction." The report called for a major federal role in the protection of American health and safety from the consumer-product related injuries. Accompanying the report was a draft of a bill to give to the federal government the responsibility to exercise regulatory authority in this area. Notably, the bill reflected a strong admonition made by the commission that *independence* of the regulatory instrument was an essential ingredient if it was to be successful [18]. Thus began a modest struggle that culminated four years later in the passage of a Consumer Product Safety Act [19].

A number of pro-consumer laws had been enacted during the late 1960s, each one of which related to a specific category of hazard in consumer interest. These included the National Traffic and Motor Vehicles Safety Act of 1966, the Flammable Fabrics Act Amendments of 1967, the Gas Pipeline Safety Act in 1968, the Radiation Control for Health and Safety Act in 1968, the Child Protection and Toy Safety Act in 1969, and the Poison Prevention Packaging Act in 1970. The National Commission on Product Safety was a reflection in part of the concern over the fragmented or "piecemeal" approach to regulation for consumer interests and in part a logical extension of the momentum of the "Consumer Decade" of the sixties.

Earlier bills had been introduced in 1970 and 1971 by Senator Magnuson and Senator Moss, identical in form to the draft bill suggested by the

National Commission, which called for a new, independent Product Safety Commission to exercise regulatory authority over the narrow spectrum
of consumer household products of concern to the study Commission. In
1971 this bill passed one House of Congress but failed in the other. Hearings were again held in preparation for reintroduction of the legislation.
Early in 1972, after hearings were completed, the staff of the Senate Committee on Interstate and Foreign Commerce introduced an entirely new
piece of legislation in the form of an unsigned and unnumbered, "Committee Print" [20]. This legislative proposal, which some took as a more
orthodox form of a numbered and sponsored act [21], went much farther
in the direction of "independent" consumer regulation than had been proposed or envisaged by the National Commission. It was a clever move in
many ways. It proposed the establishment of an independent Consumer
Safety Agency, some of whose functions were confined to consumer
products of the sort contemplated by the National Commission in Product
Safety. In this way, it reflected closely the terms of the prior legislative
attempts. In addition and most important, it would have transferred to the
new agency all of the functions then subtended by the Food and Drug Administration along with certain others. Thus, it would have had the effect
of removing the Food and Drug Administration from HEW and placing it
in a totally independent agency. Further, the bill also included a number
of features contained in a concurrent administration proposal—making
opposition by the executive branch particularly difficult. Finally, and
clearly deliberately, all of this strategy occurred in an election year when
a veto of pro-consumer legislation would be particularly unpalatable [22].

The key element of this proposal was independence of federal regulation. This draft bill included a provision, for example, under which the
new agency would report its budgetary recommendation directly to Congress, bypassing the traditional budgetary review of the Office of Management and Budget.

The bill was reported out of the Senate Commerce Committee overwhelmingly by a 17 to 1 vote. However, the sharply critical view of Senator Norris Cotton, the lone dissenter, illustrates the seriousness of the debate on the issue of independence:

I joined with the Chairman of our Committee on Commerce, Senator Magnuson
[in 1967], in co-sponsoring S.J. Res. 33 which served to establish the National
Commission on Product Safety. . . . If in 1967 I had known what I now know
about how far the final product, S.3419 [the Senate Bill finally reported out of the
Committee] would go, then my earlier support would have been something less
than enthusiastic. S.3419 goes well beyond the bounds established for the Commission pursuant to P.L. 90-146 and the recommendation set forth in its final report. As a matter of fact, during that same earlier consideration of S.J. Res. 33 I
also stated that "great oaks from little acorns grow, and whenever we scratch the
surface of a subject of legislation, immediately during the hearings that result,
from the study of legislation, there is brought to light many other steps that should

be taken. Little did I realize that the seed we planted would blossom into a patch of poison oak which will have legitimate business breaking out in a rash from fear of potential regulatory harassment and scratching for years to come if the Committee bill is enacted [23].

Ultimately a law was passed—the product of a Conference Committee that leaned heavily toward a House version, which in turn reflected the various ambitions of the National Commission on Product Safety [24]. An independent Product Safety Commission was established and the product safety interests of the Food and Drug Administration were transferred to it. However, the vast majority of the Food and Drug Administration was left intact within HEW. Independent status of the new commission was highlighted including a provision for direct reporting of the budget to Congress. Thus, although the agenda for this new agency was cut from that which some had hoped, the notion of independence received a new prominence and clearly had a large number of partisans. Several, of course, had shown their stiff opposition to this notion during the debate. Secretary Richardson of HEW had early expressed his opposition to the creation of a new regulatory agency [25] and his commissioner of foods and drugs had strongly urged that the secretary persuade the president to veto any bill that would establish a new independent governmental entity to regulate product safety [26]. Those few scientists who made themselves aware of this series of legislative initiatives generally expressed dismay over what they felt were false, public expectations of increased human health and safety that were supposed to result from new administrative practices. They felt, too, that the scientific basis for decisions would be further compromised rather than strengthened [27, 28]. Of course, those segments of industry potentially affected by these legislative measures were consistent in their opposition [23]. While the form of the legislation that was passed represented a pulling back from a full-scale push toward independence of consumer and food and drug regulation, there were some who felt that the subject of "what to do about FDA" would surely return to the front of the legislative stage [29].

Environmental Protection Agency

In assembling the arguments in favor of a more independent food, drug, and consumer-product regulator, the Senate Commerce Committee in 1972 had leaned rather heavily and explicitly on what they felt was a useful precedent. This was the creation two years before of the Environmental Protection Agency [23]. In late 1969 and early 1970, the Ash Commission [b] had reviewed the advantages and disadvantages of government by

---

[b] Presidential Commission on Executive Reorganization headed by Roy Ash, then president of Litton Industries, Inc.

independent commission and had generally opposed any further proliferation of independent regulatory entities. However, at a time when reorganization for environmental action was receiving widespread public attention, and because governmental activities aimed at environmental conservation and improvement were widely scattered throughout the executive branch, a new Environmental Protection Agency was created by Reorganization Plan [30]. This new agency was designed to be an amalgam of bureaus and departments from several federal agencies—Interior, Agriculture, HEW, AEC—some of which were traditionally charged with the development or promotion of a variety of desired elements of national life (recreational parks, electric power from nuclear fuel, assured supply of food at reasonable cost, etc.).

The intent was clearly to bring about a separation between agencies and institutions that aimed at development and those that were responsible for human protection from the undesirable or unexpected by-products of these developments. Regulation was the instrument of federal leverage and, it was argued, the strength or direction of regulation was inevitably compromised if left in the hands of agencies such as the Department of Agriculture or the Department of Interior. The presidential statements accompanying the Reorganization Plan submitted to Congress proposing the establishment of EPA listed, among the advantages of the new agency, the fact that it would ". . . insulate pollution abatement standard-setting from the promotional interests of other departments" [30]. Thus, while Senator Cotton two years later termed the supposed analogy between the independent Environmental Protection Agency and an independent Consumer Product Safety "specious and grossly misleading" [23], there certainly were some parallels and these were not lost on the proponents.[c]

Air and Water Pollution Laws

These air and water pollution categories of regulatory authorities are grouped together here, not because of common features of the pollutants themselves (although obviously there certainly are some), but rather, because it is useful to consider systematically some of the similarities and the differences among the forces that shaped these laws over time. Again, these are important as they strongly colored the manner in which the laws were eventually administered.

A few generalizations are in order: As J.C. Davies [31] and others have pointed out, public concern with pollution is strongly related to the

[c] Interestingly, several spokesmen for the White House and the Office of Management and Budget later privately expressed misgivings over the assumptions that underlay the creation of the Environmental Protection Agency. "If we had it to do over we would not have argued for that creation" was a not uncommonly heard theme.

growth of production and of affluence. Obviously, pollutants as public nuisances or problems increased in roughly direct proportion to the growth of industry and the proliferation of automobiles. At the same time, tangible political and administrative action to counter pollution is a luxury—to be afforded only after a country has reached a certain level of affluence. Thus, the evolution of the laws governing air and water pollution reflect this growing ability (as well as growing necessity) to permit public expenditures to be made in behalf of pollution control.

The fundamental emphasis or rationale for these laws has varied over time for each category and among the categories. Protection of human health has been a fairly constant consideration in the history of federal air pollution laws in the United States. By contrast, water pollution legislation has been "sold" politically on quite different issues from time to time. What is particularly interesting is to note that a particular emphasis or other has been strongly determined not by ideological considerations but as a function of administrative and congressional jurisdictions.

Pollution issues, of course, have had their champions in the public press just as did the pure food and drug causes. Rachel Carson's *Silent Spring* was a timely and clearly influential counterpart of the earlier, Upton Sinclair's *The Jungle*. What Miss Carson's book clearly succeeded in accomplishing was to establish health as the political issue upon which pesticides, air pollution, and nuclear energy regulation were to turn. Effects on ecological features and on the integrity of the general environment were raised as issues. However, as rallying points for political action, health was singled out as number one.

Thus, elixir of sulfanilamide and thalidomide incidents had their counterparts too. These included the acute air pollution episodes in London, England and Donora, Pennsylvania. Again, it was the pollution-related illness and the accelerated mortality mainly from respiratory disease upon which the public's attention was focused.

There was one notable difference between the histories of the food and drug laws and the pollution laws, however. The major, vocal constituency of antipollution legislation, the loose amalgam of pro-environmentalists, conservationists, and consumers, have had little alliance with the professional medical and health-related scientific fraternity. This, of course, is all the more striking in the face of health as the major central issue! In fact, if anything, the best of the scientific community whose careers correspond to the discipline, environmental health, have served as tempering influences as much or more than they have as advocates. Thus, it is fascinating to note the contrast between the confidence expressed in the Report of the Senate Public Works Committee that said, in essence, that we have sufficient knowledge to set automobile exhaust emission standards [32], with the great anxiety and dismay of Dr. Norton Nelson, director of the Institute of Environmental Medicine, New York University Medical Center. Dr. Nelson was commenting on the state of fundamental knowledge that existed for the purpose of air pollution standards setting during a conference on the health effects of air pollutants at the National Academy of Sciences in 1973: "We ought to apologize to someone for having reached this stage in an area of great economic and social importance with such a vague knowledge base" [33]. While health has been hotly espoused by the advocates of pollution legislation as the rationale, in fact the political issue has run *from* not *with* the major scientific spokesmen for the health sciences.[d]

Air Pollution

The first air pollution law in the United States was a city ordinance adopted in 1881 by the Chicago City Council. The target of the ordinance was smoke or particulate matter—considered at that time to be a public nuisance. In 1947 the city of Los Angeles developed an air pollution control program—a reflection of public concern over industrial odors. The following year, through a combination of peculiar topography, meteorological conditions and the emanation of airborne effluents, the town of Donora, Pennsylvania suffered a severe smog episode to which were attributed 20 deaths and 6,000 cases of illness. By 1951 Dr. Arie Haagen-Smit had unraveled the mechanism of smog formation and had singled out the automobile as the major contributor of its elements in Los Angeles.

The first federal legislation dealing with air pollution was passed in 1955—aided politically by the after effects of the Donora, Pennsylvania incident. It was a very cautious first step—leading the federal government into a *temporary* program of research, training, and demonstration. This law was extended in 1959 for four additional years.

The next several years saw a rapid escalation in concern for air pollution effects—especially on human health. In 1962 a severe air pollution episode occurred in London, leaving a trail of considerable accelerated mortality and respiratory illness. The following year, Congress passed the Clean Air Act of 1963. This law was a sharp departure from its predecessors. It expanded the level of research. However, for the first time it recognized a federal responsibility in the *abatement* of pollution, albeit indirectly. Thus, this law authorized grants to States and localities for air pollution control and abatement efforts.

A new Subcommittee on Air and Water Pollution was created in 1963

---

[d] In addition, as is seen later in chapter 3, it has at times even been politically attractive to discourage the development of more scientific information where additional research is viewed as simply delaying "good judgment."

within the Senate Committee on Public Works. The federal administrative responsibility remained where it had started—in the Department of Health, Education, and Welfare. The new Subcommittee embarked on a series of fact-finding hearings on air pollution in various parts of the nation. Perhaps the most impressive finding to emerge from these hearings was the contribution of automobile exhaust to overall national air pollution. It was estimated that the automobile contributed some 50 percent of the national air pollution problem [34]. Accordingly, Senator Muskie introduced legislation that would authorize the setting of standards for exhaust emissions from all new automobiles. This pattern and the standards were influenced by the pattern already being established by the state of California. California law had established maximum allowable emission levels for automotive exhaust components and had engaged the automotive industry to produce cars capable of meeting these standards. Following an initial recalcitrance on the part of the White House, amendments to the Clean Air Act were ultimately passed and signed by the president.

Considering changes in the law to come a mere five years later, it is interesting to note the philosophy behind this important bit of regulation. The committee report that accompanied the bill on its way to the Senate floor made the point that: "The Committee believes that exact standards need not be written legislatively but that the Secretary [of HEW] should adjust to changing technology" [35]. Further, in setting emission standards, the secretary was directed to give . . . an appropriate consideration to technological feasibility and economic costs. . . ." [35].

In 1966 a severe air pollution episode accompanying a four-day inversion was thought to have contributed to the deaths of 80 persons. This incident occurred in the midst of a period of growing public sentiment for treating the problems of air pollution. The following year presented a further turning point in federal responsibilities toward air pollution. President Johnson proposed new legislation (the Air Quality Act of 1967), which, in essence, moved halfway toward complete federal jurisdiction over local air pollution issues. The Air Quality Act proposed the establishment of regional "airsheds," which were logical from the point of view of topography and meteorology but which cut across political jurisdictions. The act called for national emission standards for major industrial sources of pollution and for the establishment of regional commissions to act as enforcement agents. The regional commissions were to be federally staffed and federally financed.

This legislation became a matter of intense debate in both Houses of Congress during the ensuing 11 months. In this process a number of strong interests were reflected in alterations of the original bill. Ultimately, the standard-setting procedure was to involve both the states and the federal government. A clear federal responsibility was to derive scientific and technical criteria to be used in setting standards as well as to document the available control technologies for treating with each of the pollutants. Standards for sulfur oxides, a matter of severe contention because of the feared economic impact, were made somewhat less stringent. Beginning concern for fuel additives such as tetraethyl lead, was signaled by a requirement that they be registered. A matter of severe controversy was California's insistence on being permitted to set its own automotive emission standards if these were more stringent than those proposed by the federal government. Finally, in spite of a brief attempt to remove it to another administrative agency (and to a different congressional jurisdiction), the air pollution program remained firmly seated in the Public Health Service of HEW and, therefore, firmly anchored to health as its rationale.

The next stage in this evolution was most significant and continues to have profound impact on a broad swath of American institutions—public and private. Again, the center of the congressional stage was Senator Muskie and the Senate Public Works Committee. The rationale for the next legislature proposals was human health—farther out in front than ever before.

The legislation reported by the [Public Works] Committee is the result of deep concern for protection of the health of the American people. Air pollution is not only an aesthetic nuisance. The Committee's concern with direct adverse effects upon public health has increased since the publication of the air quality criteria documents for five major pollutants (oxides of sulfur, particulates, carbon monoxide, hydrocarbons and oxidants). These documents indicate that the air pollution problem is more severe, more pervasive, and growing at a more rapid rate than was generally believed [32].

Whether the documentation and facts reflected in the advisors' criteria documents really indicated these conclusions was to become a matter of turbulent controversy, which continues to the present time.

The Senate Committee sought changes in the legislation that would, in effect, realize a much accelerated program of control of air pollution over any contemplated in the past. It would do so with much more direct federal responsibility (or preemption). Again, protection of human health was the visible rationale. However, in this instance, the case for human health was held to be so important that it was portrayed as worthy of pursuit to the *exclusion of all other considerations*. It was this enforced, exclusive consideration of the human health effects of air pollutants that, more than anything else, set this legislative stage off from all others. It meant that matters of technological feasibility and economic cost, for example, were excluded from consideration in decision making.

In the Committee discussions, considerable concern was experienced regarding the use of technical feasibility as the basis of ambient air standards. The Committee determined that 1) the health of people is more important than the question of whether the early achievement of ambient air quality standards protective of health is technically feasible; and 2) the growth of pollution load in many areas, even with application of available technology, would still be deleterious to public health.

Therefore, the Committee determined that existing sources of pollutants either should meet the standard of the law or be closed down [32].

Note how the exclusivity of this approach contrasts sharply with the intent of previous legislation.

The Senate Committee had grown increasingly impatient with the slow pace at which states and localities had developed and implemented air pollution control plans. Thus, the new legislative initiative proposed that the federal government establish minimum national air quality standards primarily to protect health. The criterion of adequate protection was to take into account persons particularly sensitive or susceptible to air pollutants in the calculation of the standard. However, this description was left sufficiently vague as to remain a sizable problem in implementing the law. The individual states were to be permitted the opportunity to adopt more stringent standards than the federally established levels if they desired.

New precedents were set in other areas as well. The new act singled out certain classes of pollutants that might be expected to have an adverse effect upon public health. Industries emitting these substances were obliged to furnish the federal government with technical and monitoring information in order to prove to the government that the emission practices would not jeopardize human health. In essence, therefore, the burden of proof of demonstrating safety was for the first time shifted to the polluter. Note the parallel with the earlier evolution of the Food and Drug Laws.

It was in the case of the vehicular emission standards, however, where the most abrupt and far-reaching changes took place. Administrative discretion and flexibility were provided the secretary of HEW in all cases except for automotive emissions. Here, the new law was to reserve to Congress the setting of the numerical standards for what were believed to be the major emissions. Here, more clearly than in any other part of the act, the exclusivity of health as the driving issue was unequivocally laid out. The then-existing law required the secretary of HEW to establish automotive emission standards on the basis of economic and technological feasibility as well as endangerment of health and welfare. The proposed amendments struck out any reference to economic and technological feasibility and insisted that standards be established exclusively on the basis of the contribution to human health and welfare. The prior law gave administrative flexibility and discretion to the secretary of HEW in the setting of emission standards. The new law, however, was to reserve to Congress the setting of numerical standards for automobiles considered to be the major sources of emissions. The standards themselves, were set knowingly somewhat arbitrarily. It was felt that these would be kept in place for a few years, tested against new knowledge produced from any augmented research effort, and tested against the ingenuity and ability of industry to meet them. The actual numbers were derived from essentially two documents, a preliminary unpublished paper given in June 1970 at the annual meeting of the Air Pollution Control Association by HEW scientists [36], and an article published in *Science* [37]. The former of these two papers was a summary of the analyses done within the National Air Pollution Control Administration of HEW to determine proper levels of automotive emissions to reach desired ambient air levels according to the terms of the 1967 law. The authors had necessarily made a number of assumptions concerning the expected rate of growth of pollution sources including automobiles, desired margins of safety, rates of increase of new vehicles and obsolescence of old ones, etc. The authors considered as a starting point the worst-case municipal area of the country (Los Angeles) and determined that the national standards should be stringent enough to accommodate that city.

One of the most critical yet still least understood subjects was the relationship between emissions and ambient air levels. This relationship is inevitably a complex one, influenced by geographical features, meteorology, natural levels of certain of the pollutants, etc. In the absence of information, the relationship has been generally treated as a proportional one. This matter was to be the subject of repeated argument and debate as time passed [38, 39]. With these assumptions, HEW had recommended a series of auto emission goals and a set of standards to be put into effect by 1980. The new Senate legislation adopted these standards and their underlying analyses but moved their adoption to a target five years earlier than the HEW scientists had envisaged.

In spite of the severe departure this bill represented, no overwhelming organized opposition arose. Industry, which had opposed a strong set of national automobile exhaust standards over the years, argued that there was no suitable technological accommodation on the horizon to meet the projected standards. Within the executive branch, the mandatory character of the standards was seen by some as an example of bad public policy and the particular values were viewed as reflective of poor science [40]. Yet, there was little real opposition raised either from without or within. The public momentum toward a cleaner environment including cleaner air was overwhelmingly strong. There was scarcely even any systematic attempt to consider what the new law would mean in terms of administrative challenges.[e] Accordingly in 1970 a series of amendments to the Clean

---

[e] As it turned out, it was this law more than any other that pressed the new Environmental Protection Agency to its administrative and enforcement limit and that led to severe frustration between EPA and the White House over standards setting and enforcement.

Air Act were adopted that resembled in most respects the proposals of Senator Muskie of earlier that year.

What was clear was that the politicians had deliberately adopted what they had found in their interest to adopt from among the scientific findings of the time and had proceeded to build the most conservative case possible for the protection of human health. Although this was both a wise political move and did promise by a good margin to protect health, it became increasingly apparent with time that the positions chosen were not easily defended scientifically. Within the Environmental Protection Agency, for example, where the administration of this law came to rest, the standard-setting and enforcement groups looked to the scientific element for assistance. When these latter urged moderation and laid out what the scientific evidence justified, the lawyers were less than satisfied and, in the end, chose to ignore their scientific colleagues.

The ensuing years since passage of the Clean Air Act Amendments have reflected some of the frustrations over the 1970 law—reflective of a political instrument supposedly based on scientific understanding but, in fact, pushed ahead of the level of scientific evidence. Most of the controversy has surrounded the mandatory automobile emission standards. The controversy has arisen both from the particular values chosen and from the enforced narrowness of the considerations behind their choosing.

Thus, it was mainly frustration over the terms of the Clean Air Act and a flurry of memoranda from his cabinet secretaries during the summer of 1971 that led the president in 1971 to establish a "Quality of Life Review Process" in the Executive Office to insure a government-wide, prepublication review of important new standards and environmental decisions (see chapter 4). In early 1972 the Office of Science and Technology published a report aimed at documenting the combined costs to the public and to industry of accommodating the automotive safety regulations and the automotive emission regulations [41].

As the months wore on, pressures for decisions mounted on the automobile industry to declare if and how its members would obey the law and meet the technological challenge of the exhaust emission standards. The law allowed for one year's extension in the schedule. This was granted. Yet, the industry and others claimed that the statutory standards were technologically unreachable at any cost the public would consider reasonable. With pressure from their constituents, a number of senators and congressmen began to prevail upon Senator Muskie to reconsider the legislative position on the ambient air quality standards—and the emission standards. Senator Muskie eventually responded by asking the National Academy of Sciences to perform a review of the scientific basis for setting those standards. The first part of this exercise was completed in October 1973 with an open Conference on the Health Effects of Air Pollutants. It is interesting to note, as reflected in his remarks to this gathering, Senator

Muskie's continuted strong insistence on the exclusive issue of protection of human health [42].[f]

Finally, in late 1973 there was added to the question of costs the extra set of pressures of the energy crisis. Suddenly, it became important to know which of various transportation options would represent the least use of scarce fuel. Congress was forced to pass in review all of the environmentally related issues—many of which were by this time thought by some segments to have been partly *causative* of the fuel shortage. Among the most controversial was the catalyst exhaust device—considered the only possible technological method for meeting the exhaust emission standards. By this time scientists in EPA had discovered the more than theoretical possibility that the catalytic converters could in turn emanate measurable quantities of sulfates and metal particulates that might pose an even greater threat to health than the emissions they were designed to avoid [43]. This point was further reinforced by an independent report on the health effects of sulfur oxides [44]. While this point of view was proposed by the scientific element of EPA, the regulatory element refused to hear of it. While the executive office took note, EPA officially ignored it. As a result, in November 1973 the executive branch actually represented itself in hearings before the Senate Public Works Committee with *two opposing points of view*—one from EPA [45] and the other, an "official" administration view, from the Office of Management and Budget [46]. The subject was advice on the emission standards and their relationship to the use of gasoline.

Water Pollution

Most observers date the first federal legislation dealing with water pollution to an 1899 law that prohibited the dumping of refuse into navigable waters [47]. The intent of that law, however, was to prevent hazards to navigation, not to insure the cleanliness of bodies of water. It was only quite recently that this latter interpretation was extended to the original law.

Responsibilities for controlling water pollution were traditionally viewed as belonging to localities. The evolution of federal legal authority in this field reflected the evolution of federal preemption of local, state, and later regional responsibilities. The first federal legal authority aimed specifically at control and abatement of water pollution was in 1948 [48]. This was clearly a very tentative authority and one that was expressly

---

[f] A parallel, complementary study of the cost-benefit relationships in setting automotive emission standards was requested by an additional group of senators over the opposition of Senator Muskie.

subordinate to that of the states. The 1948 law deferred to the states for enforcement powers and offered federal loans for the construction of waste-treatment plants. This theme of federal financial assistance as the major source of federal leverage was to remain a common thread throughout much of the federal legislation in this area. The public works projects fostered during the New Deal had included many waste treatment plants. The fact that these had been eagerly accepted by states and localities made the passage of the 1948 law somewhat easier [49]. One final interesting point should be mentioned. The 1948 law authorized the surgeon general to assist states in their studies and efforts toward water pollution control. That is, at the outset, federal efforts at water pollution control were allied with a felt need to protect human health. However, this alliance was to be shifted later on—not because of a fundamental ideological shift but because of a change in political jurisdiction.

The 1948 law was a temporary authority. This was extended an additional three years in 1953 [4]. The final permanent federal program was enacted in 1956 [50]. This law provided federal grants for treatment plant contruction (when the previous law had provided only for loans). It provided for an augmented program of research and it provided a vehicle for enforcement of state and local standards. However, the spirit of states' rights was very strong. Hence, the pattern of enforcement was a cumbersome one and state consent was a necessary requisite for Federal court action.

A 1961 law [51] increased the level of the granting authority, further augmented the program of research and extended pollution abatement procedures to navigable *intrastate* and coastal waters. (Previous abatement procedures applied only to interstate waters.) However, the permission of owners was required before a federal enforcement suit could be brought to stop pollution activities in those waters [51].

The slow pace of achieving control of water pollution remained a matter of concern to some parts of Congress. In 1963 Senator Muskie introduced legislation that represented a marked departure from the past pattern in which the federal government generally had deferred to the states. The fact that pollution not infrequently crossed state boundaries and often required a broader or regional pattern of control became evident. At the same time, it became generally acknowledged that municipalities and states had been unable or unwilling to mobilize the resources and the systems to halt the increasing pollution of their waters. In the 1956 act, the two polar views, states' rights and federal power, both appear. Section 1 of that law declared that it was Congress' policy to ". . . enhance the quality and values of our water resources and to establish a national policy for the prevention, control and abatement of water pollution." The same law, however, maintained the traditional view that it was also Congress' policy "to recognize, preserve and protect the primary responsibilities and rights of the States in preventing and controlling water pollution" [50].

The 1965 Water Quality Act, for the first time, put the states on notice. This new law obliged the states to set standards for ambient water quality. In the face of their failure to do so, the secretary of HEW could establish the standards [52]. (Note the strong similarity to the evolving air pollution laws.) New enforcement mechanisms were created. However, in the case of pollution of intrastate waters, the federal government was obliged to await the request of the state before proceeding to an "abatement conference."

The following year saw the enactment of a further piece of legislation, the Clean Water Restoration Act of 1966 [53]. This new law authorized a large new infusion of federal funds for the construction of waste treatment facilities (although the appropriations fell far short of the amounts authorized). A second significant event occurred in 1966. This was the transfer by executive order of the responsibility for administration of the water pollution control program from the Department of Health, Education, and Welfare to the Department of the Interior. Up to this point, health had been the prime mover and the major rationale for water pollution control. By 1965 it had become evident that the case for cleaner water could not be made on the basis of protection of human health and some felt that the pace of pollution control was slowed *because* of its alliance with the health issue [31]. Within less than half a year, however, this arrangement was rendered moot by a presidential reorganization plan that transferred the new water pollution control administration out of HEW to the Department of Interior.[g]

In parallel with and about the same time as the jurisdictional battles were being fought within the executive branch, Congress was fanning its own jurisdictional conflicts. While there have been few forays into the territory of the Muskie Subcommittee on Air and Water Pollution on the Senate side, there have been efforts to treat pollution control in different ways on the House side. Representative Emilio Daddario, beginning in 1965, held a series of hearings in which pollution was treated as an ecological rather than a health problem. From this he argued that the Department of the Interior should be the lead agency in the coordination of all federal pollution control programs. By 1968 an alliance had been forged between Representative Daddario and Senator Henry Jackson and the two advocated the establishment of a joint congressional committee on

---

[g] Actually, this was simply one of a long series of reorganizations and administrative shifts in the federal water pollution control authority within the executive branch. These were inevitably disruptive and contributed to serious discontinuities. The shift in 1966 also provoked the loss of large numbers of key scientific personnel from this program [48].

the environment. (This proposal eventually served as the basis for an additional one—establishing a Council on Environmental Quality in the Executive Office of the President.) As has been pointed out [31], these moves were directed in part against the alliance of pollution with the issue of health and favoring a move to the Department of the Interior. It was this shift of emphasis that was so marked in the case of water pollution that was not found in the case of air pollution where health has remained the unequivocal rationale.

There were amendments added in 1970 to confront specific problems such as the cleanup of oil discharges, control of sewage from vessels, and cooperation from federal agencies in the control of water pollution. The most far-reaching moves, however, came in legislation drafted by Senator Muskie's committee in 1971 and passed ultimately in 1972. What had been the Federal Water Pollution Control Administration of the Interior Department had undergone a further bureaucratic shift to the new Environmental Protection Agency in 1970. The rationale for water cleanup remained fairly disassociated from health protection. There remained the traditional dissatisfaction with the pace of achieving control of water pollution.

Under the 1965, water quality standards were to be set as the control mechanism. States were to decide the uses of water to be protected, the kinds and amounts of pollutants to be permitted, the degree of pollution abatement to be required, the time to be allowed a polluter for abatement.

The water quality standards program is limited in its success. After five years, many States do not have approved standards. Officials are still working to establish relationships between pollutants and water uses. Time schedules for abatement are slipping away because of failure to enforce, lack of effluent controls, and disputes over Federal-State standards [54].

The fundamental shift in policy this legislation represented was away from the concept of ambient water quality standards and towards one of standards and controls for sources or effluents. It would no longer be necessary to understand and document the relationship between effluent or sources of pollution and ambient levels of pollution. The new bill simply prohibited or controlled effluents. The prohibition of discharges was tempered by arranging for the prohibition to occur over a period of time and in stages. The first phase was qualified by the limitation of "best practicable technology." The second phase, to be accomplished by 1981, was to be limited only by the best *available* technology [55]. Thus, costs and considerations of benefits were effectively eliminated as was protested by Office of Science and Technology in a highly unusual paper delivered to the Senate Public Works Committee [56]. As the debate was presented to the Congress by its advocates, the rationale for water cleanup was partly, although by no means entirely, related to issues of health. Thus, Senator Muskie's speech during the debate on the bill on November 2, 1971 related both to mercury as a human health hazard and to the extinction of a variety of lower organisms as a result of oil spills [57].

References

1. Wilson, S. *Food and Drug Regulation*, American Council on Public Affairs, Washington, D.C. 1942.
2. Anderson, O.E., Pioneer Statute: The Pure Food and Drug Act of 1906, in the Government and the Consumer: Evolution of Food and Drug Laws, *Emory University J. of Public Law*, 13: 189-196, 1964.
3. Young, J.H., The 1938 Food, Drug and Cosmetic Act, in the Government and the Consumer: Evolution of Food and Drug Laws, *Emory University J. of Public Law*, 13: 197-204, 1964.
4. Janssen, W.F., FDA Since 1938. The Major Trends and Developments in the Government and the Consumer: Evolution of Food and Drug Laws, *Emory University J. of Public Law*, 13: 205-221, 1964.
5. Jackson, C.O., *Food and Drug Legislation in the New Deal*, Princeton University Press, Princeton, N.J., 1970.
6. Harris, R., *The Real Voice*, Macmillan Company, New York, 1964.
7. Bermon, A., Drug Control in Nineteenth-Century France: Antecedents and Directions,; Blake, J.B., ed., *Safeguarding the Public Historical Aspects of Medicinal Drug Control*, The Johns Hopkins Press, Baltimore, Maryland, 1968.
8. Bouvet, M., Un remède secret du XVIIIème siecle: le rob Boyveau-L.affecteur, *Bull. Soc. Hist. Pharm.*, no. 39, June 1923, 264-272.
9. Stieb, E.W., Drug Control in Britain, 1850-1914 in Blake, J.B., ed., *Safeguarding the Public—Historical Aspects of Medicinal Drug Control*, The Johns Hopkins Press, Baltimore, Maryland, 1968.
10. Trousseau, A., *Clinique medicale de l'Hotel-Dieu de Paris*, 5th ed., 3 vols. Paris, Baillière, 1877.
11. Ackerknecht, E.H., *Medicine at the Paris Hospital*, 1794-1848, The Johns Hopkins Press, Baltimore, 1967.
12. Burrow, J.G., The Prescription—Drug Policies of the American Medical Association in the Progressive Era, in Blake, J.B., ed., *Safeguarding the Public—Historical Aspects of Medicinal Drug Control*, The Johns Hopkins Press, Baltimore, Maryland, 1968.
13. Johnson vs. United States, 221 U.S. 488 (1911).

14. Young, J.H., Drugs and the 1906 Law, in Blake, J.B., ed., *Safeguarding the Public—Historical Aspects of Medicinal Drug Control*, The Johns Hopkins Press, Baltimore, Maryland, 1968.

15. Special Report of the Work on the Council on Pharmacy and Chemistry, *J. American Medical Association*, 65: 69-70, 1915.

16. National Academy of Sciences, Drug Efficacy Study.

17. Cavers, D.F., The Evolution of the Contemporary System of Drug Regulation under the 1938 Act. in Blake, J.B., ed., *Safeguarding the Public—Historical Aspects of Medicinal Drug Control*, The Johns Hopkins Press, Baltimore, Maryland, 1968.

18. *National Commission on Product Safety—Final Report*, presented to the President and Congress, June 1970, U.S. Government Printing Office, Washington, D.C.

19. Consumer Product Safety Act, P.C. 92-573, 86 Stat. 1207, October 27, 1972.

20. Product Safety Legislation [Committee Print No. 3], March 21, 1972, Consumer Safety Act of 1972.

21. S. 3419, Food, Drug, and Consumer Product Safety Act of 1972, March 24, 1972.

22. Gardner, J., Consumer Report/Congressional Battle over FDA Control Focuses on Product Safety Legislation, *National Journal*, June 10, 1972, pp. 987-997.

23. *Consumer Safety Act of 1972*, Report of the Senate Committee on Commerce on S. 3419, Senate Report No. 92-749, April 13, 1972.

24. P.L. 92-573, Consumer Product Safety Act, October 27, 1972.

25. Letter from Elliot L. Richardson, secretary of the Department of Health, Education, and Welfare, to Senator Warren G. Magnuson, January 20, 1972.

26. Memorandum from Charles C. Edwards, commissioner of the Food and Drug Administration, to the secretary of the Department of Health, Education, and Welfare, October 11, 1972.

27. Memorandum from Edward E. David, Jr., science adviser to Lewis A. Engmen, assistant director, Domestic Council, White House, June 20, 1972.

28. Letter from Philip Handler, president, National Academy of Sciences, to Representative Paul G. Rogers, July 19, 1972.

29. *Consumerism and the Legislative Response*, Robert P. Mullen and Company, Washington, D.C., November 2, 1972.

30. The White House, Fact Sheet on Reorganization Plans No. 3 and 4, July 9, 1970.

31. Davies, J.C., III, *The Politics of Pollution*, Pegasus, New York, 1970.
32. *National Air Quality Standards Act of 1970*, Report of the Committee on Public Works, United States Senate, to accompany S. 4358, Report No. 91-1196, September 17, 1970.
33. Nelson, N., Concluding remarks offered to the Conference on Health Effects of Air Pollutants, National Academy of Sciences, Washington, D.C., October 5, 1973.
34. *Steps Toward Clean Air*, Report to the Committee on Public Works, United States Senate, from the Special Subcommittee on Air and Water Pollution, October 1964.
35. *Clean Air Act Amendments and Solid Waste Disposal Act*, Report to accompany S. 306. Senate Report No. 192, May 14, 1965.
36. Barth, D.S., Romonovsky, J.C., Schuck, E.A., and Cernansky, N.P., Federal Motor Vehicle Emission Goals for CO, HC, and NO_x Based on Desired Air Quality Levels, Presented at the Annual Meeting of the Air Pollution Control Association, June 1970.
37. Lave, L.B., and Seskin, E.B., Air Pollution and Human Health, *Science*, 169-723, 1970.
38. NAS documents on relation between auto emission standards and ambient air levels.
39. EPA critique of NAS documents.
40. Memorandum from S.W. Gouse, Jr. to Edward E. David, Jr., director, Office of Science and Technology, Executive Office of the President, October 9, 1970.
41. *Cumulative Regulatory Effects on the Cost of Automotive Transportation (RECAT)*, Final Report of the Ad Hoc Committee, Office of Science and Technology, Executive Office of the President, Washington, D.C., February 28, 1972.
42. Muskie, E., Remarks presented to the Conference on Health Effects of Air Pollutants, National Academy of Sciences, Washington, D.C., October 3, 1973.
43. *Probable Public Health Impact of Equipping Light Duty Motor Vehicles with Oxidation Catalysts*, Environmental Protection Agency, November 14, 1973.
44. Rall, D.P., *A Review of the Health Effects of Sulfur Oxides*, Department of Health, Education, and Welfare, October 9, 1973.
45. Train, R.E., Testimony before the Senate Public Works Committee.
46. Sawhill, J., Testimony before the Senate Public Works Committee.
47. Rivers and Harbors Act, 1899, 30 Stat. 1152.

48. Water Pollution Control Act, 1948, P.L. 80-845.

49. P.L. 82-579.

50. Water Pollution Control Act, Amendments of 1956, P.L. 84-660.

51. P.L. 87-88, 1961.

52. Water Quality Act, P.L. 89-234, 1965.

53. Clean Water Restoration Act, P.L. 89-753, 1966.

54. *Federal Water Pollution Control Act Amendment of 1971*, Report from the Senate Committee on Public Works, Report No. 92-414, October 28, 1971.

55. Federal Water Pollution Control Act Amendments of 1972, P.L. 92-500, October 18, 1972.

56. Environmental and Economic Benefits and Costs Related to Various Water Pollution Abatement Strategies, Comments on the Federal Water Pollution Control Act Amendment of 1971, Office of Science and Technology, Executive Office of the President, November 1, 1971.

57. Senate Debate on S. 2770, November 2, 1971.

3 What is the Case for Regulation?

The particular class of government regulation discussed in this work is that intended principally to protect human health. The question, what case can be made for regulation, has in fact two parts: One concerns the impact of environmental influences on human morbidity and mortality, the avoidance of which would relieve the populace of at least some of that burden. The second part of the question follows from the first. Given an identifiable contribution of environmental influences to his ill health, what should one expect from government regulation as a particular instrument in intervening or avoiding harmful environmental influences. For example, we have consented to regulation of known or implied hazards to which we might otherwise be exposed involuntarily. For those numerous exposures to which we willingly and knowingly submit on a voluntary basis, we have generally refrained or even carefully avoided government intervention.

Contribution of the Environment to Human Ill Health and Mortality

If one examines the contribution of environmental factors (in the broad sense) to ill health in the industrialized world today, one finds a striking and compelling case to be made. There is, in brief, a large impact to be found of environmental (and social) influences on human morbidity and mortality. The opportunity, of course, afforded by the exercise of identifying specific environmental influences is the opportunity of prevention—inevitably less costly and more effective than later treatment.

In 1967 Dr. William Forbes attempted an analysis of the relationship between national health expenditures (most all of which go to personal health services) and health. His conclusions (for a period when the health expenditure was only $44 billion) was that: ". . . in the United States there is no longer any significant relationship between the money spent on health and the results achieved" [1].

One of the principal reasons given for this phenomenon was the sizeable contribution made to human mortality and morbidity by environmental conditions and social habits generally not of concern to traditional clinical medicine). More recently (and with an annual expenditure for

37

DEATH RATES IN THE UNITED STATES, 1900 - 1960

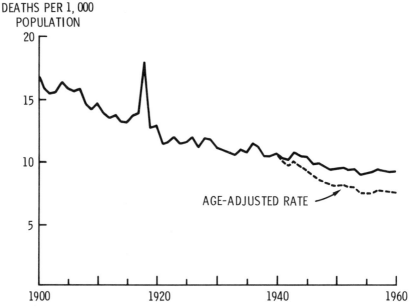

Source: Various reports of the National Office of Vital Statistics, and Burger, E.J. "Regulation and Health: How Solid is Our Foundation?" *Environmental Law Reporter*, 5, September, 1975: 50179-50187, Copyright © 1975, Environmental Law Institute.

Figure 3-1. Death Rates in the United States, 1900-60

health exceeding $100 billion), others have made similar observations [2, 3]. In 1974 the minister of Health and Welfare in Canada, Dr. Marc LaLonde, issued a frank and forthright statement on the same subject. His report pointed to the necessity for dealing with certain major and influential environmental and social influences on health if the Canadian people truly desired to make further improvements on their health status [4].

Americans (and, indeed, inhabitants of the industrialized Western world) have become used to a pattern of declining death rates over the years—even to the point, perhaps, of taking this trend for granted. Indeed, for the United States, overall death rates have declined and continued to do so through the first half of the twentieth century (figure 3-1). However, there are two phenomenon of significance that occurred during this time. On the one hand there was a shift in the patterns of causes of death. In the early years of this century, the leading causes of death were diseases caused by infectious processes including pneumonia and tuberculosis. In 1900, for example, each of those diseases accounted for 10 percent of all deaths (table 3-1). Cardiovascular diseases caused 14 percent of

Table 3-1
Leading Causes of Death in the United States, 1900 and 1960

Rank	Cause of Death	Deaths per 100,000 Pop.	Percent of All Deaths
	1900		
1	Pneumonia and influenza	202.2	11.8%
2	Tuberculosis (all forms)	194.4	11.3
3	Gastritis, etc.	142.7	8.3
4	Diseases of the heart	137.4	8.0
5	Vascular lesions affecting the CNS	106.9	6.2
6	Chronic nephritis	81.0	4.7
7	All accidents[a]	72.3	4.2
8	Malignant neoplasms (cancer)	64.0	3.7
9	Certain diseases of early infancy	62.6	3.6
10	Diphtheria	40.3	2.3
	All causes	1,719	100
	Total		64%
	1960		
1	Diseases of the heart	366.4	38.7
2	Malignant neoplasms (cancer)	147.4	15.6
3	Vascular lesions affecting the CNS	107.3	11.3
4	All accidents[b]	51.9	5.5
5	Certain diseases of early infancy	37.0	3.9
6	Pneumonia and influenza	36.0	3.5
7	General arteriosclerosis	20.3	2.1
8	Diabetes mellitus	17.1	1.8
9	Congenital malformations	12.0	1.3
10	Cirrhosis of the liver	11.2	1.2
	All causes	946	100
	Total		85%

Source: Burger, E.J. "Regulation and Health: How Solid is Our Foundation?" *Environmental Law Reporter,* 5, September, 1975: 50179-50187, Copyright © 1975, Environmental Law Institute.

[a]Violence would add 1.4 percent; horse, vehicle, and railroad accidents provide 0.8 percent.

[b]Violence would add 1.5 percent; motor vehicle accidents provide 2.3 percent; railroad accidents provide less than 0.1 percent.

the deaths in the United States and cancer caused less than 4 percent. By 1960 influenza and pneumonia were the only infectious diseases ranking in the top 10 causes of death (together less than 4 percent in 1969), while diseases of the heart were responsible for over 39 percent of all deaths,[a] and cancer for over 15 percent. It is significant that these increases were substantially greater than could be accounted for by the decreases in deaths from infectious diseases. The role of chronic degenerative diseases to morbidity and mortality has become increasingly important.

[a] Most recently, some evidence has emerged that suggests a decline in deaths from cardiovascular diseases [5].

Table 3-2
Principal Contributors to Rise in Mortality in 1967 Compared with 1960 for White Males

Cause of Death	Percentage Increase in Deaths, 1967 versus 1960
Carcinoma of the lung	22.9
Carcinoma, other, unspecified	14.2
Circulatory, other	17.0
Bronchitis	39.3
Bronchopneumonia, other	39.4
Cirrhosis	15.3
Motor vehicle accidents	14.6
Homicide	30.1

Source: Burger, E.J. "Regulation and Health: How Solid is Our Foundation?" *Environmental Law Reporter*, 5, September, 1975: 50179-50187, Copyright © 1975, Environmental Law Institute.

Note: Diseases and conditions shown are those for which the number of extra deaths comprise more than 10 percent of the total deaths from that cause.

At the same time that a shift occurred in the relative ranking of the major causes of mortality there occurred an important change in mortality rates. The trend of decreasing death rates, characteristic of the first half of the twentieth century, was interrupted in the decade of the 1950s by a flattening of the curve representing changes in age specific death rates for various age groups. In the case of males, the curve plateaued and then, in the early 1960s, changed sign and turned upward again [6, 7, 8]. (See figure 3-1.) An examination of the major contributors to the mortality, which was *in excess* of that expected from the earlier trends, leads to a number of interesting conditions. The list of diseases leading to this excess mortality, includes lung cancer, othr forms of cancer, bronchitis, cirrhosis of the liver, motor vehicle accidents, and homicide [6]. These are conditions recognized as heavily related to two groups of environmental factors—smoking and various forms of air pollution and the use of alcohol (table 3-2). That is, the health of the nation has been heavily infringed upon by what we do to eath other and what we do to ourselves—sometimes unknowingly and often knowingly.

Types of Evidence

The class of diseases known collectively as cancer is illustrative and interesting in this context. There is some evidence from laboratory experiments to draw upon concerning the carcinogenic properties of chemicals and ionizing radiation. Further, there is some useful and illuminating experience from specific exposure in occupational settings such as nickel

MORTALITY FROM ALL CAUSES
AND FROM CANCER, UNITED STATES, 1900-1960

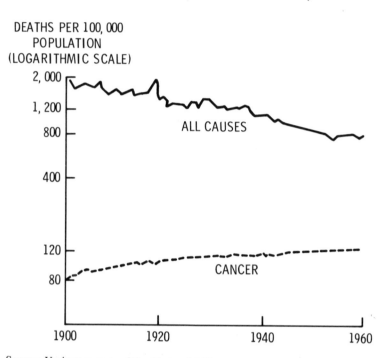

DEATHS PER 100, 000
POPULATION
(LOGARITHMIC SCALE)

Source: Various reports of the National Office of Vital Statistics.

Note: Rates since 1949 have been adjusted to the fifth revision of the "International List of Diseases and Causes of Death."

Figure 3-2. Mortality from All Causes and from Cancer, United States, 1900-60

carbonyl or dibenzanthracene. However, many of the clues to the existence of human chemical carcinogens have come indirectly and inferentially.[b] Mortality is almost always used as a surrogate measure for ill health. Morbidity statistics are highly unreliable and are difficult to use in comparative studies.

Recording of the fact of death is done with much greater reliability and care than for morbidity and cause of death is usually noted according to a reasonably standardized scheme.

Figure 3-2 shows a relative rise in mortality from cancer over with

[b] At the present writing, there are less than 20 specific chemicals singled out and confirmed as human carcinogens.

NUMBER OF DEATHS FROM CANCER OF ALL SITES, U. S. DEATH REGISTRATION AREA OF 1900, 1909-60

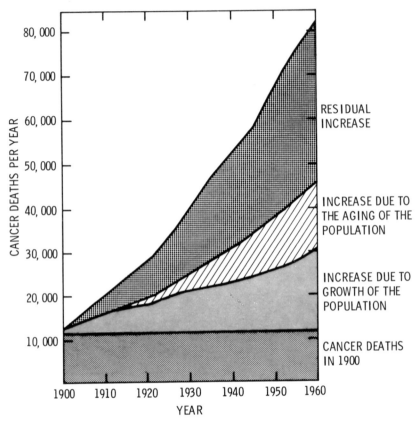

Source: *Cancer Rates and Risks*, Public Health Service Publication No. 1148

Figure 3-3. Number of Deaths from Cancer of All Sites, U.S. Death Registration Area of 1900, 1909-60

time. This suggests, perhaps, that cancer has simply "taken the place" of other causes of death. In fact, there appears to have been an *absolute* increase in cancer deaths since 1900, which cannot be explained entirely by the increase in the size and age of the population (figure 3-3).

There have been changes with time of death rates from cancer of various organ sites. The lung cancer epidemic is the most prominent. Not all cancers have risen. Deaths from stomach cancer have declined dramatically in the past 40 years. Similarly, carcinoma of the cervix of the uterus

CANCER MORTALITY IN
JAPAN AND THE UNITED STATES BY SITE, 1958-1959
AGE-ADJUSTED DEATH RATES

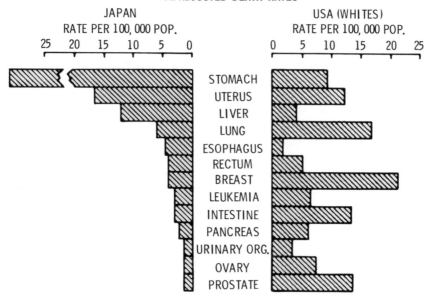

Source: Segi, M., and Kurihara, M., Cancer Mortality from Selected Sites in 29 Countries, Japan Cancer Society, Tokyo, Japan, 1962.

Figure 3-4. Age-adjusted Death Rates by Site of Cancer, Japan and United States, White Population, 1958-59

has declined in the United States. Cancer of the breast, ovary, brain, and kidney in addition to leukemia have all risen.

There are striking geographic variations in cancer mortality and these, too, are evidence of the influence of environmental factors. Figure 3-4 illustrates the variation in cancer mortality of various types of cancer in the United States and in Japan. While the total mortality rate from cancer is approximately the same for the two countries, there are striking differences for cancers of various organ systems. Cancer of the stomach is more than five times as common in Japan as in the United States while cancer of the breast, ovary, and intestine are more than five times as common in the United States as in Japan.

There are areas of the world in which the incidence of cancer of the esophagus is more than 100 times as frequent as it is in the United States.

Cancer rates for cancer of the breast, the colon, and the prostate show variations of 10- to 30-fold from country to country.

Recently, an extensive analysis of geographic variation of cancer mortality has been made on a county-by-county basis in the United States [10]. This analysis of 20 years of experience (1950-69) revealed a number of interesting patterns and associations. For example, strong associations with urban residence was found for cancer of the nasopharynx, larynx, colon, and rectum. Mortality from malignant melonoma is progressively more likely the farther south one moves in latitude (presumably related to exposure to sunlight). Most recently a study was made of the relationship between cancer mortality rates for various residential locations and industrial activity. The apparent associations between these two are provocative and may indeed suggest important determents of chronic degenerative disease [11].

Some of the most striking evidence of all, perhaps, has come from studies of persons who migrate from one part of the world to take up residence in another. There have been by now several observations confirming differences in cancer mortality between native and foreign-born populations in the United States [12]. The series of investigations known as the migrant studies, have revealed, on the average, if one moves from one part of the world to another, one tends to close the risk of cancer characteristic of his original home and adopt the pattern characteristic of his new home [13]. Again, the implication that it is "something" in the environment that has led to the observed alterations in disease and mortality patterns is a very strong one indeed.[c]

The case for intervening in hazardous environmental exposures, indeed, is a compelling one. This collective impact is more than modest. In this picture, certain particular factors stand out sharply. One is the contribution of cigarette smoking. A large fraction of the rise in cancer mortality is accounted for by an epidemic of lung cancer. By far, the single most prominent contributor to lung cancer is cigarette smoking. For example, at this writing, the figures for lung cancer and mortality from lung cancer for women are beginning to creep up toward those for men. With a 20-year latent period for lung cancer, these figures most probably reflect the rise in smoking among women that became increasingly evident two decades ago. It has been estimated that 17 percent of all deaths that occurred in 1967 were linked to cigarette smoking—a total of 300,000 deaths.

Of corresponding importance to health is the use of alcohol and the combination of alcohol and automobile driving. (Approximately half of

[c] Striking geographic variations in incidence and mortality from coronary heart disease have now also been identified [14]. In addition, migrant studies have shown similar shifts in risk with changes in domicile for coronary heart disease and stroke [15].

the accidental deaths associated with motor vehicles include alcohol as a significant factor.) These are examples of identified, serious, and technically preventable environmental influences. Typically, man exposes himself voluntarily to these with full knowledge of the probable consequences.

As well, there clearly occur from time to time accidental or unexpected exposures of certain groups to harmful materials. In 1968 in Fuokuoka, Japan, there occurred a leakage in a heat exchange in a system used to sterilize rice oil used as cooking oil. The fluid that leaked out of the heat exchanges into the oil was a mixture of the families of chemicals known as polychlornated biphenyls. The resulting illness among those who ingested the rice oil became well known [17, 18].

A large number of specific, relatively high-level toxic exposures have by now been recognized in industrial situations (although in many cases not without a great deal of searching and prior intelligence.

Much more difficult is the challenge of ascertaining the implications for health of small or trace quantities of substances found in processed foods and in the generally community environment. Their biological effects are subtle, may be important, and are characteristically very different to study directly. These are lower level exposures—sometimes of long-term or chronic duration—to substances such as pesticide residues, food additives, or air pollutants. Since the exposures or doses are typically small, their effects are easily confounded with those due to other materials to which man is exposed.

Statistically, the resulting observations in health may be low or improbable. However improbable, the biological implications may be quite serious—especially for chronic degenerative diseases.

Ionizing radiation has been known since the time of Mme. Curie to be causally associated with cancers of various types. Because the atmospheres of uranium mines were known to exhibit high radon levels and because elevated lung cancer rates began to appear among uranium miners, a study was begun in 1957 to determine the relationship between the incidence of lung cancer among uranium miners and radon measurements in the mine atmospheres. The key to this study was a life-table analysis of mortality statistics [19]. This analysis compared the expected pattern of mortality of miners in the Colorado Plateau area with the observed incidence of lung cancer mortality for various levels of accumulated uranium mine atmosphere exposures. This study required observations on 5,000 miners from 1950 to until 1968. An essential part of this study was the identifying of the particular role of uranium mine atmosphere exposure as a contributor to lung cancer over and above that cuased by cigarette smoking.

A second example has been in the realm of insecticide residues on food crops. The spraying of fruit and vegetables with antifungal and antiinsect chemical materials has always been accompanied by a fear that the residues of these chemicals would persist on the plants through their preparation for human consumption and that their residues would be hazardous to human health. These anxieties were generally well-founded for early generations of insecticides that were often acutely toxic. The advent of chlorinated hydrocarbon type insecticides such as DDT brought new problems and new uncertainties. For one thing, the residence time or persistence of these new materials was much longer than that of the older types. Further, because of their high lipid solubility, if introduced into the animal organism, they would tend to deposit themselves in the fatty tissues and remain there for very long periods. With repeated, although low-level exposures, accumulations over time of residues could be expected.

With this background, a study was initiated in 1965 to determine how widespread the accumulations in human tissues were, how large were accumulations in the fat depots, and what, if any, associations there were between these chemical residues and biological effects, including manifest disease. This study, known as the Community Pesticide Study, gathered evidence of pesticide exposures and accumulation of pesticide residues from biopsy specimens taken from surgical material and from autopsy examinations. This surveillance has run for nine years and has included observations on large numbers of subjects. There has accumulated a sizable fund of information on exposures and residues but, as yet, no clear evidence of any relationship between pesticide accumulation (for the pesticides considered) and human disease.

A third example is that of polycyclic hydrocarbons. Complex, polycyclic organic material has been associated with various forms of cancer in laboratory animals and in certain occupational settings for many years. A question has arisen as to the place of polycyclic hydrocarbons contained in the atmosphere—especially urban atmospheres—in the causation of or the contribution to human lung cancer. The answer remains elusive. The National Academy of Sciences, after an extensive review of this subject in 1972 concluded from epidemiological evidence that, while cigarette smoking was a ". . . major factor in the causation of lung cancer in man, it does not account completely for the increased incidence of this disease. . . . It appears, then, there is an 'urban factor' in the pathogenesis of lung cancer in man" [20]. Again, a major element in this judgment was the separation of the complex of factors associated with dwelling in an urban area from a large influence of cigarette smoking [20].

Again, major air pollution episodes as in Donora, Pennsylvania or London, England have been associated with measurable increases in accelerated mortality among those who have impaired cardio respiratory function. Typically these are discrete, sometimes tragic, but self-limited events. It is more difficult to judge the implications of low levels of gaseous and particulate matter in the general community atmosphere.

Those exposures we have consented to bring under regulation are not uncommonly of the latter variety—low in level, frequent or constant in occurrance, responsible for subtle and improbable biological effects. Notably, these are exposures to which we submit *involuntarily*. The case for regulation, then, is a complicated one. The exposures and the resulting efforts on health may not necessarily rank among the most serious of environmental influences. However, they typically are involuntary exposures and we have set our social threshold for these at a higher level than we have for voluntary hazards.

The distinct messages from this examination are the following:

1. There are, without question, contributions made by environmental chemical and physical agents to human ill health, including mortality.

2. Under conditions of sufficiently high doses, biological effects can be exhibited. (These are not uncommonly the conditions of the experimental laboratory.)

3. There have occurred from time to time a number of distinct, generally high-level, accidental human exposures where cause and effect relationships between the exposure and a disease condition were often demonstrable.

4. Occupational environments are often the settings for relatively high-level exposures to chemical and physical agents.

5. Apart from the above, much of the relationship between involuntary exposures to environmental substances and human ill health of the general population is of a subtle character. This is not meant to detract from the social importance of these hazards but only to point out the relative difficulty in defining their magnitude since they are in many cases dwarfed by substances to which man voluntarily exposes himself and are made manifest only by the most painstaking and indirect of experimental observations.

References

1. Forbes, W.H., Longevity and Medical Costs, *New England Journal of Medicine*, 277: 71-78, 1967.

2. Burger, E.J., Jr., Health and Health Services in the United States, A Perspective and a Discussion of Some Issues, *Annals of Internal Medicine*, 80: 645-650, 1974.

3. Fuchs, V., *Who Shall Live*, Basic Books, New York, 1975.

4. Lalonde, M., A New Perspective on the Health of Canadians, A Working Document, Minister of National Health and Welfare, Ottawa, Canada, 1974.

5. Walker, W.J., Coronary Mortality: What is Going On? *J. American Medical Assn.*, 227: 1045-1046, 1974.

6. National Center for Health Statistics, *Leading Components of Upturn in Mortality of Men: United States, 1952-1967*, Vital and Health Statistics, Series 20- No. 11, DHEW Pub. No. (HSM) 72-1008, Health Services and Mental Health Administration, Washington, D.C., U.S. Government Printing Office, September 1971.

7. National Center for Health Statistics, *Mortality Trends, Age, Color, and Sex, United States, 1950-1969*, Vital and Health Statistics, Series 20-No. 15, Health Resources Administration, Rockville, Md., November 1973.

8. National Center for Health Statistics, *Mortality Trends for Leading Causes of Death: United States, 1950-1969*, Vital and Health Statistics, Series 20-No. 16, Health Resources Administration, DHEW, Rockville, Md.

9. Rall, D.P., A Review of the Health Effects of Sulfur Oxides, Submitted by the secretary of HEW to OMB, October 9, 1973.

10. Hoover, R. Mason, T.J., McKay, F.W., and Fraumini, J.F., *Geographic Patterns of Cancer Mortality for U.S. Counties*, Epidemiology Branch, National Cancer Institute, National Institutes of Health, Bethesda, Maryland, 1975.

11. Hoover, R., and Fraumeni, J.F., Jr., Cancer Mortality in U.S. Counties with Chemical Industries, *Environmental Research*, 9:196-207, 1975.

12. Lilienfeld, A.M., Levin, M.L., *Cancer in the United States*, Cambridge, Mass., Harvard University Press, 1972, 546 pp.

13. Haenszel, W., ed., *Epidemiological Approaches to the Study of Cancer and Other Chronic Diseases*, National Cancer Institute, Monograph No. 19, Washington, D.C., U.S. Government Printing Office, 1966.

14. Gordon, T., Garcia-Palmieri, M.R., Kogan, A., Kannel, W.B., and Schiffman, Differences in Coronary Heart Diseases in Framingham, Honolulu and Puerto Rico. *J. Chronic Disease*, 27: 329-344, 1974.

15. Kagan, A., Harris, B.R., Winkelstein, W., Jr., Johnson, K.G., Kato, H., Syme, S.L., Rhoads, G.G., Gay, M.C., Nichman, M.Z., Hamilton, H.B., and Tillotson, Jr., Epidemiologic Studies of Coronary Heart Disease and Stroke in Japanese Men Living in Japan, Hawaii and California: Demographic, Physical, Dietary and Biochemical Characteristics, *J. Chron. Dis.*, 27: 345-364, 1974.

16. *Chemicals and Health*, Report of the Panel on Chemicals and Health of the President's Science Advisory Committee, National Science Foundation, Washington, D.C., September 1973.

17. Tskamoto, H., Makisumi, S., Hirose, H., et al. The Chemical Studies of Toxic Compound in the Rice Bran Oils Used by the Patients of Yusho, *Fukuoka Acta Medica*, 60: 496-512, 1969.

18. Polychlorinated biphenyls—Environmental Impact, A Review by the Panel on Hazardous Trace Substances, *Environmental Research* 5: 249-362, 1972.

19. *Uranium Miners*, Report to the National Academy of Sciences, National Research Counsel, Division of Medical Sciences, Ad hoc Advisory Committee to the Federal Radiation Council, Washington, D.C., January 27, 1971.

20. *Particulate Polycyclic Organic Matter. Biologic Effects of Atmospheric Pollutant*. Committee on Biological Effects of Atmospheric Pollutants, National Academy of Sciences, Washington, D.C., 1972.

4

What Is in the Public's Best Interest?

An answer to the question, what is in the public's best interest, is a point central to the regulatory enterprise. What segment of the public is to be protected? How much protection or safety is sufficient or desirable? Should health be considered exclusively as a public interest by itself, or should it be weighed or balanced alongside other public desires? When do the interests of protection of the public from hazards outweigh the public desires of freedom of choice such as the freedom to use or eat some product?

All regulatory decisions of any consequence (including nondecisions) will leave some parties affected and aggrieved. Most often cited on the opposite side of the balance sheet from health is the economic impact of regulation. Although given somewhat less notice publically, standards and regulations, on occasion, have also led to the exchange of one type of hazard for another.

There are a number of public policy issues implicitly affected by regulatory patterns. However, many of these issues have not been explicitly considered or have not been systematically treated in the development of legislation or in its subsequent administration. Hence, there have emerged some inconsistencies, several unsettled but important public policy questions, and something of a mosaic of presumptions as to what serves the public interest best.

Because of the complexity of the issues and because of the heterogeneous character of the nation's populace and of its interests, it is unlikely that simple answers will be satisfactory. Yet, since this question of proper emphasis in behalf of the public interest is so important and because it is, at heart, a political issue, it deserves a more systematic and a better informed public consideration.

Philosophy and Meaning of Risk (and Risk Taking)

The laws (that is, Congress) have treated the subject of the proper philosophy of risk taking at different times for various settings and for various substances. The food and drug laws, as they have evolved, have focused increasingly on the issue of human health and safety alongside the earlier issues of purity and avoidance of fraud. Although some members of Congress from time to time have urged that preservation of health be treated as an exclusive issue, the laws themselves and the agencies that administer them acknowledge (although sometimes weakly) the existence of other issues. The risk philosophy governing the federal laws dealing with occupational safety and health standards permit generally higher level exposures in the case of occupational workers than for members of the general population. The Clean Air Act, as has been seen, insists on the exclusiveness of the issue of human health and requires that automobile emissions and primary air quality standards be set to protect fully the public's health. In part, it is the exclusiveness of this charter of protection of health (to the exclusion, that is, of other considerations) that makes it particularly difficult to fulfill. In addition, however, there remain some overwhelming uncertainties that stand in the way of any clear-cut action to protect health. For example, environmental, physical, and chemical agents can both precipitate a disease process and can also aggravate or exacerbate diseases that already exist.

From the evidence drawn from a variety of epidemiological and laboratory investigations, environmental (in contrast to host) factors are strongly implicated as contributors to a number of disease processes. However, the nature of the contribution in many cases appears to be other than a direct one-to-one relationship between an environmental agent and a susceptible host (as is characteristic of infectious disease). Thus, the relationship between the London or Donora smog episodes and the augmented mortality rate from respiratory disease appears to have been one in which the environment precipitated excess or accelerated mortality but was not the primary cause. In theory, indirect contributions of environmental agents to ill health may occur by bringing about a weakening of the resistance of the host to disease(s) or by combining in an additive fashion with other agents to lead to disease. This, of course, increases enormously the complexity of the task of gathering the intelligence necessary in order to establish the true causal or contributory relationship between the environmental factors and disease, and it clearly complicates the task of delineating a clear pattern of risk. Thus, where most of the legal instruments and administrative patterns of regulation implicitly assume a definable threshold of effect that can be related to dosage or degree of exposure to the environmental substance, such a concept is very difficult to sustain or confirm in many cases.

A second and related feature of environmental contribution or causation of disease that complicates the picture is that of nonspecific physiological and biochemical effects. Increasing refinements in biological measurement, which have accompanied a corresponding evolution in analytic methods, are capable of detecting smaller and smaller quantities of trace substances in the environment. Partly as a result, a growing number of instances have arisen in which subtle, nonspecific biological changes have been associated with environmental alternations. The problem in this case is that as measurements of biological responses become more sensitive and more reflective of basic cellular events, they tend to be more nonspecific in relation to the type of environmental insult. Several or even a very large number of environmental agents may provoke the same biochemical alteration. The measured changes also become less specific and more difficult to relate to the ultimate health of the individual. That is, the link between a single, biochemical or cellular alteration and a recognized disease process truly threatening the health of man is by no means always clear [1].

A third type of complication arises from the fact that a single environmental agent (such as carbon monoxide or lead) may lead to more than one set of physiological or biochemical alterations. Thus, lead can exhibit changes in red blood cells, in the central nervous system and can alter the composition of bone. There are, effectively, a series of thresholds—one for each of the alterations produced.

Simplicity of the legal concepts, in many cases, are not matched by simplicity of scientific concept. Regulatory laws imply definable thresholds and "adequate (definable) margins of safety." Because the contrast between these two is so great, the philosophy of the present air pollution law, for example, may not be tenable [2]. In practice, the scientific understanding of the biological mechanisms of the diseases in question is simply too imprecise.

Who Is to Be Protected?

The answer to the question, who is to be protected, clearly is a social decision. However, it should rest on a foundation of biological understanding sufficient to guide an informed judgment as to the nature of the risk from which protection is to be sought, the statistical probability of the risk, the seriousness of the disease process, etc. Again, although it is treated simplistically in the regulatory laws, the problem of defining the population to be protected is a very complex one.

Most of the regulatory laws make no attempt to delineate the levels of human susceptibility that are to be met through regulation. Characteristically, the population is treated legally as if it behaved uniformly and were homogeneous in its reaction to environmental influences—both of which are untrue. Instead, this matter is generally left to the chief administrator as an area where he is invited to use his discretion. There are clearly exceptions, however, in which the administrative agency is specifically directed to place its efforts in behalf of one or more particular groups. Thus, the secretary of labor is impelled to set standards and to make regulations in order to protect occupational workers. The secretary of comemmerce is directed to protect in some settings the safety of children.

The Amendments to the Clean Air Act of 1970 represent something of an unusual case. This act directs the adoption of national ambient air quality standards ". . . necessary to protect the health of persons." The legislative history of this act made it clear that persons whose health is to be protected include "particularly sensitive citizens . . ." [3] The act excludes persons dependent on a "controlled internal environment," such as an intensive care unit or a newborn nursery. The act is meant to include persons whose preexisting diseases or lowered resistance makes them particularly susceptible to the effects of air pollution. The line is a difficult one to draw, however. Thus, for example, the phenomenon of accelerated mortality among persons hospitalized with severe chronic bronchitis or emphysema where air pollution was statistically associated with the accelerated process might by the law be considered outside the intended envelope of protection. At the same time, it is likely that subtle biochemical and physiological changes will be found among ambulatory but susceptible groups within the population who are exposed to natural background levels of certain air pollutants [4]. Again, effective thresholds may be difficult or impossible to define in many cases.

The question of how to treat unusually susceptible members of the general population in setting environmental standards remains generally unanswered—both for air pollutants and as well as for other environmental agents. No single response will satisfy the question. The definition of susceptible groups to pollutant exposures in any detail is a sizable task. The biological variability among the unusually susceptible (as among normal healthy human beings) can be considerable. Further, some categories of decreased resistance or increased vulnerability to disease are reasonably straightforward, understood, and justifiably considered when calculating risk taking. For example, among persons vulnerable to air pollutants, asthmatics, those suffering from chronic respiratory disease, and those with severe heart diseases can be identified. The aggravating effects of air pollutants to the severity of these conditions are least partially recognized. On the other hand, there is little on which to base a rational judgment concerning the relationship between air pollution and several other disease processes such as various types of anemia or categories of malignant disease where air pollution might again be aggravating.

An even more difficult problem arises, however, when one considers the particular susceptibilities associated with voluntarily chosen hazards. For example, cigarette smoking has been clearly identified as a very strong contributor to chronic obstructive lung disease and to lung cancer. The relationship between cigarette smoking and lung cancer is so strong that it has tended to overpower the effects of other substances such as urban air pollutants [5] or the atmospheres of uranium mines [6] in their contribution to lung cancer. In similar fashion, carbon monoxide occurs in high concentrations in cigarette smoke. The body burden of carbon monoxide (measured as carboxyhemoglobin or as carbon monoxide concentration in the exhaled air) from cigarette smoking is roughly proportional to the smoking history and is a large factor alongside the increment that may be added by community air pollution [7, 8].

Thus, it is for reasons such as these that E.J. Cassell wrote a short time back in commenting on air pollution laws:

Generally speaking, laws are drawn to correct things which people have come to think are problems. Because a constituency must be developed among both the society and its legislators that believes that the problem must be solved, the development of legislation is often difficult and time consuming.

. . . the toxicologists have clearly shown us that the urban atmosphere contains a great many toxic materials with considerable potential for harm, and epidemiologists have clearly shown us that the environment contributes to disease. Almost without exception, whatever index of adverse effect on health is employed, a harmful effect of the polluted environment can be demonstrated for man.

But, and very importantly, the more specifically one attempts to pin the adverse effect on a single constituent of the atmosphere, the weaker the evidence becomes. To put it another way, air pollution clearly and consistently can be shown to have an effect on health, but the effect on populations for specific air pollutants in the urban atmosphere consistently escapes us [9].

In part, this dilemma between legal expectation and scientific reality is a reflection of the limited fund of scientific information. In part, too, it is a matter of severe misreading by those who draft the laws of the degree of complexity inherent in these issues. Simplistic (especially rigid) legal responses will not square with science in this case.

A further question of this type, how safe is safe, concerns the adequacy of margins of safety built into regulatory standards and regulations fairly arbitrarily. Given the present state of scientific understanding of the mechanisms of environmentally related diseases and of the spectrum of human variability, it is unrealistic to expect other than arbitrary judgments. No other type is really possible. Thus, the margin of safety for tolerated levels of pesticide residues on food crops has for years been set at 1/100 the dose known to be toxic in experimental animals [10]. There is nothing particularly significant about that figure. Similarly, and equally arbitrarily, the margin of safety for exposure to ionizing radiation for members of the general population was established many years ago at ten times that permitted for occupational workers [11]. It has become a fairly common practice to select some arbitrary fraction of an experimentally derived, "no-effect" level as a practical limit for exposure [12]. The problem, of course, is that a true no-effect level or threshold may not exist or may be impossible to determine experimentally. Hence, the resort to arbitrary limits should be viewed as an expedient method of giving some useful estimates. However, the use of numerical values should not imply certainty or rigor of the estimates.

Issues Related to Human Testing

A matter of both public and scientific concern has been the relationship of testing of chemicals such as drugs in laboratory animals and investigations in humans in controlled clinical situations. Specifically, the question is frequently asked, how much preliminary animal testing is enough before sufficient information is available to permit clinical testing in humans.

The following lead article appeared in the *Washington Post* in October 1974:

Pharmaceutical manufacturers are testing potent new medicines in thousands of humans every year even before they complete experiments designed to show if the same chemicals are carcinogenic in laboratory animals. . . .

Most always, companies experimenting in humans while animal tests are still under way are complying fully with FDA's regulations. The FDA's General Guidelines for Animal Toxicity Studies require a company starting human testing to notify the agency that it is doing so, but neither to have first completed animal testing nor first to have obtained approval before moving to humans [13].

This story points up an issue for which there has been little public understanding and for which there is not a clear, simple answer. Yet, the subject is important enough to deserve a rational explanation. Practically speaking, the issue has arisen essentially only in the case of therapeutic drugs. As voluntary subjects, humans are purposefully exposed on occasion to a variety of substances under highly controlled experimental laboratory conditions. However, it is only in the case of drugs that human investigations are conducted regularly, according to a recognized and systematic series of stages and on a scale large enough to produce statistically valid samples. Drugs, by definition, are meant for human administration. Further, they are purposely given in doses large enough to provoke biochemical and physiological or pharmacological alterations. It is desirable and, at times, even essential that the biological behavior of a drug within the organism be understood as thoroughly as possible before making it available for general use in the therapeutic practice of medicine.

A variety of types of preliminary information are sought. A new drug entity is examined for its manifest or gross toxicity. The pattern of metabolic handling of the drug by the organism is elucidated. This implies investigations to determine how it is absorbed, what biochemical transformation it undergoes within the body, how and in what organs it is stored, and how it is excreted. Third, details of is toxic or adverse side effects are required in order to appreciate the limits of its useful or safe dosage, how it may interact with other drugs, and how it may behave in a weakened or diseased organism. Some of this information can be obtained from animal studies. However, there is sufficient interspecies variation to observe that animal experimentation alone is never sufficient to offer the biological insight necessary to judge a new drug. Animals never completely substitute for humans where it is human experience that is ultimately desired.

A second important constraint necessitates the mounting of trials in humans in order to understand adequately the behavior of drugs. Here one is concerned, not for the unexpected and undesirable toxic side effects, but for the intended pharmacologic effects. That is, the desire here is to understand as thoroughly as possible the efficacy of a drug in countering or containing a disease process. The experimental steps consist of making detailed measurements and observations of the pharmacologic changes provided by the drug (seen as alterations in the biochemical and physiological functions of the body). By observing these in detail in the setting of controlled, statistically valid trials, one can determine the effect on the disease processes for which the drug was intended. Again, humans have no real substitutes in animal models. Efficacy is determined ultimately only by trials in humans—both normal subjects and patients with the disease to be treated. The utility of an insecticide is determined by field trials. The usefulness of a new food additive can be ascertained without any exposure of human subjects. The effectiveness of a therapeutic agent, however, is determined only by observations made in humans—including patients.

The question, then, is how much preliminary animal experimentation is enough in order to insure safe trials in humans? There are generally strongly felt pressures—often in opposing directions—that would favor, one the one hand, extreme caution, and on the other, as much as possible an acceleration of the drug-development process (including the process of biological testing). There are economic pressures in the pharmaceutical industry that generally favor an acceleration of the process of moving a new drug into the marketplace from preliminary research through development, with the least delay possible. Similarly, there are public and professional pressures that urge that the potential of newly developed therapeutic advances be brought into medical practice as soon as possible. Attention has been focused by members of the medical profession from time to time on a possible "innovation" lag by which new therapeutic advances are thought to be introduced into the United States after they have appeared in other countries. For example, in February 1972 a group of physicians and scientists headed by the late Robert Dripps, vice-president for medical affairs of the Unittversity of Pennsylvania, argued in a letter to Representative Paul Rogers that ". . . the procedures by which new drugs are evaluated and approved for use in this country [are] causing us to fall behind in this important area of medical science" [14]. The argument contends that, because of the precautions of the FDA-directed regulations of drugs, the United States is deprived of new pharmacologic agents relative to the experience abroad [15].[a]

On the other side of the balance sheet are those biological scientists who urge caution in the process of investigation and approval of new drug entities. Finally, there is a segment of the public that has come to fear voluntary exposure to unsafe drugs in the same way as it fears involuntary exposure.

The present pattern of investigation of new drug candidates comes from amendments to the Food, Drug and Cosmetic Act of 1962. These direct the developer of a potential new drug to provide to the Food and Drug Administration the results of a number of investigations according to a prescribed sequence. The developer of a new drug petitions the Food and Drug Administration for permission to examine the new chemical in humans as an experimental or investigational drug. His petition is supposed to include ". . . adequate information about the preclinical investigations, including studies made on laboratory animals, on the basis of which the sponsor has concluded that is reasonably safe to initiate clinical investigations of drugs" [17]. The regulations outline the stages of investigation of the drug as an investigational entity. The schedule of investigation includes three stages or phases. Phase 1 begins with first introduction of the drug into man (normal human subjects) and is used to collect data from humans on toxicity, metabolism, absorption, elimination, and other physiological actions. I* is also during phase 1 that information is gathered to determine pharmacological action and to ascertain the preferred route of administration. Phase 2 is one of initial trials in a limited number of patients (by contrast to normal, healthy subjects). The first two phases may overlap and additional animal data may be called for. Phase 3 represents a full-scale but controlled clinical trial in patients.[b]

The dilemma in this case seems to be one of rigidity of interpretation rather than necessarily one of substance. In the first place, experiments using laboratory animals as subjects can never be expected to give thor-

[a] The Panel on Chemicals and Health of the President's Science Advisory Committee examined the patterns of drug development and marketing in the United States in comparison with those in the United Kingdom, Germany, France, and Italy. This panel found no evidence of any significant disparity or specific deprivation in the United States. Further, variations in timing and in R&D activities appeared to be related to marketing considerations or local medical attitudes, at least as much as to regulatory practices. [16].

[b] In a few cases in recent years an additional phase 4 of testing has initiated during which a drug is followed over long periods in large numbers of patients. This stage of surveillance is not specifically called for in the law.

oughly adequate insight into the human disease-producing potential of chemical substances including drugs. The possibilities are too numerous. The variation among species is in many cases, too great. The observations made in animals are, necessarily relatively crude. Symptoms, for example, which are by definition subjecture findings, are excluded. Further, the elaborateness of animal trials could, in theory know no boundary and could, if permitted, delay human studies unreasonably.

The possibility of inadvertent carcinogenesis by drugs leading to neoplastic disease in patients has been of special concern. At the present time, not all new drugs are evaluated for their carcinogenic potential. It has been estimated that if animal trials designed to determine carcinogenic properties were enforced on the evaluation of all new drugs that the development of new drugs could be seriously retarded with a consequent deprivation to the public of useful therapeutic entities [16]. Because of the long latent period involved in chemical carcinogenesis—20 or more years in humans and generally a measurable fraction of an animal's lifetime—investigation of a potential new drug could be held up for two to three years for carcinogenesis testing in rodents. Nevertheless, the potential of chemical carcinogenesis is a real one and cannot be dismissed.

One type of resolution for this dilemma is to consider new drug entities from the point of view of their expected benefits and to tailor the evaluation of their side effects and hazards according to these benefits. Thus, to take an example, an anticancer drug for an adult form of cancer (which characterizes most neoplastic disease) would generally be given to patients in older age groups. The amount of information concerning animal toxicity required for a potentially heroic treatment of a fatal malignancy would seem reasonably to be less than that required for a new expectorant or tranquilizer. In these cases, the expected therapeutic benefits would be of a lesser degree and there would seem to be no defensible reason not to undertake a meticulous, preclinical examination in order to avoid the occurrence of chronic and irreversible lesions or side effects.

Animal tests and human tests should be viewed as complementary, not simply as serial elements, in the evaluation of drugs. In numerous cases, insight gained from either category dictates directions for new research in the other. Thus, the best policy in this case from both the points of view of scientific investigation and protection of health would be one of flexibility—reflective of the nature of the expected benefits to be derived from the drug product eventually and of the kinds of scientific information felt to be most useful.

Pros and Cons of Phased or Staged Introduction of New Products

It is frequently argued that we would be relieved to a greater extent from the unexpected adverse side effects on health of chemicals if therapeutic drugs, food additives, cosmetics, and other consumer products were introduced into use gradually or in a phased manner. The rationale is that the period of phased introduction would also be one of surveillance where biological effects of the material upon a sufficiently large but carefully watched human population could be observed and monitored. In this way, the biological implications for the general population could be at least understood, anticipated, and perhaps avoided.

This notion, on the surface, is an attractive one. It is clearly not possible to learn all there is to know of the toxicological effects of household chemicals or food additives from animal laboratory studies. Neither is it possible to ever be fully apprised of the complex of subtle biological effects of therapeutic drugs from the limited observations on small groups of human subjects in closely controlled clinical trials. It is simply physically impossible to anticipate and look for all possible physiological and biochemical changes that might occur. Further, as pointed out above, the duration required for the development of a disease process may simply be very long. Accordingly, detection of unexpected or low-probability events or alterations that follow long latent periods may require surveillance of known, exposed populations.

This issue is really of two parts: When during this process of evaluation of the biological effects of a new chemical product should marketing be permitted; and when or to what extent should surveillance be continued after marketing begins? Again, universally applicable rules are probably impractical and not particularly useful. However, some guidelines can be offered.

A major consideration is that of good "denominator" information. That is, in order to make observations on an exposed population (exposed, that is, to a particular food preservative or tranquilizer, for example), there must be on hand some information that would set apart or identify the exposed population. In most cases, the identification and follow-up of a group of persons known to have been subjected to specific exposures are exceedingly difficult. It is possible with prescription therapeutic drugs—partly because the very act of prescribing is a kind of accounting system. Yet, even here, the problems of surveillance have appeared enormous and very little drug surveillance in any rigorous sense is traditionally carried out. The experience of the Food and Drug Administration in its attempt to carry out postmarketing surveillance of adverse drug reactions from among drug-taking patients has been exceedingly discouraging—principally because of the very difficult task of identifying with reasonable certainty those persons who are, in fact, taking particular drugs.

This is vital information. Without it, observations on human subjects cannot be compared with known, unexposed, or controlled groups and it becomes essentially impossible to interprete the observations. The National Academy of Sciences acknowledged this difficulty in their review of adverse drug-reaction reporting systems. In fact, th only really reliable information collected after marketing has begun on previously unsuspected adverse reactions from therapeutic drugs has been from carefully controlled intensively monitored, in-hospital studies [19].

Compared to therapeutic drugs, the problem of postmarketing surveillance of other consumer products in any scientific sense is overwhelming. If a product distributed for general use (household cleaner, food coloring agent, cosmetic), there is essentially no practical method known for singling out and identifying persons who are exposed and for separating theee exposed from the nonexposed. If one attempts to introduce a non-drug product gradually to a known group of persons who could be kept under surveillance for a period, one raises a number of new and difficult ethical questions. In brief, it appears unlikely that large-scale testing (implied by gradual introduction with human surveillance) can be justified for other than therapeutic drugs, since the costs would be enormously high and the presumed benefits (counteracting the possible risks) would be generally much less. These reasons prompted the Panel on Chemicals and Health of the President's Science Advisory Committee to recommend that ". . . large-scale testing of the sort implied in staged introduction is not ordinarily defensible for substances other than medicines because the possibility of benefit is not sufficiently clear, personal, informed, consent is less likely, and adequate monitoring is virtually impossible" [16].

Criteria Governing the Introducion of Products into the Marketplace

Regulatory laws governing the manufacture or distribution or use of new products imply some utility or efficacy for the products. The laws historically have been concerned with factors thought from time to time to detract from their utility. As was discussed in chapter 2, the early food and drug laws were primarily concerned with preventing impurities and false claims and, more recently, with hazards or unsafe materials. Similarly, pesticide regulations have included features concerned with avoidance of residues on crops that might prove to be deleterious to health.

Classically, purity is the item on which regulatory laws seek assurances first. This was the first concern of food and drug laws. However, health and safety generally joined the list later.

There are two criteria, both of which bear explicitly on the subject of benefit or utility, that deserve some additional consideration. One is efficacy or demonstrated utility. New or already marketed therapeutic drugs both require evidence of effectiveness in each case. While there was concern for avoidance of fraud during the early part of the twentieth century, the present regulatory provision requiring proof of efficacy date only to 1962. Effectiveness or efficacy is established through a series of laboratory and clinical investigations. At the present time, there are no corresponding requirements of efficacy for pesticides or for food additives (as regulated materials) nor, by definition, are there any for industrial chemicals or ingredients in other products.

A major argument in favor of a prior demonstration of efficacy is that such a judgment would limit the number of chemicals in use, and therefore, would limit man's exposure to a correspondingly smaller chemical universe. The argument continues by noting that with a smaller list of chemical materials to contend with, it is possible to understand more about each one and to exercise more suitable controls over chemical exposures of man and the environment.

However, there is a counterargument that also applies to health. Substances that appear innocuous at one point in time may turn out to be implicated by a new scientific finding at a later period. With a limited portfolio of chemicals for any purpose, it is possible for widespread exposure to an offending agent to occur before a hazard is recognized. Larger numbers of alternative chemicals simply reduce the population at risk to each one—if it becomes a risk. Had thalidomide been the only tranquilizer available, presumably larger numbers of women of child-bearing age would have been exposed to that drug.

An argument of a different sort can be raised in favor of early determination of efficacy. Here, it is assumed that at some point it is desirable to know and understand the real utility of the product (without at the moment saying why that is important). In practice, it is repeatedly apparent that once a product is introduced into use, it is often very difficult or impossible to return to question the true utility or efficacy of the item. This is not only true for drugs but is the case for medical and surgical procedures generally. Apparent dependence upon these items discourages rigorous questioning of their worth, and ethical questions surrounding the denial of an "apparently" useful treatment often prohibit it. Another example of this sort can be found in pesticides. Insecticides and herbicides have been associated with gains in production in food and fiber in large numbers of specific instances. There are usually a number of variables outstanding in each instance (fertilizer use, resistance of pests, rainfall, etc.) and the exact utility function of the pesticide is difficult to determine. Furthermore, pesticides have been relatively inexpensive technological adjuncts. This fact has made possible the generous (perhaps, overly generous) application of pesticides by farmers. Although intuitively it is supposed that some applications have exceeded a critical or necessary level to achieve "suitable control," it is difficult to ascertain what a critical level is in many cases. At the present time, we are said to be dependent upon pesticides to maintain our present level of agricultural productivity. However, the particular marginal productivity of pesticides is not really known and is very difficult to determine [20].

A second criterion that has been suggested as appropriate for limiting the introduction of chemicals is that of betterment. This can be looked upon simply as further refinement of efficacy. The limitation would be more stringent. For example, it has been suggested that a new pesticide or food additive should not be registered unless it has been demonstrated to have desired characteristics not now possessed by other materials on the market. A further step would be to permit (through regulation) new and demonstrably better products to displace older and less desirable substances. This, of course, is precisely the course of events that it is supposed occurs through the operation of market prices. The addition of this element to regulation would accelerate the process of displacement and, so the argument goes, insure a scientific basis for the action as a result of experimental evidence.

These ideas are not novel and there is some precedent in regulatory practices and policies in other countries. For example, in the United Kingdom it is government policy to oblige food processors (who are the users of food additives) to demonstrate in a test situation that a proposed food additive has clear advantages over those possessed by similar substances already in use.

This suggestion of a criterion of betterment (or relative efficacy) is one that deserves serious, informed public debate. Health is by no means the sole issue at stake. A major consideration is one of diversity. Demand for demonstrated utility—especially for products where the public is generally a poor judge or where someone such as a physician intervenes in decisions for the public—would serve the public interest well. Thus, although there remain some detractors [21, 22], in the author's judgment, we are better served by the more limited list of medicines of demonstrated efficacy than by a longer list that contains large numbers of substances of unproven usefulness.

The question raised, however, especially when advocating a criterion of betterment, is reduction of diversity. Diversity here means a portfolio of available products with similar qualities. To elect to preserve in the marketplace only the most efficacious or the best, as demonstrated by experimental trials, may not always be found to be in the public's interest. It has already been suggested that, where two or more similar substances are available, there is less relative dependence on any one among them. It is easier to take vigorous regulatory action when one becomes suspect or is found to represent a risk. With alternatives, a shift can be made to other substances. The judgments of the federal government toward restrictions on the use of polychlorinated biphenyls took account of the fact that substitute materials were available except for those used in electrical equipment [23].

A second argument in favor of diversity reflects the variability of applications. In some cases, one drug of a class of similar drugs is found to be effective clinically where the others are not. People do vary in their responsiveness to drugs. In a similar fashion, the appearance or intensity of side effects of drugs varies from patient to patient—sometimes dictating a strategy of titrating various levels or of trying various drugs. While these are generally exceptional situations, they are sufficiently important and prominent to make substitutes an attractive prospect.

Balance in Decision Making: Serving the Public's Interest

If one chooses any one of the many regulatory decisions made in the past several years in the name of the protection of health, one finds a common characteristic. They are all no-win decisions in the sense of never fully satisfying all parties in each case. The restrictions placed on the sale of DDT, while they pleased those concerned with the integrity of the environment, found aggrieved parties among farmers who felt that they had lost a major agricultural tool, among farm workers who found themselves suddenly confronted with highly toxic substitutes, and among all of the myriad of economic interests who had formerly profited from the sale and use of DDT. The banning of cyclamates from among artificial sweeteners made diabetics and others who depended upon a low carbohydrate intake particularly unhappy. It also provided sufficient economic unhappiness among various canners and packers to lead to a bill in Congress for their compensation or indemnification.

These examples are fairly straightforward. There have, in addition, however, been examples of regulatory action that, while aimed at protecting health, have inadvertently led to the trading of one hazard for another. Congress' mandating of automobile emission standards in the amendments to the Clean Air Act in 1970 was done to hold down the ambient air levels of these pollutants *exclusively* to protect health [23]. It was clear at the time this law was passed that there were limitations associated with the technologies available to aid in the abatement of automotive exhaust emissions (although the law specifically denied any consideration of this constraint in judgment making). Accommodation to the final mandated automotive emission standards would require the use of a series of anti-emission controls and devices on automobiles—the principal one of which is a catalytic exhaust control device (or devices in serial arrangement).

These have been viewed as the necessary technological element in order to reduce emissions of hydrocarbons, oxidants and nitrogen oxides. What became apparent only latterly was the high probability that catalytic converters would accelerate the conversion of sulfur contaminants in gasoline to sulfates in aerosol or particulate form leading to a new and perhaps even more unhealthy automotive emission [24].

A second and better known example of a hazard exchanged for another hazard through regulation occurred with the banning of DDT and its replacement by organophosphate insecticides. These latter, while not possessing the high physical and chemical stability of DDT in the environment, are much more toxic acutely and, therefore, have posed severe occupational problems.

A third example concerned the government's actions and statements concerning phosphate-containing detergents. While the federal government exercised no regulatory action in this case, its point of view did encourage the development of a number of chemical substitutes for phosphate compounds in household detergents. One of the unforeseen results has been in an entirely unrelated area—the flameproofing of children's clothing. The Commerce Department under the terms of the Flammable Fabrics Act was charged with the development of standards and procedures for flameproofing children's sleepwear. With the disappearance of phosphate detergents came a number of substitutes for phosphates, some of which contained acutely toxic and corrosive substances and all of which were found to compromise the flameproofing qualities of materials.

These examples simply amplify the point. Regulatory decisions made by independent agencies are narrowly conceived, are rewarded generally by the major constituency of the agency, but are, therefore, not reflective of the broad set of issues ultimately affected by the impending action. The commissioner of the Food and Drug Administration, was chastised from time to time by members of Congress for employing an economist on his staff. The economist was spoken of as a fringe benefit by the congressmen. There has rarely been an example of regulatory decision making in behalf of health by the Environmental Protection Agency in which a full spread of the issues surrounding the decision or the multiplicity of efforts expected by each of the optimal avenues was anlytically explored before the decision was made. In brief, balancing in any real sense is not generally done when reaching these regulatory decisions. Worse, it appears impossible to achieve in the face of the generally narrow constituency of the agencies involved.

Yet, balance in decision making *is* in the public's best interest: "Regulatory procedures should ensure balanced consideration and balanced decision in regulatory actions. This implies consideration of both direct and indirect consequences that will flow from each of the possible actions"

[16]. To make the point more forcibly, we are at particular peril if these decisions are not made broadly or if they do not reflect a balance of important considerations, *even though health may be the nominal end point.* It was this thought that led Bert Dinman, an expert in environmental health, to remark at the National Academy of Sciences that ". . . it should be clearly understood that the fiscal resources available to the country are finite. . . ." [25]. One part of the peril is, of course, inappropriate or frankly bad decisions. Another is subversion of the administrative process by other agencies of the government borne out of frustration.[c]

References

1. Hatch, T., Concepts of Threshold Limits. Present Applications and Future Needs, Background paper prepared for Task Force on Research Planning in Environmental Health Science. See, *Man's Health and the Environment—Some Research Needs*, U.S. Department of Health, Education, and Welfare, National Institutes of Health, Washington, D.C., U.S. Government Printing Office, 1970.

2. Finklea, J.F., Conceptual Basis for Establishing Standards, Remarks presented to the Academy Forum on Air Pollution, National Academy of Sciences, Washington, D.C., October 1973.

3. *National Air Quality Standards Act of 1970,* Report of the Committee on Public Works, United States Senate, September 17, 1970, Report No. 91-1196, U.S. Government Printing Office, Washington, D.C.

4. Carnow, B., Sulphur Oxides and Particulates, Invited discussion presented at the Academy Forum on Air Pollution, National Academy of Sciences, Washington, D.C., October 1973.

5. *Particulate Polycyclic Organic Matter,* Committee on Biologic Effects of Atmoshperic Pollutants, Division of Medical Sciences, National Research Council, National Academy of Sciences, Washington, D.C., 1972.

6. *Public Health Service Uranium Mines Report,* Division of Medical Sciences, National Academy of Sciences, Ad Hoc Advisory Committee of the Federal Radiation Council, Washington, D.C., 1971.

7. *Air Quality Criteria for Carbon Monoxide,* U.S. Department of Health, Education, and Welfare, National Air Pollution Control Administration, Washington, D.C., March 1970.

---

[c] The example of the White House's attempt to lift regulatory decision making out of the independent agencies to a higher authority is given in chapter 7.

8. *Effects of Chronic Exposure to Low Levels of Carbon Monoxide on Human Health, Behavior, and Performance,* National Academy of Sciences, Washington, D.C., 1969.

9. Cassell, E.J., Towards an Optimum Environment, Chapter 16 in Lee, D., ed., *Environmental Factors in Respiratory Disease,* New York, Academic Press, 1970.

10. Title 21, Food and Drugs, Part 120, Tolerances and Exemptions from Tolerances for Pesticide Chemicals in our Fresh Fruits and Vegetables, *Federal Register,* p. 1493, March 1955.

11. Little, J.R., Environmental Hazards. Ionizing Radiation, *New England* 275: 929-938, 1966.

12. National Academy of Sciences, *Principles for Evaluating Chemicals in the Environment,* Washington, D.C. 1975.

13. Mintz, M., and O'Brien, T., The Guinea Pigs, Nobody Knows if Drugs Tested on Humans Will Cause Cancer, *Washington Post,* October 24, 1971.

14. Dripps, R.D., Correspondence addresses by Dr. Dripps along with 20 other co-signers to Congressman Paul G. Rogers, February 29, 1972.

15. Gilgore, S.G., Controls Style New Drugs, Emphasis on Side Effects Hinders Progress, *The New York Times,* July 2, 1972.

16. *Chemicals and Health,* Report of the Panel on Chemicals and Health of the President's Science Advisory Committee, September 1973, Science and Technology Policy Office, National Science Foundation, U.S. Government Printing Office, Washington, D.C.

17. Food, Drug and Cosmetic Act as amended, CFR 130-3, May 1964.

18. *Report of the International Conference on Adverse Drug Reaction Reporting Systems,* National Academy of Sciences, Washington, D.C., 1971.

19. Boston Collaborative Drug Surveillance Program: Drug Surveillance—Problems and Challenges, *Pediatric Clinics of North America,* 19: 117-129, 1972.

20. Headley, J.C., Productivity of Agricultural Chemicals, Paper presented at the Economic Research Service Symposium on Economic Research on Pesticides for Policy Decision-Making, Washington, D.C., April 27-29, 1970.

21. Wardell, W., Therapeutic Implications of the Drug Lag, *Clin. Pharm. Therap.,* 15: 73-96, 1974.

22. Peltzman, S., The Benefits and Costs of New Drug Regulation, Paper presented to the Conference on Regulation of the Introduction of

New Pharmaceuticals, Center for Policy Study, University of Chicago, Chicago, Illinois, December 1972.

23. *National Air Quality Standards Act of 1970,* S. 4358, Report of the Committee on Public Works, U.S. Senate, Senate Report 91-1196, September 17, 1970.

24. Letter and Report from the secretary of health, education, and welfare to Senator Jennings Randolph on the Potential Health Hazards from the Use of Catalytic Converters, November 14, 1973.

25. Dinman, B., Presentation to A Forum on Air Pollution, National Academy of Sciences, Washington, D.C., 1973.

5

Information for Regulatory Decision Making

At the heart of good decision making in any setting is good information for the decisions. This point takes on added emphasis where decisions are made about complex, multivariate political issues and about subjects that are technically complicated. Although it may appear too elementary to be worth repeating, good information is especially important for decisions that represent large expenditures and investments, are far-reaching in time, and that tend to rearrange large segments of national life. Those qualifications clearly apply to regulatory actions undertaken in the name of human health. Standards for emissions of pollutants from automobiles, decisions to restrict the distribution or manufacture of a food additive or an intermediate substance in the manufacture of a chemical product, are examples of actions that inevitably have multiple consequences (economic, biological, effects on other government policies and programs, etc.). The expenditures implicated by regulatory decisions are often exceedingly large ($63 billion in the case of the Clean Air Act [1]). Regulatory actions are thought of as definitive with consequences extending for sizable periods into the future. In some cases (such as the provisions of the Clean Air Act) large areas of life are purposely rearranged. Manufacturing plans for automobiles, for example, demand three to five years of anticipation or lead time in order to bring about the necessary mechanical and tooling operations to accommodate altered designs.

The point is, since both the intended effects and the unintended side effects of regulation are so important, regulatory decisions deserve a suitable foundation of information. Hence, it is not unreasonable to pose the question, in practice, what is the nature of the information base available for and used for regulatory decision making? What is the quality of the scientific fabric for what are obviously scientific questions relating environmental exposures to human ill health? What is known of efficacy or benefit in each instance where risks are said to be desirably matched against benefits?

The fact is that, in spite of the importance of good information and good scientific information, in an uncomfortable number of instances suitable information is lacking. Present air quality standards and air emission standards for such pollutants as nitrogen oxides and sulfur oxides rest on very little information. Nitrilotriacetic acid, a chelating agent suggested as a potential replacement for phosphates in washing detergents, was not introduced into use in the United States originally because of warnings by the Department of Health, Education, and Welfare on the basis of only preliminary or pilot scientific studies. Knowledge of the biological side effects of artificial sweeteners and of a number of pesticide residues is exceedingly sparse. Dose-response relationships and mechanisms of biological behavior are generally not known or understood for doses or exposures ordinarily present in the environment. The recent attempts to arrive at a decision over the use of tetraethyl lead as a fuel additive represent an example.

The cost of performing the necessary research to insure an adequate base of scientific knowledge for decisions is large enough to be a measurable and debated budgetary item in terms of national accounts. Yet, the absence of knowledge appears, in the long run, to be much more expensive and clearly encourages bad public policy. Regulatory actions are typically expensive.

Second, errors in regulatory judgment are typically expensive errors and often raise questions of compensation or indemnification. Cranberry growers were compensated in 1968 when HEW condemned a harvest of cranberries because of pesticide residues just prior to Thanksgiving. Canners and fruit packers nearly succeeded in having special legislation passed in 1972 aimed at compensating them for losses they laid to the banning of cyclamates. In 1974 poultry growers were nearly successful in having enacted a law to compensate them for the enforced slaughter of a large number of chickens upon the finding of high residual levels of Dieldrin.

Third, political and legislative processes tend to err on the side of protection of health in the face of a lack of information. The Delaney amendment to the Food, Drug, and Cosmetic Act and the mandated automobile air pollution emission standards are of this sort. As pointed out elsewhere, although protection of health is the goal, it is not always clear that health is bettered and some injudicious regulatory decisions may have an effect opposite to that nominally intended.

Fourth, expenditures implicated by regulatory actions in the name of protection of health are, by definition, not available to be spent in behalf of health in other ways. This, of course, is important if the expenditures are not productive.

Finally, with regulatory action taken on the basis of shaky or nonexistent scientific evidence, the public credibility in the integrity of the regulatory system is jeopardized or is made more fragile. The emission standard chosen for nitrogen oxides, based to a large extent upon a single set of observations made on school children in Chattanooga, Tennessee, is an example [2]. This bit of epidemiology had been designed as a pilot or preliminary experiment—not as a definitive investigation. The principal measurement was that of absence from school due to respiratory illness presumed to be associated with measured levels of atmospheric nitrogen oxides. It was eventually realized that the body of scientific data undergirding a major emission standard was very thin indeed. At the same time, some sizable uncertainties arose as to the validity of the physical measurements of nitrogen oxides in the original experiment. As a result, the originally proposed standard was called into serious question and eventually revised [3,4]. Such a process can be expected to erode rather than build public and professional confidence in the process of decision making for regulation.

In sum, then, two kinds of processes occur—both reflective of a poor scientific basis for decisions. One is lost opportunities for preventive measures to protect human health. Without proper intelligence, true opportunities are not recognized or are not appreciated until a disaster has occurred that brings an issue forcibly to the public's attention. The other process is that of injudicious decisions leading to a type of hysteresis or overkill. Government and private actions taken nominally to protect health on the basis of an implied hazard may, in fact, have little real impact on health.

What Kinds of Information Are Needed

Most of the emphasis in this chapter (and, indeed, the focus of most of the public's attention) is on the scientific basis for judgments of risk or hazard to human health. In fact, a variety of kinds of information logically should be available for regulatory decisions. Regulatory decisions for the public's good must reflect a consideration, not only of health, but of a breadth of issues—economic, legal, social, institutional, and biological. To be considered fully, each of these areas must be represented by a body of information that allows sufficient insight for judgment. While this present description relates in particular to the quantity and quality of scientific information—especially that concerned with biological properties—it should be understood that the legacy of information on a variety of issues is typically in very short supply.

Although it may appear elementary to point out, knowledge of physical quantities of substances considered as potential or recognized environmental hazards is of great importance. Yet, while it is important to have, it is often correspondingly difficult to find—especially for commercial products. The federal government relies on manufacturers in the private sector to a great extent to supply figures describing quantitative output, and in many cases, manufacturers are reluctant to reveal their output. While the U.S. Tariff Commission keeps accounts on production of substances generally (on the basis of reports supplied by manufacturers), in cases where there are fewer than three suppliers, these figures are kept confidential and are not available for government or any other use. The total production of polychlorinated biphenyls in the United States had emanated from a single manufacturer who, until the middle of 1972, steadfastly refused to make this information publically available.

If a regulator is to make appropriate judgments about the likelihood of human exposure, some information concerning the routes of commercial and physical diffusion of substances as a result of man's activities must be available. That is, one needs to be informed on the patterns of distribution and use and of the ultimate disposal of manufactured chemicals, for example, in order to come to any sensible judgment as to the likelihood of impingement upon human beings. As we will see shortly, a very strong case can be made for efforts to map sources and quantities of materials which become environmental pollutants or redistributed trace substances. Further, one would like to discuss as quantitatively as possible their patterns of rates and routes of use through human activity or dispersal or diffusion as through seepage or leaching in the environment. Except for such occurrences as large-scale, accidental spillages, models designed to elucidate environmental sinks and patterns of migration will be essential if even rough estimates of human exposure are to be thoughtfully made. Yet, as desirable or essential as such an exercise might be, it has been performed only rarely. Two recent attempts, which grew out of studies done by the Office of Science and Technology, concerned cadmium [5], as a naturally occurring trace element, and polychlorinated biphenyls [6], as a synthetic chemical compound. In fact, the major impediment to such an exercise is a profound lack of information necessary to assign numerical coefficients to a model. The total of a substance produced as a synthetic chemical is not always available. The patterns of manufacturing processes are not always simple to describe. Yet, such information is essential if one is to distinguish between milligram or ton quantities in man's environment.

It is common to profess that decisions reflect considerations of risks matched against benefits. In spite of this profession, in fact the ability to engage in risk-benefit analysis in any rigorous or systematic way is severely limited by lack of information about both risks and benefits [7]. Estimation of efficacy or utility is commonly thought of or suitably represented by behavior in the marketplace. "If a material or product is purchased, it must be worthwhile," goes the admonition. Yet, in fact, the market test is by no means always an accurate reflection. Sufficiently free market systems do not operate in every instance. Physicians, for example, effectively make surrogate judgments for patients in the case of therapeutic drugs. Consumers (and physicians, for that matter) are often poor

Table 5-1

New Product Introductions in the Ethical Pharmaceutical Industry, 1950-70

Year	Total New Products	New Single Chemicals	Duplicate Products	Compounded Products	New Dosage Forms
1950	326	28	100	198	118
1951	321	35	74	212	120
1952	314	35	77	202	170
1953	353	48	79	226	97
1954	380	38	87	255	108
1955	403	31	90	282	96
1956	401	42	79	280	66
1957	400	51	88	261	96
1958	370	44	73	253	109
1959	315	63	49	203	104
1960	306	45	62	199	98
1961	260	39	32	189	106
1962	250	27	43	180	84
1963	199	16	34	149	52
1964	157	17	29	111	41
1965	112	23	18	71	22
1966	80	12	15	53	26
1967	82	25	25	32	14
1968	87	11	26	50	21
1969	62	9	22	31	12
1970	105	16	50	39	23
Total	5,283	655	1,152	3,476	1,583

Source: Paul de Haen. *Ten Year New Product Survey*, 1950-1960 and Paul de Haen, *Non Proprietary Name Index*, vol. VI (New York: 1967 and 1970).

judges of true efficacy. Clearly, one indication of the disparity between the assumed efficacy and the scientifically demonstrated efficacy of therapeutic drugs is the number of drugs removed from the market and the declining number of new entrants since 1962. Table 5-1 illustrates the decline in the total number of new drugs marketed in the United States from 1950 to 1970. Without question, the number of all new pharmaceutical products introduced each year fell—beginning, perhaps, somewhat before 1962—and has continued to fall to the present. It was Congress' intent that the number of drugs on the market would be governed according to some measure of their true biological utility in the physician's armamentarium of treatment procedures. Following the amendments in 1962 to the Food, Drug and Cosmetic Act, the National Academy of Sciences was engaged to assist in a review of what was known of the efficacy of all prescription drugs. The Drug Efficacy Study divided all prescription drugs into 30 groups and each group was reviewed by a separate panel of scientists and was graded according to the degree of confidence in the effectiveness based on scientific evidence available. A major conclusion reached by the participants in the Drug Efficacy Study was that of generally poor quality or effective lack of scientific information upon which one could base a judgment of efficacy.

Many of the presentations submitted by manufacturers in support of the claims made for the use of their drugs consisted of bulky files of reports of uncontrolled observations and testimonial-type endorsements. The lack of substantial evidence based on well-controlled investigations by experienced investigators was conspicuous. Moreover, searches of the medical literature indicated that there existed little convincing scientific evidence to support many of the cited indications for the use of drugs that are currently in good standing in medical practice. There is every good reason to believe that industry is aware of the need for, and seeks to obtain, the best scientific endorsement of its products. The failure, therefore, must be attributed to the difficulty that industry has in commanding the needed clinical facilities and the services of experienced investigators. This is not a fault of industry alone, but rather is a reflection of a serious gap in the programming and management of the national effort in therapeutic research [8].

This admonition is important in part since there is probably better information concerning utility and efficacy of therapeutic drugs than there is for any other chemical product. Although the lack of efficacy or benefit information may seem less urgent than some others, it emerges as a major factor in certain instances. Decisions may be made from time to time that have the effect of banning or supplanting a product for which a true dependence has been developed over the years. Without adequate knowledge about the true nature of this dependence, and of the consequences and costs related to doing without it, it becomes virtually impossible to relate any assessment of implied or known hazard to one of benefit in any studied manner. Except for pharmaceutical products, there is no real incentive at the present time for documenting the characteristics of utility or benefit. Further, once a pesticide or a drug has reached the market and has achieved a wide and even respected use, it becomes exceedingly difficult and ethically troublesome to examine questions of usefulness and benefit in any scientific fashion.

Most public and regulatory attention for pesticides, food additives, cosmetics, and therapeutic drugs is focused on questions of hazard to human health and safety. There is generally assumed to be a legacy of information that relates human exposure to biological effects that bear directly on or have implications for human health. In fact, especially for chemical substances, the body of scientific data and recorded human experience is a highly variable one, depending upon the substances involved as well as the quality of the information. In many instances, the quality of the scientific fabric available for determination of risks is very thin. This picture prompted H. Guyford Stever as Science Adviser in his Foreword to the Report on Chemicals and Health to remark that ". . . to a great extent our ability to understand the biological effects of chemical substances such as pesticides, food additives and therapeutic drugs has not kept pace with our technological ability to develop and use new substances'' [7].

The fund of scientific understanding of the relationship of human health to exposure to environmental agents accrues from a variety of research activities. They include laboratory investigations on experimental animals, toxicology, pharmacology, and biochemistry. They include fundamental studies of disease processes. They include controlled studies in the laboratory on humans. They embrace, also, observations (often over a period) of the effects of known exposures to limited groups of humans (such as occupational groups) and to members of the general population (epidemiology). This research runs the spectrum from clearly basic studies (such as studies of the mechanism of the clearance of foreign particles from the lung) to clearly applied investigations (testing or screening of pesticide products to determine if there is a tendency to provoke birth defects in experimental animals). Some (but not all) of the research can be directed or targeted. Some of it is of short duration but a portion represents a lengthy dedication and a necessary investment toward future earnings.

Perhaps most of all, this segment of research deserves an increase in sophistication and a level of scientific insight commensurate with the capacity of the scientific method of the day. In brief, where much of this research in the past has been preoccupied with elementary observations of gross biological effects (numbers of animals killed by a specific dose, enumeration of obvious tumors, etc.) there is a strong need for a level of research aimed at *understanding* why and by what mechanisms specific environmental agents exert their effects. That is, research needs to be aimed not so much at simply the *counting* of biological abnormalities but an appreciation of the underlying biological behavior of the environmentally related diseases. Leon Golberg has frequently noted the disparity between the standard or set mechanical exercises characteristically used to ''test'' the biological effects of food additives in experimental animals and the level of sophistication that science and, in particular, present-day toxicological research is capable of offering to this endeavor [9].

In many instances, regulatory agencies have increased their demands for information from manufacturers and developers of new regulated products prior to granting permission for sale and distribution. In some cases those demands have reflected the pace of science, which continues to raise new questions at the same time that it answers old ones. In many other cases, information is sought to ''cover'' the reviewer of a petition for a new drug within the FDA or is volunteered to ''cover'' a manufacturer in anticipation that the data will be solicited. This pattern has tended over many years to substitute thick reports containing multiple observations of low-order *tests* for investments in research that would lead to appreciation and *understanding* of the biochemical and physiological phenomena being studied. There has been a strong tendency to substitute a voluminous but mechanical "printout" for an intelligent and scientifically sophisticated "thinkout" [10]. It is only through the acquisition of this type of understanding that the real significance of gross toxicological observations for human health can be gained.

It is important to note here that this increase in the level of sophistication of environmental health research need not represent a corresponding increase in the cost of the research. In fact, it is likely that in many instances work performed to elucidate mechanisms of biological action of an environmental substance may be less expensive than a saturation type portfolio of multiple standard testing procedures.

It has become very common in recent years to focus much scientific attention on three specific disease processes—cancer, genetic alteration, and birth defects or congenital abnormalities—and to ask routinely if somewhat blindly whether chemical substances were carcinogens, mutagens, or teratogens. As a consequence of this emphasis, insightful scientific concern for other disease processes that might result from human exposure are at times ignored or given less than appropriate attention. Judgments as to the hazard of nitrilotriacetic acid (NTA) as a substitute for tripolyphosphates in household detergents have turned on the question of whether that chemical was or was not a carcinogen. The question of carcinogenesis first arose when the National Cancer Institute was asked by the surgeon general, Dr. Jesse Steinfeld, if on the basis of the information available NTA could be carcinogenic for humans. The "information available" consisted essentially of a broad-ranging yet fairly nonspecific series of animal studies, none of which was designed specifically to provide insight into the potential of NTA to produce neoplastic disease. The interpretive response from the National Cancer Institute was that NTA, on the basis of the experiments performed, could not be ruled out as a carcinogen [11]. At the same time, the major chemical characteristic of NTA is its relatively strong chelating properties, that is, its ability to combine in a chemical complex with a variety of metallic elements. Biologically, this property could lead NTA to alter the dynamics of a number of trace elements in the human organism—some of which are essential for the functioning of vital enzymes. Although this property was given modest attention through some pilot experiments conducted by another part of the National Institutes of Health, it was not considered with the seriousness of cancer.

A series of problems have arisen secondarily to investigations into the biological effects of environmental agents. These are findings that, by themselves, are not known to be specific in their relationship to disease or whose ultimate interpretation is unclear. A large number of biochemical abnormalities have been found to be associated with exposure to exogenous agents. Alterations in liver biochemistry, for example, have been found partly as a result of improvements in the resolution and accuracy of biochemical measurements. However, the interpretation of these measurements is often very unclear. An example from another area is even more controversial. It has not been clear how properly to interpret the finding of histologically benign tumors. There is no general agreement within the scientific community as to the natural history of many histologically benign tumors and of progression (if any) of benign to malignant transformations. Of corresponding importance is the fact that in practice, neoplastic-like lesions in experimental animals used to test the biological properties of chemicals are often not categorized with any sophistication according to histological characteristics. Thus, characteristically, all tumors found are considered as potentially malignant and are interpreted as indicators of the human malignant disease known as cancer. The well-known series of experiments in which hormonal contraceptive agents were administered to beagle dogs and shown to produce mammary tumors were of this sort. A large number of instances of hepatic enlargement and tumors represent a further example. There is little information concerning the natural progression of hepatomas, for example. There is, in brief, a very strong argument for a level of research intermediate between the most fundamental of studies on living phenomena and the clearly directed research or applied testing common to much of the regulatory field.

The pressures of the world of regulation for immediacy similarly color the research efforts of the regulatory agencies. Research performed or supported by the Environmental Protection Agency has in practice of necessity had to pass a test of immediate relevance to that agency. This has often ruled out all but the most nonsophisticated and scientifically superficial types of investigations. Regulatory agencies have tended to focus their research efforts strongly in the direction of problems immediately at hand and to reduce support for investigations whose results will be necessary several years in the future. Thus, there is a serious need for new knowledge of sort that is intermediate in nature between basic biology on the one hand and research that is closely related to immediate regulatory questions on the other. In practice, it is this research area, intermediate between basic and applied studies, that is important, that is viewed as the government's own responsibility, and it is this area's obligation that has been poorly fulfilled up to now.

There are, in addition, a number of special challenges within this area of science. In much of clinical toxicology or for most diseases of bacterial or viral origin there is generally found a fairly straightforward and identifiable relationship or concordance between exposure to an offending agent and the occurrence of a lesion or disease. In a large number of instances of pathological conditions related to environmental chemical or physical agents, such a neat, one-to-one relationship between agent and specific lesion does not obtain.

A very common, generally poorly understood problem is that of threshold of effect for low doses or levels of exposure to environmental agents. Doses of a large number of environmental substances in the general community environment are typically low in comparison to levels used in laboratory experiments and for which the published literature may contain some insight. Without a sufficient understanding of the mechanisms of a number of the diseases involved (such as cancer), it becomes difficult or impossible to know whether a critical threshold of effect exists in many cases and, if it does, at what level of exposure (both duration and intensity) it is to be found. There have been a few general approaches to this particular problem. One has been to investigate the mechanisms of the disease in question so as to predict dose-response behavior for low doses. A second has been to proceed totally theoretically by constructing models of possible interactions between offending agents and susceptible cellular or molecular targets [12, 13, 14]. A third approach has been to examine experimentally the low end of dose-response relationships. Here, the practical problem arises from the statistical challenge of searching for improbable events. The sample size of experimental animals necessary to lend suitable validity to negative results is very large. Fact that this statistical problem was largely ignored in very large numbers of older experiments renders many of them of little value in present-day attempts to assess the carcinogenic properties of large numbers of chemical substances [15]. This particular challenge was the origin of the large-scale animal experiments mounted at the new National Center for Toxicological Research administered by the Food and Drug Administration.

Environmental exposures may provoke a series of biochemical or physiological alterations. These may or may not be significant as true pathogenic (disease-causing) alterations. Both the intensity and the number of alterations may vary according to the strength or dose of the exposure, the duration over which the exposure occurs, development by the organism of resistance or repair (after previous exposure, for example) as well as other factors. Alterations can occur sequentially as well. This may mean, for example, an effective threshold for each of several alterations. Exposure to lead provokes alterations in several organ systems including bone, red blood cells, and the central nervous system. Exposure to polyvinyl cloride (or to its components or impurities) has been associated with both lesions of the hand (acrosteosis) and a type of malignant tumor of the liver (hemangiosarcoma).

Substances including pollutants found in the general environment may combine or be additive with similar substances of both endogenous as well as exogenous origin. The human organism normally produces carbon monoxide at a rate of 0.42 ml/hour—most of it from the catabolism of hemoglobin. The principal paramenters that influence body CO stores are production, uptake via the lungs from environmental sources, dilution in the body stores, and excretion. A resident level of carboxyhemoglobin (the form in which carbon monoxide combines with hemoglobin in the blood) of 1 to 2 percent in nonsmoking urban dwellers is not uncommon. Cigarette smoking increases this level by 2 to 6 percent, depending on the intensity of smoking and upon whether the smoker does or does not inhale. Any carbon monoxide from the ambient atmosphere (as from motor vehicle exhaust) is additive to the already burden and, in fact, may be dwarfed by it. A similar pattern is seen in the case of lead. Inorganic lead from lead paint, for example, which is taken into the organism, is added to the body burden, which comes about as a result of a natural level of lead in foodstuffs of plant origin (and ultimately from the soil in the earth's crust).

An additional, related challenge is the understanding and definition of susceptibilities and susceptible populations. This is a complex issue both politically and biologically as discussed in the last chapter [16]. In the first instance, as for all biological phenomena, there exists the characteristic of normal biological variability for essentially healthy members of the population. Description of this variability requires that it be investigated and mapped for each disease and for each offending agent in question. However, this has been done only rarely as a systematic exercise. A second problem of biological variation occurs among persons rendered especially susceptible because of preexisting disease, old age, previous disease or damage, etc. A third and related problem arises in those instances where the reserve or resistance to an offending agent may be reduced by an already excessive body burden from some other source. The place of lead from automobile exhaust as an addition to the lead body burden of urban-dwelling children who are exposed to lead-based paint is of this sort [17]. The amendments to the Clean Air Act in 1970 were clear in their intent of protecting the health of both normal and and susceptible persons [18]. Yet, a suitable definition of susceptibility is still forthcoming.

Finally, a number of the diseases themselves that are or are feared to be caused or promoted by environmental substances are chronic diseases. Periods of latency between exposure and manifestation may be exceedingly long (15 to 20 years for many cancers, for example) compared with 3 to 30 days for many of the diseases of microbiological origin. This area of investigation of chronic degenerative diseases, therefore, is governed by marked challenges for that reason alone. Latent periods for experimental animals typically occupy a similar fraction of the animal's life as do the corresponding periods for humans. This prolongs the period of experimentation, limits the immediate rewards to the experimenter and, in recent years, has given extra incentive to searches for substitute, faster, *in-vitro* tests of certain important biological end points [19].

A corollary problem is that of finding suitable animal models of human disease. A sophisticated approach to toxicological testing in behalf of man's health should include animal experiments in which animal models of human diseases are available. This means the use of not only normal animals but animals stressed by a variety of factors as test subjects. Although it has been found possible to provoke most human disease in one or more animals (or the disease occurs naturally in one or more animals), this is not universally true. Thus, this subject deserves a concerted, dedicated effort of its own.

A special challenge is that of epidemiology. It is elementary, yet essential, to point out there are differences in biological behavior between man and other animals. Epidemiology or systematic observations on human populations are useful for several reasons. Desirably, confirmation of theoretical constructs of disease or of the results of animal experimentation should come from observation in humans. At the same time, sophisticated epidemiological studies can provide useful insight that can in turn generate new hypotheses and additional animal experiments. This has generally been the pattern of many of the human disease epidemiological studies pursued by the National Cancer Institute. Human epidemiology also provides clues concerning specific exposure as well as effect in much the same way as physical measurement and monitoring is used to describe physical distribution in the environment. The Community Pesticides Study administered by the Environmental Protection Agency has been of this sort.

While chronic disease epidemiology is acknowledged as an exceedingly important instrument in fact finding and in understanding of the biological effects of environmental agents, its rise continues to remain limited. To a great extent, the doing of epidemiology is itself limited by the relative unavailability of certain kinds of reliable data. Certain types of data that would be useful or even essential are simply not available because of lack of appropriate instruments for collecting them. For example, the notion of screening human beings for all diseases in the face of a large or unending number of environmental contaminants is untenable. Accordingly, there are advantages in narrowing the population at risk and under observation to those who are known to have been exposed to known contaminants. To do this requires some specific data-collecting instruments for selecting population and methods for following persons to the point of definite biological end points, including death. Without these fairly straightforward yet essential aids to data collecting, this area of research becomes exceedingly time consuming and tedious or even impossible to accomplish. While these data collection needs have been recognized for some time, they are yet to be supplied.

In the realm of collection of data, existing sources are thought to be adequate for cerain types of studies although modifications are necessary in the institutions that collect the data in order to make them useful. For example, the social security system could be a useful device for following a variety of persons over a number of years. There exist certain registries for the maintenance of data on specific disease processes. There are, for example, a number of cancer registries that are considered satisfactory or that could be improved. There is a need for a corresponding registry for congenital malformations. The attractive notion expressed above of singling out and following over a period a population of persons subjected to known environmental exposures is presently possible only in unusual circumstances and then with great difficulty. In part, this is due to the high degree of mobility of the population. In part, too, it represents a seeming conflict between the twin desires of achieving useful scientific goals and maintaining personal privacy. As a consequence, the practice of following a cohort of persons to death is achieved only rarely.

An additional but major problem in epidemiology of chronic diseases relates to availability of suitably trained scientists. In part this is a reflection of the very long period necessary for epidemiological studies to mature and to lead to scientific results and to publication. As a result, rewards in academic departments—traditionally given for publication of results in professional journals—are not liberally available to chronic disease epidemiology. This paradox, a sizable research task to be accomplished (and even a liberal amount of money to aid in its accomplishment), has not been matched by sufficient numbers of suitably trained professionals. This situation has led several to recommend that public subsidization be provided to the training of nonphysician professionals in chronic disease epidemiology [20].

Finally, there is a question of forecasting or of "looking around the corner." The universe of environmental physical and (especially) chemical agents is exceedingly large. Clearly, the rate of technological production and alteration has outstripped the rate of accretion of biological understanding. Because of this enormous disparity, it has generally been difficult or impossible to make intelligent and systematic choices as to where to begin to attack the total list. In practice, biologists, those who are charged with setting priorities for research, are overwhelmed by the apparent size of the universe. Priorities and choices have generally been set by chance findings rather than in any systematic fashion. Scientific interest in asbestos was spurred on by the finding of asbestos fibers in the ambient atmosphere and in water. Hepatic angiosarcomata were discovered in unexpected numbers and clustered among certain occupational workers leading to previously unasked biological questions about vinyl chloride. Residues of some insecticides and of diethylstilbesterol were found unexpectedly in foodstuffs, thereby secondarily setting research priorities for biology and medicine. If one is to hope to "be ahead of the news," to anticipate and to guide the effort of scientific research into environmental diseases in any systematic fashion, there must be developed and used some particular tools for forecasting and assessing.

A very few pilot attempts in this direction have been made. The National Cancer Institute has embarked upon a specific exploration along with the Stanford Research Institute of the ranking of the members of the universe of chemical substances. The ranking is done according to a probability of human exposure plus some insight concerning inherent biological effects. This pilot attempt appears to hold the promise of ranking over a range of approximately 10^{18}.

The National Cancer Institute's patterns of cancer mortality and morbidity (country by country) was mentioned earlier. Again, this holds out the promise of specific yet systematic clues pointing toward areas of needed information and research [21].

A potentially fruitful avenue is based upon the observation that knowledge of physical and chemical properties of chemical substances is generally much more complete than is biological knowledge. Theoretically, it is possible to infer certain types of environmental behavior (persistence, adsorption on particulate matter, migration, and leaching, etc.) from a knowledge of certain physical and chemical properties. Again, it appears possible to devise an index (or indexes) that would give some estimate of the probability of human impingement or human exposure. A series of these indexes (with suitable qualifications) could then be used to select from a universe of substances those that conceivably could become a hazard to health. Again, these might be used to derive research priorities.

Finally, there appears to be considerable merit to the notion of environmental forecasting—technological forecasting for the purpose of pointing up future instances of concern for environmental health. Both new technologies and growth in scale of established technologies are of interest. Here the idea of most attractiveness is to apply some of the traditional industrial tools of technology forecasting in order to predict forthcoming technological developments in direction and in size that could, in turn, indicate new materials in use, new distributions of materials, or greatly augmented uses of materials that themselves could represent environmental hazards. The methodology of industrial technology forecasting should be of value in the environmental field but, as yet, has received only rudimentary application. To be most useful, an environmental forecasting effort would of necessity be a scientifically insightful and critical instrument for assessing new technological and developmental directions.

Responsibility for Providing Information for Regulatory Decision Making: Public versus Private Roles

The Information used by government agencies in their role as standard setters, regulators, and enforcers comes from a variety of sources. The scientific research that generates this information is underwritten or performed by a number of different laboratories and agencies—public and private. The patterns vary among the substances regulated and according to a variety of government and corporate policies, incentives, etc. In some instances, such as therapeutic drugs, private manufacturers supply essentially all of the information upon which government agencies base regulatory decisions. In other instances, such as air pollutants, the government generally assumes all of the task of doing or underwriting the research.

It is convenient in discussing this issue to divide the universe of chemical substances into three categories:

Commercial Products Subject to Regulation. Examples are pesticides, food additives, and therapeutic drugs. In each case, the pattern has developed of requiring from a developer or manufacturer of a new product the information upon which the manufacturer bases his claim of safety and freedom from hazard. As pointed out earlier, in the evolution of the Food, Drug and Cosmetic Act and the federal Insecticide, Fungicide and Rodenticide Act, the onus of demonstrating safety prior to permission for marketing was clearly placed on the manufacturer. Thus, for new products subject to regulation, it has generally been assumed it was the manufacturer's responsibility to perform or underwrite the research and testing from which this information was obtained.

Nonproducts, Substances Subject to Regulation Considered in the Public Domain. Air and water pollutants are clearly of this sort. Here, the federal government has generally shouldered the burden of the research for regulation.

Commercial Products Not Subject to Regulation. Industrial chemicals, many of which are used as intermediate substances in the manufacture of other materials, are of this sort. Here there is essentially no requirement or enforceable responsibility nor any real incentive to engage in research and assessment of the sort required as the basis for regulatory decisions.

Polyvinyl chloride and polychlorinated biphenyls (both substances recently the subject of concern as hazards to health) were of this sort. As a result of a lack of any party's responsibility, this class of materials is generally little studied.[a] Substances from this class are generally brought to the laboratory at the same time they are brought to the public's attention as real or implied problems—often as a result of a chance finding or a recognized accident. Thus, alkyl mercury in bodies of water, in fish, and as a hazard to humans became the subject of some study after it was found as an unexpected contaminant [22]. Investigations into the biological effects of polychlorinated biphenyls were initiated after finding a hazard in the industrial environment [23] and then after this family of chemicals were found to be a contaminant in animal feed and in food for human consumption [24, 25].

Biological research and testing to determine the health hazards of chemical materials is performed by a number of different institutions— private and public—and these programs of research are supported from a diversity of sources. The patterns vary widely according to the class of substance under consideration. Thus, knowledge about the unintended side effects of a pesticide typically is generated by a different group of laboratories than those engaged in research on air pollutants or therapeutic drugs.

The federal programs of environmental health research are divided for the most part among three agencies (Health, Education, and Welfare, Energy Research & Development Agency, and the Environmental Protection Agency). In addition, there are minor programs in each of several other agencies such as the Department of Agriculture and the Department of Defense. That is, the government's programs are "distributed" among several agencies—representing a portfolio of programs and a spectrum of research—from relatively basic to relatively applied. The largest portions include the research program on biology and medicine of the ERDA (formerly the AEC) and the research sponsored by the National Cancer Institute. In addition to the National Cancer program, certain other parts of the National Institutes of Health (National Institute of Environmental Health Sciences, National Heart and Lung Institute) are contributors to this field as are certain other bureaus and programs within HEW (the Food and Drug Administration and the National Institute of Occupational Safety and Health, for example).

In practice, the programs of the National Cancer Institute and the ERDA dominate federal activities. Of the total federal investment in environmental health research for chemical and physical agents, roughly half

---

[a] A pending piece of federal legislation, the Toxic Substances Control Act, was designed to fill this very gap in both knowledge and regulation.

is spent in behalf of research on ionizing and nonionizing radiation and most of this is under the control of the ERDA [7]. The significance is to be found in the fact that the remaining half is divided among all of the chemical substances considered as potential hazards. As the PSAC Panel on Chemicals and Health noted, "There is a heavy emphasis on radiation research—most of it on effects of ionizing radiation and most of this by the AEC" [7]. The panel members found this a distinct imbalance considering the relative magnitude of the regulatory tasks and the legacy of existing scientific information in each case.

In 1972 a careful review was undertaken of all of the government programs of environmental health research [26]. The purpose of this survey was to determine the magnitude and character of the investment in this area of research, to ascertain how the programs were distributed among several agencies, and to determine how this research was divided among several substantive categories. In order to determine the amount of effort devoted strictly at an understanding of the effects of chemical and physical agents on biological organisms in a narrow sense, certain categories of research were singled out. These reflect research done to promote understanding of absorption (or entry) of environmental substances into the human organism, metabolism, distribution, along with mechanism of biological action, modification, interactions with other substances, and biological consequences or end points. These figures most closely approximate the most meaningful and the most sophisticated of environmental health research (table 5-2). From figures such as these, the distribution and areas of emphasis can be seen. The programs of the two regulatory agencies concerned with chemical substances, the FDA and the EPA, are relatively poorly funded while, again, the AEC and the National Cancer Institute contained the lion's share of the task. If, as a further refinement, that research concerned solely with mechanisms of biological action (perhaps an indicator of the degree of scientific sophistication of this research), the total investment here is quite meager, amounting to $11.9 million in FY-1972. Eighty percent of this research is supported by the National Institutes of Health (64 percent of it within the National Cancer Institute).

Table 5-3 illustrates how these federal funds were divided among grants, contracts, and intramural (within government) research.

The private (manufacturing) sector invests heavily in certain aspects of environmental health research. Much of this is focused on the particular topics of therapeutic drugs and on pesticidal chemicals. (Since these are not classified nor refined in the same way as are the figures for the government, comparability is difficult.) Table 5-4 illustrates the relative magnitudes of these research programs. These figures include expenditures for both basic and applied studies, research and development to-

Table 5-2

Federal Research Effort Aimed at Understanding the Human Biological Effects of Physical and Chemical Environmental Agents

Agency	Total—Physical and Chemical Agents, Human-directed Biological Research Only[a]			
	Physical ($'s Million)	Chemical ($'s Million)	Total ($'s Million)	Percent of Total
EPA	2.8	7.3	10.2	11.8
AEC	25.1	2.7	27.8	32.2
HEW	6.9	26.2	33.1	38.6
NCI	(0.8)	(11.6)	(12.4)	(14.5)
NIEHS	(1.6)	(10.0)	(11.5)	(13.4)
NIOSH	(2.7)	(2.8)	(5.6)	(6.5)
FDA	(1.8)	(1.8)	(3.6)	(4.2)
DOD	6.2	0.6	6.9	7.9
Other	4.9	3.2	8.1	9.5
Total	46.0	40.0	86.0	100.0

[a] These amounts do not include the appropriation for the Pharmacology/Toxicology Program of the National Institute of General Medical Sciences (see p. 36H).

Note: See [6].

Table 5-3

Distribution of Federal Support for Environmental Health Research (Percent)

Agency	In-house	Percent Contract	Grant
AEC	0	100	0
EPA	59	37	4
DOD	74	25	1
HEW:			
NIOSH	60	30	10
NCI	0	51	49
NIEHS	27	3	70
FDA	53	47	0
Average	39	42	19

ward new product opportunities as well as that dedicated to an understanding of pharmacology and side effects. They may also represent some nondrug research (such as that aimed at hardware and technological items).

The development of a new therapeutic agent follows a pattern generally dictated by the Food, Drug and Cosmetic Act. The progress of develop-

Table 5-4
Industry-financed R&D on Drugs for Human Use, 1968-71
($'s million)

1968 *Actual*	1969 *Actual*	1970 *Actual*	1971 *Budgeted*
449.5	505.8	565.8	625.3

Source: Data from the Pharmaceutical Manufacturers Association.

Table 5-5
Expenditures for Toxicology and Metabolism by Members of the Pesticides Industry, 1967, 1970, and 1971
($'s million)

1967	1970	1971 *Estimated*
8.5	11.2	12.0

Source: Original data drawn from a study performed for the National Agricultural Chemical Association.

ment proceeds through investigational or experimental stages through to the point of satisfying the requirements for a "New Drug Application." While the general pattern of these investigations is governed by the law, the choice of particular studies is made as a result of negotiations between the government (FDA) and the manufacturer.

Pesticides are generally produced by large chemical manufacturers, which also develop and manufacture a variety of chemical products. During the process of developing these products, manufacturers are obliged to supply the government (Department of Agriculture and the Environmental Protection Agency) with information on chemical analytic techniques for measurement, residues expected on plants, and, in the case of materials used on food crops, biological effects and side effects. The investments made by industry in behalf of biology, including toxicology of pesticides, are much more modest than those made by the pharmaceutical industry (table 5-5).

Food additives represent a special class. Again, these are typically the products of large chemical manufacturers. However, the scale of their production is generally very small and their total volume represents a very small fraction of the total production of the industry. In some other cases they are produced by small, specialty manufacturers. In either case, the incentive to perform much prior research and testing is not overwhelming. Again, the FDA requires certain minimal pieces of information before permitting their enregistration. Much of this work is performed by independent testing laboratores on contract to the manufacturer. The quality and the sophistication of this work has varied considerably.

Other regulatory laws are less explicit in their obligations for research and for background information for safety. Household chemical products and consumer products are governed by the Federal Hazardous Substance Act. The power of this law comes from the use of the project label, which is supposed to denote a hazard. However, the onus in this case lies with the government to demonstrate that a specific product is not safe and, as others have pointed out, the government is poorly equipped to engage in research sufficient to establish safety in any systematic fashion [7]. For industrial chemical substances as products, there is essentially no specific obligation on the part of any party to engage in research and to supply information on biological effects and safety. The National Institute of Occupational Safety and Health is the government's focus for research on materials that may be hazards in the occupational environment. The scale of effort in this area remains small. For industrial quantities of chemical substances that may find their way into the general environment, there is no systematic provision and research and investigations are mounted on the basis of perceived need or crisis. As the PSAC panel pointed out, "It should not be surprising, therefore, that the storehouse of knowledge on the biological effects of materials such as polychlorinated biphenyls are as recently gathered as they are" [7].

Consequences: What Is the Quality of the Information?

The storehouse of information for decisions for environmental health is very poorly stocked—both in quality and in quantity. With the balance of federal research heavily weighted in the direction of the biology of ionizing radiation, it is not surprising to find that the legacy of information is much better supplied in radiobiology than for chemical substances and pollutants. In spite of the seemingly compelling case for good information for regulatory decision making, in spite of the evident opportunity for prevention of ill health, through regulation, the amount of information available from research for judgments and decisions is strikingly poor. The challenge of this task of research has not been taken up to any extent proportional to the importance of the issue nor commensurate with the capacity of science to contribute to this endeavor.

The legacy of scientific information gathered reflects a great deal of research that is superficial or nonsophisticated in character. In addition, much of the information used for decision making represents "frontier science." That is, it has been very common, for a variety of reasons, to reflect unconfirmed, preliminary results from laboratory experiments in regulatory action. It has been not at all common for the results of experimental studies to be "rushed into action"—sometimes through the zeal of an individual investigator, sometimes because of a probing press that has uncovered an important scientific result that "demands" regulation, sometimes because of a beleaguered government agency that finds it uncomfortable to deliberate on information, however tentative. A number of regulatory decisions in recent years on such substances as cyclamates, diethylstilbesterol, and 2,4,5-T reflected the results of frontier science. The classical doing of science includes a great deal of critical review and interpretation of results by peers of the investigator. Further, experimental results are viewed as only really valid when they have been independently obtained by other investigators. The frontier science phenomenon bypasses this important element of scientific confirmation and interpretation considered of vital importance in maintaining the quality of scientific investigation.

The body of scientific information reflected in government regulation is, therefore, often unmatured and is without benefit of critical interpretation as to its real meaning. It is not at all clear that the public's best interest is served by forcing or allowing regulatory decisions to be made on the basis of tenuous and tentative knowledge. It is commonly said that decision makers must come to a decision in the face of even halfway or incomplete information. One possible decison, which is probably not elected with sufficient frequency, would be to seek additional knowledge. In addition, however, and most important, there is a strong need for some new and imaginative instruments to foreshorten yet preserve the traditional role of peer review and interpretation of otherwise unmatured and preliminary scientific data for regulation.

References

1. *Cumulative Regulatory Effects on the Cost of Automotive Transportation—Final Report of the Ad Hoc Committee,* Prepared for the Office of Science & Technology, Executive Office of the President, Washington, D.C., February 28, 1972.

2. *Air Quality Criteria for Nitrogen Oxides,* Environmental Protection Agency, Washington, D.C., January 1971.

3. Ruckelshaus, W., Testimony before the U.S. Senate recommending a change in the automobile emission standard for nitrogen oxides, April 17, 1973.

4. *NO$_x$ Analysis Report,* U.S. Environmental Protection Agency, Office of Air Quality Planning & Standards, Durham, North Carolina, September 21, 1973.

5. Environmental Impact of Cadmium: A Review by the Panel on Hazardous Trace Substances, Office of Science & Technology, Executive Office of the President, *Environmental Health Perspectives,* Experimental Issue No. 7, 253-323, 1974.

6. Polychlorinated Biphenyls—Environmental Impact, A Review by the Panel on Hazardous Trace Substances, *Environmental Research,* 5: 249-362, 1972.

7. *Chemicals and Health,* Report of the Panel on Chemicals & Health of the President's Science Advisory Committee, Science & Technology Policy Office, September 1973.

8. National Academy of Sciences, *Drug Efficacy Study,* Final Report to the Commissioner of the Food and Drug Administration, Washington, D.C., 1969.

9. Golberg, L., Safety of Environmental Chemicals. The Need and the Challenge, Presented before the Panel on Chemicals and Health of the President's Science Advisory Committee, Washington, D.C., February 7, 1971.

10. Golberg, L., Intentional Food Additives and Chemical Residues in Food, Background document, Task Force on Research Planning in Environmental Health Science, National Institutes of Health, Department of Health, Education, and Welfare, 1970.

11. Department of Health, Education, and Welfare, Report and conclusions concerning the use of nitrilotriacetic acid and other substitutes for phosphates in laundry detergents, September 15, 1971.

12. Mantel, N., and Bryan, W.R., Safety testing of carcinogenic agents. *J. Nat. Cancer Institute,* 27: 455-470, 1961.

13. Albert, R., and Altschuller, B., *Considerations Relating to the Formulation of Limits for CONF-72050, National Technical Information Service,* Springfield, Virginia, 1973.

14. Friedman, L., *Problems of Evaluating the Health Significance of Chemicals in Foods,* Proceedings of the 5th International Congress on Pharmacology and the Future of Man, San Francisco, California, 1972.

15. *Report of the Secretary's Commission on Pesticides and Their Relationship to Environmental Health,* U.S. Department of Health, Education, and Welfare, December 1969.

16. Finklea, J., The Conceptual Basis for Environmental Standards,

Academy Forum on the Health Effects of Air Pollutants, National Academy of Sciences, Washington, D.C., February 7, 1973.

17. Environmental Protection Agency, *Preamble to Final Lead Regulations,* Washington, D.C., October 1972.

18. The Clean Air Act as amended, P.L. 604, 91st Congress, 1971.

19. News release, National Cancer Institute, Development of *In-vitro* Test for Cancer.

20. *Man's Health and the Environment. Some Research Needs,* National Institute of Environmental Health Sciences, National Institutes of Health, Department of Health, Education, and Welfare, 1970.

21. Hoover, R., Mason, T.J., McKay, F.W., and Fraunini, J.F., *Geographic Patterns of Cancer Mortality for U.S. Counties,* Epidemiology Branch, National Cancer Institute, National Institutes of Health, Bethesda, Maryland, 1975.

22. Hazards of Mercury, *Environmental Research,* 4: 1-69, 1971.

23. Schwartz, L., An Outbreak of Halowax Acne ("Cable Rash"), *J. Amer. Med. Assoc.,* 122: 158-161, 1943.

24. *Polychlorinated Biphenyls and the Environment,* Interdepartmental Task Force on PCB's, COM-72-10419, National Technical Information Service, Springfield, Virginia, May 1972.

25. Polychlorinated Biphenyls—Environmental Impact, A Review by the Panel on Hazardous Trace Substances, *Environmental Research,* 5: 249-362, 1972.

26. *Report of the OST-CEQ Ad Hoc Committee on Environmental Health Research,* Washington, D.C., June 1972.

6 The Law versus Science in Regulation

At the outset, this title may appear misleading. Research aimed at uncovering and understanding hazards is generally thought of as supportive of the legal instruments directing government in regulation. Indeed, such a complementary relationship, to a great extent, does in fact exist. At the same time, however, there have emerged in recent years a number of areas where science and the laws of regulation are not totally matched—provoking, at times, severe problems of public policy and of administration.

In Theordore Lowi's view, regulation by the federal government, beginning with the Interstate Commerce Commission, is more than simply an extension of the executive branch. It is, he insists, a larger delegation by Congress leading to the establishment of a minigovernment—legislative, executive, and judicial [1]. As regulatory authorities in the name of human health have evolved, several trends can be discerned. (The history of certain of the major laws is discussed in chapter 2.) One has been a clear tendency to extend regulation to more and more classes of items—products, effluents, industrial processes, uses of products such as pesticides, etc. Another has been an increasing specificity of the laws governing regulation. In part, this latter has been a response to critics of earlier laws who have pointed out what appeared to be weaknesses in administration thought to be attributable to lack of sufficient detail and specific guidelines [2]. A third important trend in recent years has been that of Congress' mandating certain of the specific standards for regulation. This may be viewed as simply an ultimate extension of the trend toward specificity. On the other hand, it may also properly be considered as desire on the part of Congress to retract some of the discretionary power that body formerly had provided to administrators of regulatory agencies. This combination of broadening and intensifying the regulatory tools while, at the same time, solidifying the details in the law has had a marked effect on the relationship between science and regulation.

Rigidity of Legal Formation

Relative to science, the legal framework of regulation tends to be highly structured and often rigid. This should not be surprising and, in fact, there are a number of advantages to a specific, tight, legal structure. For example, a highly specific construction leaves little room for equivocation. All parties to the law entertain similar interpretations. The industries regulated are able to determine in advance what obligations they have toward the regulatory agency. Clarity and specificity are probably desirable from a purely legal standpoint as they go far toward insuring an orderly process. However, specificity brings with it a quality of rigidity. The regulatory laws dealing with food and drugs and air pollutants are generally considered to have a foundation in some body of scientific findings and understanding. Typically, in fact, laws are written as a reflection of the state of scientific knowledge at the time of their writing. What they often do not accommodate is the dynamic character of science. Science, by definition, is a continuously changing affair—raising new hypotheses, characterized by new and unexpected empirical findings.

A very large number of the crisis-ladened regulatory decisions of the past few years have had the common characteristic of conflict between an older decision and new scientific finding. The herbicide 2,4,5-T was one of a family of phenoxy herbicides developed in the 1940s. Although relatively few toxicological investigations were mounted, all of the evidence available at that time pointed to a family of chemical substances of very low toxicity. In 1964 the National Cancer Institute of the National Institutes of Health began a large-scale screening experiment to determine (in a preliminary manner) the potential of several pesticides to provoke birth defects, cancer, or genetic alteration. Quite unexpectedly, 2,4,5-T emerged from this pilot study with a sufficiently positive result as a teratogen as to provoke further confirmatory studies and regulatory action. All three of the new tests performed on this chemical represented scientific questions that had not been posed previously.

In a similar fashion, the nonnutrient sweetner cyclamate was subjected to animal testing in a way that revealed, unexpectedly, bladder tumors in the experimental test animals used. Both the findings and the hypothesis that cyclamates might lead to the formation of tumors were simply not considered by scientists years before when these compounds were first entered into use. Mercury metal has long been considered very inert in the environment. Because it was inert, inorganic mercury as a byproduct of industrial processes was disposed of simply by dumping it into bodies of water. Only latterly and unexpectedly, was it discovered that this elemental mercury was alkylated naturally by organisms in the environment and that the resulting methyl mercury was many times more biologically "available" and highly toxic. A fourth example is the family of chemicals known as polychlorinated biphenyls (PCBs). PCBs were first developed commercially in the 1920s specifically because of their peculiar and highly advantageous physical and chemical properties. They were highly stable—even at high temperatures. Further, they demonstrated a particularly high dielectric capacity and good electrical insulating properties. The combination of these characteristics made PCBs particularly useful in situations where fluids were needed in conjunction with very high temperatures (e.g., heat exchangers) and in electrical equipment (transformers) where there was danger of arcing and fire. One of the unexpected findings in the case of PCBs was their discovery in a remarkably widespread pattern of distribution in the environment approximating that of DDT. Another was a series of accidental leakages of PCBs into foodstuffs and animal feeds, which led to identifiable human disease [3].

In each of these cases the judgments of a previous decision to permit development, marketing, and use were rather abruptly overturned by new scientific insight.[a] In many cases, however, there has been no truly appropriate legal accommodation to a changing scientific foundation.

Approvals of New Drug Applications for therapeutic drugs and registrations for pesticidal chemicals generally assume a very long if not unlimited period of certification. If the expected duration of approval is not unlimited, it is at least thought of as long enough to permit manufacturers to capture their expected profits. In order to insure this, regulatory laws generally have not provided for easy alteration of the original permission. When alteration does occur, it, too, is looked upon as a definitive, drastic, and usually irreversible decision. The Federal Insecticide, Fungicide and Rodenticide Act permitted a pesticide permit (termed a registration) to be rescinded only by processes known as cancellation or suspension. Because these were considered very serious moves, they were chosen reluctantly and only rarely. (Suspension, the more drastic of the moves, had been exercised by 1973 only five times thoughout the entire life of the law.) In fact, of course, the law was drafted originally with this built-in inhibition to reversal of registration precisely in order to discourage capricious decisions and consequent economic perturbations.

A problem, however, arises in trying to accommodate new and unexpected scientific findings. Typically, the new science that would perturb an old decision is of preliminary character. The experiments on 2,4,5-T were screening experiments. When methyl mercury was found in fish, that discovery had to be interpreted in the perspective of an unknown background of mercury occurring naturally in the environment.

If government action is to be a reflection of good science, a definitive regulatory decision should often be delayed until confirmatory or more definitive results can be obtained, or until the results obtained can be understood and interpreted. Yet, as discussed in chapter 5, a great deal of the science reflected in regulation is of preliminary character.

Scientifically, therefore, the character of the threats implied by the

---

[a] In the absence of a Toxic Substances Control Act, there has been no single regulatory authority exercised over industrial chemical substances such as the polychlorinated biphenyls. PCBs were subject of a review by the government, however, in 1972 leading to voluntarily imposed restrictions.

scientific findings is often highly uncertain. In the past, in cases of implied threats, where many have argued for banning or for other hard lines of regulation and others (notably those with economic interests at stake) have argued just as fervently for no action, scientific judgment would often urge that a proper response would be the gathering of additional information. This logic often dictates a *temporary* restriction on the use or manufacture of a material pending the gathering of additional information or the interpretation of the results. However, because of the characteristic rigidity of many of the regulatory laws, temporary restrictions have not generally been available as options. The Panel on Herbicides of the President's Science Advisory Committee recognized the defect in the pesticide laws in 1971 and recommended change in the legislation to make provisions for a temporary restriction [4]. Partly as a result of that recommendation, the new pesticide law, the Federal Environmental Pesticide Control Act of 1972, permitted the reclassification of a pesticide from "general-use" to a "restricted-use" category [5]. This classification decision, which can be elected fairly simply by the administrator of the Environmental Protection Agency and which does not carry with it the stigma of outright ban, can be used as a temporary restriction.

A second example of legal rigidity versus a dynamic science is the problem of standard "protocols" for testing. The laws governing the regulation of chemical products have generally placed upon the manufacturer the burden of gathering the information necessary to establish safety. That is, the research and testing necessary to determine safety are performed or underwritten by the industry petitioning for permission to market. In some cases, the experimental procedures are not prescribed in the law but rather are left to the discretion of the manufacturer. (This is generally true in the case of therapeutic drugs although the general phases of animal experimentation and clinical testing are spelled out.) In several other cases, the law obliges the government agency to develop a series of "standard" testing procedures the manufacturer must follow in gathering this background information. Again, there are perceived benefits of this pattern for some parties.

Standardized testing prescriptions that the manufacturer simply fulfills offer the rewards of stability and predictability. A manufacturer can plan that part of the task of development of a new product with a fair degree of certainty and he can demonstrate to the regulatory bureaucracy that he has completed all that he was asked to do. Again, too, all of this makes for an orderly legal process. However, the imposition of standard "protocols" for research has been an invitation to bad science. In several cases, it has led to the mounting of research and testing that were simply inappropriate for the substances under investigation or for their eventual applications. This pattern of "routine" or "standard" testing exercises is clearly in many cases both scientifically and monetarily wasteful.

The origin of this pattern is fairly clear and involved the government's obligation to make decisions for a mounting list of chemical substances that found their way into an increasing variety of complex applications. Hence, for pesticides and food additives, for example, it became attractive in view of expediency and orderly administration to designate a series of standard or routine procedures that manufacturers were obligated to fulfill. The simple fulfilling of these steps became the administrative hurdles to overcome in seeking registration or certification. As well as a pattern of administration procedure, this pattern of "standard" tests has found itself written into the regulatory laws themselves, from time to time [6].

Scientifically, such a process has at times proved meaningless. It has encouraged the substitution of mechanical steps for what should be a raising of specific scientific hypotheses. Investigations should be based on some insight into the specific chemical and physical properties of the substance in question, on whatever preliminary information there may be concerning biological effects, and on some astute guesses as to the probability and routes of exposure to man. The following example may illustrate the point. In an effort to find substitutes for phosphate-containing detergents, a number of manufacturers developed alternative detergents composed of caustic and other salts in some case, and chelating agents in others. Both the environmental and human biological effects that could be expected from tripolyphosphate would clearly be very different from those resulting from caustic or saline "builders," as they are called. A "routine" or "standard" set of tests applied to all of these materials would be scientifically meaningless as they would be unlikely to offer any real insight into the biological mechanisms involved and would afford no real understanding of hazards, if any, that these substances might represent.

Leon Golberg has commented in several instances on this standard test phenomenon versus real scientific understanding:

Flexibility of approach to safety is a slogan to which all pay lip service. In practice, however, any unorthodox system gives rise to problems of interpretation, usually because the background of experience is so slender. 'Playing it safe,' that is sticking to established routine, is unfortunately often the best commercial policy, even though it may yield little of value scientifically . . . Even today the tendency exists to substitute a mass of data for quality, a mechanical, technical approach for expert, intelligent appraisal—in brief 'print out' for thinkout [7].

Golberg has been impressed with what he has considered an "incentive to negativity"—a fear on the part of government agencies of discovering unexpected and awkward facts and an incentive on industry's part to produce only negative results.

. . . Science has moved on. In certain respects, however, the phase of mechanical performance of set exercises in animals has persisted to the present day . . . so much so, that even now it is possible to complete the investigations necessary for clearance knowing virtually nothing, and understanding even less, about the intrinsic biological properties of a compound [8].

Unfortunately, the traditional pattern persists. Both the House and the Senate versions of the Toxic Substances Control Act contain key provisions that direct the administrator of the Environmental Protection Agency to prescribe "test protocols for such substances or classes of substances . . . necessary to protect against measurable risk to health or the environment. . . ." [9, 10]. The implications of the new legislation are the development of a series of testing patterns or procedures for large classes of industrial chemical substances that have never before been subjected to biological investigation. Fortunately, the advice of the National Academy of Sciences has been solicited and an overseeing Toxic Substances Board is called for in the legislation. However, the principal objection remains. The legislative process has still failed to come to grips with the character of the scientific investigation, which must be undertaken if any real biological understanding is to be forthcoming for environmental chemicals. This demands flexibility, not standard or class-related protocols. It demands the application of reasonable scientific insight, not the institution of seemingly orderly and categorical but scientifically meaningless investigations.

Administrative Discretion versus Mandated Standards

One important trend in recent years has been that of Congress' direct mandating of standards for regulation in behalf of health and the environment. In place of a general commission and delegation of authority, in certain cases Congress has specified the precise levels of pollutants to be permitted in the environment or the levels of contaminants to be allowed in foods. There are at present two outstanding examples, the automobile emission standards in the Clean Air Act of 1971 [11] and the amendment to the Food, Drug and Cosmetic Act, which directs the banning of a food or animal feed additive if it has been shown ". . . to cause cancer in man or experimental animals" (Delaney Clause) [12].

Both of these acts are subjects of continuing discussion but much comment has already been added to the debate. There are certain additional comments worthy of consideration, however, which relate to the scientific aspects of this type of legislation and also those which link science and the political science.

Another example of a congressional mandate is the occasional injunction against any trace or residue of a pesticide material considered harmful. For several years, the Food, Drug and Cosmetic Act, required that residues of pesticides used on crops be entirely absent from foodstuffs at the time of harvest. As the science and technology of chemical analysis advanced and as monitoring became more sophisticated and widespread, pesticide residues began to appear that were formerly undetected. This represented a clearly untenable situation in which an advancing technology began to overtake a rigid legal arrangement. In 1965 a committee of the National Academy of Sciences recognized this conflict and recommended that "zero tolerance" (no measurable amount of residue tolerated) and "no residue" registrations be replaced by categories of "negligible residue tolerances." This new category explicitly recognized that residues might result from pesticide use but limited these to levels believed to be insignificant for human health [13].

This appears to have been an appropriate accommodation in the case of pesticides. There is still, however, a less than satisfactory legal acknowledgment of the continuing and relentless improvements in analytic technologies and monitoring that will surely make manifest what many had considered as absent.

Ironically, and from a scientific point of view, one of the undoubted consequences of this pattern of mandated standards is a removal of any incentives to perform further scientific investigation. Once a substance has been considered carcinogenic, albeit on the basis of preliminary evidence, further work, which might confirm or further elucidate the preliminary finding, is not pursued. There has been little further investigation of DDT since its use was restricted.

A recent (and exaggerated) example of this same phenomenon of disincentive toward further scientific investigation was found in an amendment offered by Congressman Delaney to the appropriations bill for the Food and Drug Administration. The House Appropriations Committee had recommended a sum of $200,000 for studies with respect to the Delaney amendment. This recommendation was based explicitly on the poor quality of the scientific information behind a number of regulatory decisions. Congressman Delaney offered an amendment prohibiting the spending of any part of the appropriation for studies of the Delaney Clause (except for those studies already in progress). Said Delaney at the time he introduced his amendment:

I see this type of funding as just another attempt by the FDA to delay their enforcement of the present law which is on the books since 1958. . . . For years FDA has sounded like a broken record. Once again Congress and the general public hears the general plea for financial backing to determine if proper benefit to risk factors can be established. And while the testing goes on, hazardous chemical additives remain in our food supply. . . . I emphasize that we must not have any further Government studies on the Delaney amendment at the double expense of the consumer's pocketbook and his physical well-being. We would all fair better if studies ceased or were curtailed and the law enforced against dangerous cancer causing substances [14].

Such an exhortation is reflective of a mood that insists it is "time to stop studying and get on with the business of regulating." Yet, even that admonition rests on an assumption of *some* scientific backing for the regulatory posture chosen. In fact, it presumes the scientific foundation to be adequate. In fact, as discussed earlier, the scientific fabric available for regulatory action if remarkably thin. It is clearly not adequate and, in some cases, it is close to nonexistent. However, worst of all, a prohibition or a disincentive to further exploration of the truth of the type advocated by the most recent of the Delaney amendments is clearly antithetical to any honest scientific ethic.

There is an additional reason to question the trend toward congressionally legislated standards.[b] Mandated standards are clearly examples of Congress' lifting the regulatory decision process out of the hands of the executive branch and placing it in its own. In this regard, it represents a reversal of the traditional pattern of increasing delegation of authorities to executive branch agencies but rather is a pulling back of certain decisions into its own house. Some have recognized and applauded this move as a part of a broader pattern in which "social" decisions are reserved to the Congress leaving only the technical views and enforcement to the executive agencies [15]. The adovcates of this point of view consider the agency bureaucracy as insufficiently broad (which it is) and ill-prepared to consider questions such as how much of a given recognized hazard the nation's inhabitants should be willing or permitted to suffer. The technical issue of the nature of the biological risk, they insist, should be the extent of the judgment demanded of an FDA or an EPA.

This general principle has had remarkably little national debate. Its protagonists seem to assume we already know for sure much that regrettably is quite uncertain. Regulatory agencies typically do take a narrow view of the scene they survey. In fact, this is probably symptomatic of some of Congress' own pressures. It appears entirely wrong to act by removing authorities from these agencies, thereby further weakening and narrowing them. Rather, they should be appropriately strengthened and supported to perform the broad tasks these important decisions demand. It is this uncertainty and freedom from strict codification that James Q.

---

[b] Although only two examples are cited, there has been pressure from time to time in Congress to extend the Delaney principle of total prohibition to certain other disease processes in addition to cancer.

Wilson insisted was so necessary an ingredient in preserving effective power of a regulatory agency [16].

Questions of Benefits, Utility, and Dependence and the Law

As discussed in the previous chapter, the major emphasis in laws governing the regulation of chemical products has been on hazards and the protection from hazards. Generally, questions of efficacy or usefulness have not been dealt with in the law but typically have been referred to the marketplace. One of the notable results of this single-minded legal mandate has been that good information about utility and efficacy at the time of decision making is often (or even generally) unavailable or it is of such poor quality that it is not of any real use [17].

This assertion of paucity of scientific information about efficacy or utility for therapeutic drugs made by the National Academy of Sciences has been challenged from time to time [18]. Some have suggested that the cost incurred in documenting biological effectiveness and efficacy for drugs is so great as to outweigh its usefulness as it tends to limit the rate of introduction of new drugs into the marketplace [19, 20]. This point of view rests heavily on an argument favoring consumer assignment of benefits and utility of pharmaceutical products [20]. In fact, this point of view is subject to fundamental challenge. Further, the judgment of professionals (practitioners) is often much less informed than one might like to believe. A.C. Cochrane [21] has commented at length on the lack of decent random controlled clinical trials of a variety of "established treatments of choice" (including drugs). He attributes to this type of noneffective expenditure a large fraction of costs of health care in Great Britain for which no increase in health can be expected. In the United States, perhaps the most recent examples of drug therapy, which have been accepted on reasonable theory, established through years of use with apparent benefit and ultimately discredited through controlled studies were the family of oral antidiabetic agents [22, 23], and a series of drugs designed to lower blood lipid levels [24].

Polychlorinated biphenyls represent a prominent exception, perhaps, where the importance of utility of an existing product was particularly evident in the course of decision making. Only 5 percent of all transformers are filled with PCBs. However, those PCB-containing transformers are generally located in confined spaces where it is most important to prevent fires and explosions. It seems probable that some of the very properties that rendered these compounds particularly useful in industry and commerce (high degree of physical and chemical stability) contributed to their persistence and, hence, ubiquity in the environment. The finding of PCBs in the environment and the incidents of accidental human exposures provoked a number of reviews of the scientific knowledge about the impact on the environment and the effects on the health of humans and on other animal species [25, 26]. In addition, in order to arrive at a studied and appropriate regulatory stance, the federal government assembled an interagency Task Force on PCBs in late 1971. Part of the work undertaken by this Task Force was the study and documentation of the utility and true benefits of polychlorinated biphenyls and the ascertaining of the ways, if any, the country had become dependent on PCBs. The Task Force attempted to supply information to answer the question, what penalties would the nation face if it were forced to do without PCBs? As a part of this question, the Task Force explored all of the instances where other materials might be substituted for PCBs.

The Task Force, realizing this, appreciating the possibility of penalties associated with the removing of these substances (there were dire predictions of fires and explosions offered by those who discouraged regulatory action) entered upon a systematic examination of utility, benefits, and substitutes. The National Bureau of Standards was engaged to undertake this review in a systematic fashion.

This analysis examined four major categories of PCB uses (dielectric fuilds for capacitors and transformers, industrial fluids for hydraulic, gas turbine and vacuum pump uses, heat transfer fluids, and plasticizer or miscellaneous uses). What emerged from this analysis was a documented story underlying the particular importance or dependence on PCBs in electrical applications and the lesser importance or possibility of substitutes in other applications. This analysis in brief, played a key role in the government's final pronouncements on polychlorinated biphenyls.

The story is related here, since, as an example of systematic analysis of benefit, it is a relatively rare event. Its accomplishment required an extra effort in addition to the usual reviews that stand behind regulatory decisions. There was no legal mandate for this analysis. Its accomplishment in this case was probably somewhat more palatable since it was commissioned by an interagency steering group and was not solely the persuasion of a single agency charged narrowly with protection of health and environmental integrity.

A second but abortive attempt at the documentation of utility in recent years concerned household washing detergents. The Council of Environmental Quality during the spring and summer of 1971 became the focus for a series of interagency meetings on phosphates and detergents in an attempt to derive an appropriate federal policy and public stance in the face of a proliferation of products offered on the market as substitutes for phosphate detergents and in the face of an ever lengthening list of state and municipal laws banning phosphate-containing detergents.

While there appeared on the market a number of phosphate-free and low-phosphate detergents, it was not really clear that these represented net benefit or net peril. Certain of these were associated with severe esophageal damage when accidentally ingested by children. Some were predictably harmful to washing machines. Notably, the utility or washing power of these substitutes was uncertain. The CEQ attempted to engage the National Bureau of Standards in a comparative study of the phosphate-containing and the low- and no-phosphate detergents. In this case, the National Bureau of Standards balked—noting that, because of the very large number of variables involved (water hardness, pH, washing conditions, type of dirt, etc.), no meaningful results could be forthcoming without a carefully controlled study. The NBS estimate of the task necessary to perform an adequate study (the Bureau of Standards refused to enter into any but a full-scale investigation) was one year and $500,000.

In this case, there appeared to be insufficient time or inclination to engage in any systematic or rigorous examination of utility and the decision process remained essentially ignorant on that matter. A CEQ memorandum of May 1971 summarizing the meetings on phosphates and detergents noted that there was "substantial question of washing effectiveness for low- or non-phosphate detergents," no widely accepted standards or test procedures for evaluating effectiveness," and "Commerce [Department] attempts to get effectiveness information from industry unsuccessful thus far" [27].

A fundamental question raised during the course of these interview discussions about detergents and phosphates was that of the federal government's responsibility to be concerned with utility and efficacy. Although the 1962 drug amendments had settled the issue for therapeutic drugs, there remained considerable uncertainty about what should be done for other products in commerce. As an addendum to this story, it should be noted that in none of the draft bills contributed during this period on detergents, phosphates, and water quality was the subject of utility and efficacy treated.

Appeals and Adjudication

Virtually all regulatory laws contain provisions that offer parties aggrieved by decisions the opportunity to have them reconsidered in another (usually higher) setting through appeal. The statutes provide for these safety valves and, in most cases, provide specific directions as to which routes of appeal are available. Generally, those who desire to question further an administrator's decision have two options for appeal—administrative and judicial. One of the marked trends of the past few years has been a frequent resort to the appeals processes for major decisions. The trend has been such a prominent one that some have looked upon the administrators' original decisions as purely academic exercises, knowing that the ultimate decisions will be reached in procedures to follow—often through the courts. There are a number of factors that have contributed to this trend. It has several important consequences—especially for those decisions of a highly technical and scientific nature.

In the case of most regulatory laws, Congress has determined that the administrator of an executive branch agency is charged with determining the need for a new environmental standard for rule making or for restricting or banning a product from use. Generally, these determinations are arrived at through a systematic consideration of scientific and technical information relating to an implied or recognized hazard. The agency's next responsibility is to make known its *intentions* to the public in the form of a proposal published in the *Federal Register*.[c] This public announcement of a tentative decision is provided to allow for comment from that part of the public that is interested in the forthcoming decision. Its publication marks the beginning of a period for this reaction at the end of which the administrator is supposed to review the received comments and then announce a definitive decision.

With the announcement of a definitive decision, interested and aggrieved parties have available to them opportunities to have the decision reconsidered in additional forums. These opportunities vary in detail among the various statutes. However, in all cases, judicial review through appeal to the courts is provided and is usually looked upon as the truly final step.

Prior to judicial appeals, in many cases an appellant can request a public hearing or a special scientific review, or even both. These prejudicial reviews are sometimes considered together under the term, administrative process. While they are not always considered as processes of appeal in the strict sense, they clearly fulfill this function of second-guessing or "reviewing" what otherwise would have been a chief administrator's definitive decision. This complex of decision and appeal typically consumes a very lengthy period (years) and makes for confusion in trying to follow the course of the decision process.

Perhaps the best examples illustrative of this decision-by-appeal phe-

---

[c] In some cases, such as the finding of an "imminent hazard" the administrator can proceed directly to a public annonnuncement. In certain others, he is not obliged to include this intermediate step of proposal.

nomenon are to be found among recent pesticide decisions. (This may be so because the formal provisions for administrative and judicial appeal are especially clearly drawn in the statutes governing pesticides.)

In October 1967 the Environmental Defense Fund petitioned the Department of Agriculture to cancel and suspend all registrations for products containing DDT. A month later (and partly as a reflection of this petition) the Department of Agriculture issued a Pesticide Regulation Notice to manufacturers of DDT in which it announced its intention to cancel DDT registrations for uses on shade trees, tobacco, around the home, and in aquatic environments. This proposed move, which would take place within 30 days if no appeals were received, represented Agriculture's estimate of the degree of restriction that could be brought about without undue disruption. Cancellation of these uses of DDT would reduce the total usage by as much as one-third. (At that time, nearly 70 percent of the DDT used in the United States was used on cotton.)

Within five days following the Pesticides Registration Notice, the secretary of agriculture issued a public notice in the *Federal Register* of the intent to cancel all nonessential uses of DDT (in addition to the four mentioned above). Rather than a notice to take specific action, this latter was an invitation to the public to provide advice on what were nonessential uses. Nevertheless, seven manufacturers potentially affected by any restriction appealed this decision and requested that there be invoked a scientific advisory committee and a public hearing. (One of those petitioning for a scientific advisory review subsequently withdrew his petition.)

There then ensued a period of interesting litigation during much of 1970 and 1971 when many of the elements of frustration and conflict concerning decisions and appeals were raised. This particular round of events led eventually to the full playing out of the administration appeals procedures (public hearing and a new advisory committee review).

On August 18, 1970 the secretary of agriculture issued a Pesticide Regulation Notice announcing his intention to cancel uses of DDT in livestock, lumber, forest trees, and in over 50 food crops [28]. This was viewed by the Department of Agriculture as a continuation of the review for nonessential uses. Prior to this action, a group of four petitioners (Environmental Defense Fund, the Sierra Club, the National Audubon Society, and the West Michigan Environmental Action Council) joined in a petition to Secretary of Agriculture Hardin to ". . . take immediate action to ban the use of DDT" [29]. This was a request for immediate action (suspension) without delay during the process of appeals. The arguments were two-fold: evidence of irreparable damage to the environment and evidence linking DDT to human cancer. The petitioners asked the secretary to "(1) suspend the registration of all economic poisons that contained DDT and, (2) issue Notices of Cancellation for all registered economic poisons that contained DDT'' [29].[d]

In June 1970 the Department of Agriculture announced its refusal to order an immediate suspension of the general use of DDT, basing the decision on considerations of both hazards and benefits:

The scientific evidence now available does not establish that the use of DDT constitutes an imminent hazard to human health [a requisite for invoking a suspension order]. Scientific evidence indicates that there are some adverse effects upon certain species of fish and wildlife or the environment.

DDT has indisputably important and beneficial uses in connection with human health and agriculture, and there are not yet available suitable substitutes for all essential uses.

The use of DDT should continue to be reduced in an orderly, practical manner which will not deprive mankind of uses which are essential to the public health and welfare [30].

The petitioners had, one month before, taken this case to the U.S. Court of Appeals in the District of Columbia, seeking in particular, a judicial judgment against the secretary of agriculture for having failed to yield on their petitions to suspend and to cancel. The August cancellations, covering about 3 million pounds per year (approximately 10 percent of the total domestic use in the United States and 2.5 percent of the total United States production) followed.

The next step in litgation was an order from the Court of Appeals to the administrator of EPA[e] in January 1971 to issue a Notice of Cancellation for the remaining DDT uses and either to suspend them or indicate his reasons for refusing to suspend them [31]. This action by the court was significant—not only because of the nature of the decisions but in particular because the arguments used in deriving the opinions illustrate how scientific information and public views are reflected by the courts. First, in the majority of opinions, it was stated that:

. . . when Congress creates a procedure that gives the public a role in deciding important questions of public policy, that procedure may not lightly be sidestepped by administrators. The cancellation decision does not turn on a scientific assessment of hazard alone. The statute leaves room to balance the benefits of a pesticide against its risks . . . The statutory scheme contemplates that these questions will be explored in the full light of a public hearing and not resolved behind the closed doors of the Secretary [31].

[d] A note of explanation would perhaps be helpful. Of the two legal processes of restricting the manufacture and distribution of a pesticide, cancellation and suspension, the second, suspension, is the more definitive and forthright ban (contrary to what the terms themselves might convey).

[e] In October 1970 the Environmental Protection Agency was established and formally assumed most of the pesticide registration activities from the Department of Agriculture.

Later in this opinion, Judge Bazelon offered:

We stand on the threshold of a new era in the history of the long and fruitful collaboration of the administrative agencies and reviewing courts. For many years, courts have treated administrative policy decisions with great deference, confining judicial attention primarily matters of procedure. On matters of substance, the courts regularly upheld agency action, with a nod in the direction of the "substantial evidence" test, and a bow to the mysteries of administrative expertise. Courts occasionally asserted, but less often exercised, the power to set aside agency action on the ground that an impermissible factor had entered into the decision, or a crucial factor had not been considered. Gradually, however, that power has come into more frequent use, and with it, the requirement that administrators articulate the factors on which they base their decisions.

Strict adherence to that requirement is especially important now that the character of administrative litigation is changing. As a result of expanding doctrines of standing and reviewability, and new statutory causes of action, courts are increasingly asked to review administrative action that touches on fundamental personal interests in life, health, and liberty. These interests have always had a special claim to judicial protection, in comparison with the economic interests at stake in a ratemaking or licensing proceeding. . . .

When administrators provide a framework for principled decision-making, the result will be to diminish the importance of judicial review by enhancing the integrity of the administrative process, and to improve the quality of judicial review in those cases where judicial review is sought [31].

This opinion is fascinating, of course, for several reasons. Perhaps more than anything else, it revealed a view from the courts of their augmented responsibilities for making what had formerly beeen considered as administrative decisions and judgments. In Judge Bazelon's opinion, the courts were obliged to do this because of a vacuum of background information from the administrators. The dissenting view in this case argued that ". . . in effect, the Court is undertaking to manage the Department of Agriculture" [31].

It was this judgment, ordering the remaining cancellations and suspensions that provoked a Notice of Cancellation of the remaining DDT pesticides by EPA and, in turn, a series of 33 appeals [32]. Thirty of these requested public hearing and 3 called for a scientific advisory committee as a part of the administrative process accompanying their appeal. Both of these ultimately came into being.

The expert advisory committee was requested in February 1971, and was appointed in April with a very broad charge ". . . to consider all relevant scientific evidence concerning DDT, and to prepare a report and recommendations as to the scientific issues raised by the use of DDT." The report of this committee was submitted to the EPA administrator within about four months. Its completion came just a month after the public hearings on DDT had begun. These latter consumed six months and the testimony they generated filled 10,000 pages of transcript.

In the present context of the questions of law and science juxtaposed, it is particularly interesting to consider the limitations of these procedures as vehicles for orderly decision making in technological areas. The scientific advisory committee, by its own admission, was assembled quickly with a very short deadline. The introduction in its report betrayed some degree of frustration over these limitations:

Based upon the breadth of the charge and the pressures of a fixed time deadline for its report, the Committee has elected to depend upon the two most comprehensive recent reports on DDT . . . for the evaluation of much of the prior scientific information concerning this compound. This has allowed the Committee to concentrate its efforts upon obtaining and evaluating whatever new information has become available since these reports [33].

Thus, the scientific evidence in this case was necessarily quickly gathered and quickly weighed.

The public hearing proved even more fascinating in this regard. The hearing examiner, Edmund Sweeny, actually prohibited the introduction of the report of the expert DDT Advisory Committee into the proceedings and the record of the hearing. The parties to this hearing who had appealed the government's decision (in essense, the industries petitioning for review) argued that it was improper to introduce into the hearings a hearsay document (". . . this is nothing more than the collective opinion of a number of people. . . .") that could not be cross-examined [34]. The hearing examiner rested his point of view on a different argument. It was his definitively expressed view (and ruling) that the framers of the Federal Insecticide, Fungicide and Rodenticide Act (the law governing the regulation of pesticides), which made provision for the public hearing and the advisory committee, intended that these two vehicles be clearly separated. It was his interpretation that this law explicitly imposed an ". . . intentional legislative restriction of the legal competency of such a report in any other hearing" [35].

Therefore, although certain elements of the Advisory Committee Report were introduced into the hearing record as individual pieces of information by some of those who testified, the record itself ultimately lacked the report proper. This, of course, was a remarkable and manifest limitation of the administrative appeals process to receive and systematically consider scientific and technical information. The hearing examiner conceived of this hearing as an adversary proceeding and thus it remained. It was argued that the advisory report should not be admitted since it would be impossible to cross-examine the document. This hearing examiner held up this argument even in the midst of the willingness of the participants in the hearing to make former members of the advisory committee themselves available for examination and cross-examination.

This experience was clearly a fresh one when a new pesticide law was introduced in 1971. Again, both public hearings and scientific reviews were provided for as avenues available to those wished to appeal an administrator's decision. However, the rules governing the hearing are more explicit. Any party to the public hearing may request, as a part of the hearing, that questions be referred to a Committee of the National Academy of Sciences. Interestingly, the law requires that the report of this scientific committee be made a part of the hearing record.

William Ruckelshaus followed the completion of the public hearing on DDT with a statement of his own factual conclusions, his own opinion, and an order concerning the substantive issues that had begun the exercise—cancellation and suspension. He began by noting that the public hearing, the final stage of the administrative review, was the culmination of approximately three years of intensive inquiry into DDT. His summary and opinion, speaking for the most part to the scientific aspects, considered it bizarre (as certainly others must have) that the hearing examiner concluded that whether DDT was or was not a carcinogen or a teratogen was a "matter of law." He commented at some length on the exclusion of the advisory committe's report from the hearing record—believing that the exclusion was done in error.

The 2,4,5-T issue was again exemplary of the extended process of deferring decisions to later appeals and further reviews.

In October 1969, after several months of simply not acknowledging the new research results and in the face of sizeable public pressure, the federal government undertook several regulatory actions at the same time. These were all announced by the president's science adviser Dr. Lee DuBridge. At the same time, he turned to the President's Science Advisory Committee for some advice and assistance in evaluating these new (if tentative) screening results. A Panel on Herbicides of the President's Science Advisory Committee undertook a review of a number of herbicides. Part of that review was included in a published report on 2,4,5-T in March 1971 [36].

In May 1970 a new set of notices of cancellations and suspensions was issued for products containing 2,4,5-T. Four manufacturers challenged these decisions and proposed actions and requested the establishment of a scientific advisory committee. This committee met first on February 1, 1971 and reported its findings to the administrator of EPA. During the course of these procedures, certain other petitioners, aggrieved over what they considered as a lack of sufficiently definitive action, sought suspensions for all of the remaining registered uses of 2,4,5-T. That is, a total and immediate ban was their goal. The court's action in this instance was to remand the case to the Environmental Protection Agency for further consideration with a deadline that corresponded approximately to the completion of the advisory committee's deliberations. Thus, in this case, there was a judicial avenue of appeal being pursued concurrently with an administrative appeal.

The administrator's review of the advisory committee's report in this case provoked his judgment that (1) the advisory committee had done an adequate job of inquiry into the scientific background concerning the hazard of 2,4,5-T. In this, the committee had judged the hazard not to be excessive or imminent. But, (2) the advisory committee provided no information as to the benefits that 2,4,5-T brought with it with continued use. In addition, the staff of EPA provided the administrator with some eight scientific questions that had not been raised or resolved by the advisory committee's review.

Thus, a public hearing was sought on 2,4,5-T—both by certain of the manufacturers who took issue with the cancellation prospect for 2,4,5-T as used on rice, and by the Environmental Protection Agency itself. The EPA in this case sought to derive a public mandate—an informed and alert constituency on the matter of all of the other and remaining uses of 2,4,5-T. This last point, calling forth a public hearing before or without a specific appeal by an outside interested party, is possible because of a change in the law. The new pesticide law passed in 1972 permits the administrator, himself, to seek a public hearing.

These complex and lengthy procedures had added much less of substance to decision making than their attention would have suggested. Neither have they succeeded in augmenting public confidence in decision making. The process has been disorderly and has seemed even more. The terminology has been and continues to be confusing. The Environmental Pesticide Control Act of 1972 improved this situation to some extent. It is now the administrator's "notice of *intent* to cancel" rather than notice of cancellation that makes way for the appeals and the advisory committee review and public hearing.

The delay in reaching a definitive decision has seemed prolonged and, in fact, has been lengthy in many cases. The final decree of EPA on DDT came only after three years of intensive review. It is likely that only those few persons who followed this scenario with great care would now remember the terms of the initial government decision that provoked the ensuing appeals, reviews, and public hearings.

The agenda for an agency decision (the initial step in the process) is perceived as undesirably narrow. A public hearing permits a broadening of the list of items that may be raised for discussion. In fact, as was illustrated in the DDT case, the agenda of a public hearing may at times be unexpectedly narrowed. In part, frustration arises not over the particular substance of the decision process but because the process is simply out of sight. Public hearings appear to offer a forum for public disclosure of a portion of the decision process, a mechanism for some public contribution and interaction with it. It is, of course, to this participatory process or "pluralistic government" that some have been sharply critical in recent years. These critics have perceived an incompatability between a government based on law and a pluralistic process, and they view the latter as simply a process of ratifying bargains struck by competing interest groups [37]. The only point to be made here is that the processes of administrative (and judicial) appeal, as they have been used, have been less than adequate vehicles for systematic consideration of scientific information and ideas. Since these regulatory decisions rest ultimately on a base of scientific and technical information, there is a clear defect in the decision process.

Independent expert review of the broad spectrum of issues surrounding regulatory matters—including scientific issues—is certainly appropriate. In fact, the agencies would clearly do well to engage in more rather than less of this. A forum for public comment and public understanding of the ingredients of the decision process is highly desirable. The important caveat in this case is that expert advisory committee reviews and public hearings should *precede* rather than follow the chief administrator's decision. They should be part of the decision process. Where Judge Bazelon observed that the importance of the judicial review would be diminished by the strengthening of the administrative decision process [33], it can be said that the administrative review process would be reduced in importance if this review were incorporated into the original decision.

References

1. Lowi, T., *The End of Liberalism,* W.W. Norton and Company, Inc., New York, 1969.
2. Davis, K.C., A New Approach to Delegation, *The University of Chicago Law Review,* 36 (4): 713, 1969.
3. *Polychlorinated Biphenyls and the Environment,* Interdepartmental Task Force on PCB's, Washington, D.C., COM-72-10419, National Technical Information Service, U.S. Department of Commerce, May 1972.
4. *Report on 2,4,5-T,* A Report of the Panel on Herbicides of the President's Science Advisory Committee, Office of Science and Technology, Executive Office of the President, March 1971.
5. Federal Environmental Pesticide Control Act of 1972, Public Law 92-516, October 21, 1972.
6. S.426, Toxic Substances Control Act of 1973.

7. Golberg, L., Intentional Food Additives and Chemical Residues in Food, Background document, Subtask on Food and Water Toxicology. Task Force on Research Planning in Environmental Health Science, National Institute of Environmental Health Sciences, National Institutes of Health, Research Triangle, North Carolina, 1969.

8. Golberg, L., Safety of Environmental Chemicals—The Need and the Challenge, Presented before the Panel on Chemicals and Health of the President's Science Advisory Committee, Washington, D.C., February 7, 1971.

9. S.426, Toxic Substances Control Act of 1973.

10. H.R.5356, Toxic Substances Control Act of 1973.

11. The Clean Air Act as amended, 84 Stat. 1690 (1970).

12. Food Additives Amendment, Food, Drug and Cosmetic Act, 1958.

13. National Academy of Sciences, Report on "No Residue" and "Zero Tolerance," Pesticides Researchers Committee, Washington, D.C., July 1965.

14. *Congressional Record,* Vol. 119, No. 93, June 15, 1973, p.H. 4811.

15. Turner, J.S., The Delaney Anticancer Clause: A Model Environmental Protection Law, *Vanderbilt Law Review,* 24: 889-902, 1971.

16. Wilson, J.Q., The Dead Hand of Regulation, *The Public Interest,* 25: 39-58, 1971.

17. *National Academy of Science, Drug Efficacy Study,* Final Report to the Commissioner of the Food and Drug Administration, 1969.

18. Peltzman, S., Testimony given before the Subcommittee on Monopoly of the Committee on Small Business, U.S. Senate, March 14, 1973.

19. Friedman, M., Frustrating Drug Advancement, *Newsweek,* January 8, 1973.

20. Peltzman, S., The Benefits and Costs of New Drug Regulation, Paper prepared for a conference on The Regulation of the Introduction of New Pharmaceuticals, Center for Policy Study, The University of Chicago, December, 1972.

21. Cochrane, A.C., *Effectiveness and Efficiency. Random Reflections on Health Services,* The Nuffield Provincial Hospitals Trust, London, 1972.

22. Universities Group Diabetes Program, A study of the effects of hypoglycemic agents on vascular complications in patients with adult-onset diabetes. *II. Mortality results, Diabetes* 19: Suppl 2, 1970.

23. Knatterud, G.L., Meinert, C.L., Klimt, C.R., Osborne, R.K. and Martin, D.B., Effects of Hypoglycemic Agents on Vascular Compli-

cations in Patients with Adult-onset Diabetes, *J. Am. Med. Association* 217: 6, 1971.

24. Clofibrate and Niacin in Coronary Heart Disease, The Coronary Drug Project Research Group, *J. Am. Med. Association,* 231 (4): 360-81, January 27, 1975.

25. Polychlorinated Biphenyls—Environmental Impact, A Review by the Panel on Hazardous Trace Substances, *Environmental Research* 5: 249-362, 1972.

26. *Perspective on PCB's,* Proceeding of a Conference on PCB's, Environmental Health Perspectives, Experimental Issue No. 1, April 1972.

27. Internal memorandum, Status Report of Phosphates, Council on Environmental Quality, May 1971.

28. U.S. Department of Agriculture, Pesticide Regulation Notice 70-19, August 18, 1970.

29. Appendix to Petitioner's Brief in Environmental Defense Fund v. Hardin, 428 F., 2d 1093 (1970).

30. U.S. Department of Agriculture, Statement sent to U.S. Court of Appeals for the District of Columbia, June 1970, in the case of Environmental Defense Fund v. Hardin, U.S. Court of Appeals, District of Columbia Circuit, 1970, 428 F., 2d 1093.

31. Environmental Defense Fund v. Ruckelshaus, U.S. Court of Appeals, District of Columbia Circuit, January 7, 1971, 439 F., 2d 584.

32. U.S. Department of Agriculture, Pesticide Regulation Notice 71-1, January 15, 1971.

33. Report of the DDT Advisory Committee to William D. Ruckelshaus, administrator, Environmental Protection Agency, September 9, 1971.

34. Environmental Protection Agency, Public Hearing on DDT, volume 57, p. 6495, December 21, 1971.

35. Environmental Protection Agency, Public Hearing on DDT, volume 58, p. 8900, February 1972.

36. *Report on 2,4,5-T,* A Report of the Panel on Herbicides of the President's Science Advisory Committee, Executive Office of the President, Office of Science and Technology, March 1971.

37. Auerbach, C.A., Pluralism and the Administrative Process, *The Annals of the American Academy of Political and Social Science,* 400: 1-13, 1972.

7

The Political Constituency of Regulation

"The regulatory agencies are, in a sense, the foremost institutionalized advocates of the public interest" [1].

This quotation is probably reflective of a good deal of honest intention and some truth. Regulatory functions have, beginning with the establishment of the Interstate Commerce Commission in 1887, sought to protect at least some segment of the public's interest (or the interests of some segments of the public) against some other set of private interests. Debates over how best to achieve a proper balance between private power and the public interest have continued for a long time. As Grant McConnell noted, "a curious feature of American politics in the twentieth century is the absence of any established body of doctrine that may be taken as an orthodoxy on the selected problem of private power" [2].

It is, of course, in an attempt to bring some order to this question, to establish and institutionalize some rules for achieving such a balance, that the series of more or less independent regulatory commissions and agencies of the federal government was established. Congress, in the case of each of so-called "Big Seven" [3] independent regulatory commissions—the Securities and Exchange Commission, the Civil Aeronautics Board, the Federal Communications Commission, the Federal Power Commission, the Federal Trade Commission, the Interstate Commerce Commission, and the National Labor Relations Board—delegated a set of authorities. These delegated authorities are partly administrative, quasi-legislative and quasi-judicial. The same pattern essentially was followed in the health-related regulatory agencies. The Food and Drug Administration derives its life from the statutory authorities (principally the Food, Drug and Cosmetic Act), which directs the agency to engage in rule making, to enforce the rules, and to establish a pattern of administration that will support regulation.

Who Makes Up the Constituency of Regulation?

The constituency of these agencies is all-important. The character of the constituency goes far toward determining the pattern of activity of the agency in a democratic government. Regulation in behalf of health is no exception. Here it is important to make a distinction between the constituency that is interested and knowledgeable about an agency's activities and the segment that is not only knowledgeable but influential or that has "access."

Those interested and alert to the regulation of food additives and therapeutic drugs, of environmental pollutants, of pesticides, or of radioactive materials clearly include those who are regulated. If one accepts the Food and Drug Administration's estimates of the pervasiveness of its regulatory activities ("38 cents out of every consumer dollar was spent for an FDA regulated item in 1972"), and unless the majority of these industries are highly oligopolistic, this interested and affected industrial segment is clearly sizable. It is their "clientele," of course, that is so often pictured as having "captured" the regulatory process.

The other major segment of the interested constituency of regulation are the conscious beneficiaries of regulation. These beneficiaries presumably include essentially everyone (although, perhaps, not always to the same extent). In spite of this universality of effect of environmental and consumer regulation, it has only been recently that those particularly interested in the protection afforded by regulation have grouped and organized themselves as environmentalists and consumerists. As is well known, this is an active and well-informed segment of the public. Some must have mused that the degrees to which these organized members among consumerists and environmentalists are informed and active may be disproportionately large compared to the actual members involved [3].

Having accounted for those who take an active interest in health-related regulation, it is useful to take account of those who are not. The striking fact here is that the scientific community has absented itself traditionally and to a remarkable degree from this debate. This is, of course, particularly unfortunate. The quality of the science behind regulatory standards and decisions is clearly a function of the amount of attention paid to this subject by the members of the scientific community. Unfortunately, the best and the brightest of the scientific estate have not been heavy contributors [4].

**The Effect of Separating Protection and Regulation in
Independent Agencies**

In parallel with a trend of an increasing number of regulatory authorities in the name of health (and of an increasing complexity of the patterns of regulation) has been a furtherance of the push toward independence of the regulatory endeavor. Independence is generally conceived of as a separation between the promotion and the protection aspects of government. This trend, begun early in the history of regulatory activities, has accelerated its pace in recent years. The original Interstate Commerce Commission when established in 1887 was allied with the Department of Interior to the extent that the latter agency was given authority to approve the number and composition of the commission's personnel (except the secretary to the commission). Further, the commission's annual reports were to be submitted to the secretary of the interior. In 1899 total independence of the ICC was established.

Similarly, in the health field, the nation, through Congress, has demanded that an institutional distinction be made between those agencies of the government responsible for encouraging productivity in agriculture or favoring the development of new drugs and those responsible for protection from these products and their by-products.

In 1970 the federal government established the Environmental Protection Agency as a new entity composed of bureaus and departments dedicated exclusively to protection and drawn from several agencies: Interior, Agriculture, HEW, AEC.

The parallel and related proposals for consumer-product legislation have all touched more or less strongly on this aspect of independence of regulatory authority. The President's National Commission on Product Safety in 1970 concluded:

Statutory regulatory programs buried in agencies with broad and diverse missions have, with few exceptions, rarely fulfilled their missions. . . . The reasons for their weaknesses include lack of adequate funding and staffing because of competition with other deserving programs within an agency. . . . Identification of the regulator with the regulated must be avoided if Federal consumer safety programs are to succeed [5].

One of the major legislative proposals during the last session of Congress, the Consumer Safety Act of 1972, would have removed the Food and Drug Administration from its present parent, the Department of Health, Education, and Welfare, and made it the nucleus of a new, independent regulatory activity [6]. The FDA was thought to be compromised, partly by its having to compete with other programs from within HEW for budget and attention, and partly because of a traditional fear of too close an approximation to its clients (e.g., the industries it regulated). The proponents for this legislative move argued that a Consumer Protection Agency, administratively singled out and given independent status, would better serve the public's interest than would a Food and Drug Administration.

The arguments favoring the separation of protection from promotion are undeniably sound in the first approximation. There can be no doubt about the conflicts of interests (public vs. public as well as public vs. private) that obtain when both functions are subtended under the same ad-

118

ministrative roof. However, the analysis usually stops there and public
expectation is characteristically directed toward the solitary if not totally
satisfying results of this administrative separation. The belief is fostered
that all major ills of the system will be cured if only a dichotomous bureaucracy can be arranged. It is here that one finds serious flaws in practice—wide divergencies between expectation and achievement. This gap
between expectation and reality in regulation for health, which is a reflection of how regulation is done, derives ultimately in great part from the
character of the constituency of the regulatory agencies. Hence, an analysis of this subject should go beyond the single separate-promotion from
protection-and-all-will-be-well view and consider higher order effects of
this separation.

What are some of the by-products of separation of promotion from
protection? A major one is the exaggeration of the narrowness of the constituency that attends the regulatory business. In part, of course, the act
of separation is designed to decrease the access or influence of the clientele of regulation even though the constituency *interested* in regulation
might remain unchanged. As R.C. Leone suggests, the relative isolation
of independent government regulatory bodies may mean that only "selective political pressures" may affect them. Leone goes on to argue that the
inherent immunity of the regulatory process is reinforced further by some
unexpected factors such as public frustration with the overwhelmingly
complex administrative bureaucracy of regulation [1].

It is, perhaps, not so much the character of the constituency of environmental and health regulation that is objectionable but rather its exclusiveness. H. Seidman has commented that when "constituencies are narrowly based and used by a common interest in preserving tangible economic privileges granted to them by law, it is the independent agency or
bureau which is most likely to be seized upon as the vehicle for safeguarding and advancing those interests" [7]. The active support of the regulatory agencies' affairs tends to be focused narrowly on the *promotion* of
regulation. Those agencies are captured, not by their traditional clientele
(the industries or elements they regulate) but by those simply intent on
regulation for its own sake.

There is, as a result, little enthusiasm for broad views of issues by the
regulatory agencies. Simply fulfilling the regulatory law is thought to be
sufficient to accommodate or serve the public's interest. Balanced decisions, consideration of alternatives, analysis of economic consequences
and of effects on other governmental and national priorities are not encouraged by these regulatory agencies. As their administrators know full
well, a systematic job of balancing options and alternatives for decisions
may not find favor or bring reward from the hotly proregulation constituency.

Science vs. Political Science

Again, it is perhaps most important for the present analysis that the constituency of regulation notably does not include the scientific community.
Scientists generally are not included among those either with interest in or
with access to the regulatory bodies—in spite of the seemingly strong reliance on scientific inquiry and information that, one would intuitively
think, would lie behind environmental and health regulation. Clearly, the
absoluteness implied by this statement will be seen as an exaggeration. In
fact, the degree of exaggeration is not great.

Regulation for health has not been a strong focus for the best scientific
minds of the country. Regulation is characteristically controversial, making it unhappy territory for traditional academics. It is seen to be heavily
populated by lawyers and filled with political overtones. Those scientists
who have approached have, on occasion, found themselves unwittingly
surrounded by the turmoil of public controversy and emotion and badger-
ing by the public press. Further, the quality of the scientific enterprise behind regulation in the past has not seemed particularly sophisticated or
challenging—inevitably bordering on applied science. (The irony here, of
course, is that it is precisely this sophistication of scientific insight that is
needed in this area.) Finally, and perhaps most important in programmat-
ic terms, is the perceived lack of research monies from the regulatory
agencies. This, too, is a circular argument. The more that scientists absent themselves from the affairs of regulatory agencies, the less support
these agencies will be able to gather internally for their own research and
development program at the time of budgetary reviews.

This characteristically narrow, pro-protection and scientist-less constituency of regulation is reflected in Congress as well. Congress has, in
some quarters, been sensitive to a public clamor to stop studying and start
regulating and to a view that science has already produced enough information upon which to base regulations. There may even be a suggestion
that too much scientific information makes regulation more difficult and
complicates an otherwise orderly administrative process. Representative
Fountain, for example, has borne down more than once on the FDA—
insisting that the Food and Drug regulator preoccupies itself too much
with science and insufficiently with regulation [9]. This, of course, is a
remarkable example of antiscience, which can ultimately only detract
from the public's best interest. New and especially unexpected scientific
findings can indeed be expected to render regulatory decision making less
orderly and more complex. Yet, to enforce ignorance and deny the truth
in behalf of orderly administration will only serve ultimately to discredit
the regulatory process. An even more striking and somewhat frightening
(although little noticed) congressional reflection of this phenomenon was

the amendment offered in the House of Representatives in 1973 to prohibit further scientific investigations of the Delaney Clause discussed in the previous chapter described earlier [9].

Just as there are reflections in Congress of the character of the constituency of environmental and consumer regulation, the executive branch similarly reflects this constituency. The administrators of the agencies concerned with the environment and with foods and drugs and consumer products have been acutely aware that their public rewards accrue from action and not from study. Accordingly, research and science in behalf of standards and rule making in the name of health protection have received a strikingly low priority in the conduct of much of the business of these agencies. This fascinating choice between science and political science has been most marked in the affairs of the Environmental Protection Agency. The deliberations and analyses leading to decisions on standards, on proposed rule making, and on decisions to proceed toward enforcement have frequently not included the Office of Research and Development or the other scientific resources of that agency. This was true for such major decisions as those for DDT and the herbicide 2,4,5-T.

There is an additional explanation for this lack of support for the government's acquisition of scientific information for regulatory decision making. This explanation rests on the recognition that the possession of information is synonymous with the possession of power. Information is a strategic instrument. To some extent, he who controls the information for regulation controls the regulatory activity. Therefore, it is to the advantage of the parties most directly concerned with the character of regulation (both industry and the consumerists-environmentalists) to supply the government with the information for its decisions rather than to encourage the government to develop its own resources.

Perhaps the most striking manifestation of ths disregard for science and for research is seen in the program budgets for the regulatory agencies. Notably, for those "independent" health-related agencies, the support for science has been remarkably low, and in the case of the Environmental Protection Agency has approached extinction.

The Environmental Protection Agency, which was first brought into being in 1970, has enjoyed a steadily and rapidly mounting total budget for pollution abatement and environmental control activities. Between fiscal years 1970 and 1973, this agency's total budget increased from $1 billion to $7.4 billion (table 7-1). The majority of this money has been dedicated to waste-treatment plant construction for the control of water pollution as well as for assistance in the abatement of air and other pollutants. During this same period, the total R&D budget of that agency will have gone from $75 million to $177 million. The important fact to note is a very small and declining percentage of the total budget is spent in behalf of information (2.4 percent in 1973).

Table 7-1

Environmental Protection Agency Budget Figures for the Entire Agency and Those for Research and Development within EPA, Fiscal Years 1970-73

Fiscal Year	Total Budget[a] ($'s Million)	R&D Budget[b] ($'s Million)	(Percent of Total)	Health Research[b] ($'s Million)	(Percent of Total)
1970	1,046	75	7.2	34.5	3.3
1971	1,289	137	10.6	9.8	0.8
1972	2,447	122	5.0	15.8	0.7
1973	7,421	177	2.4	15.5	0.2

Source: Burger, E.J. "Regulation and Health: How Solid is Our Foundation?" *Environmental Law Reporter*, 5, September, 1975: 50179-50187, Copyright © 1975, Environmental Law Institute.

[a] Budget of the United States, various years.
[b] Budget of the United States, Special Analysis, various years.

Table 7-2

Food and Drug Administration Budget Figures for the Entire Agency and Those for Research and Development within FDA, Fiscal Years 1962-73

Fiscal Year	Total Budget ($'s Million)	R&D Budget[b] ($'s Million)	(Percent of Total)	Health Research[c] ($'s Million)	(Percent of Total)
1962	23.0[a]	2.4	10.4	2.4	10.4
1963	29.1[a]	3.9	13.5	3.9	13.5
1964	35.8	6.3	17.6	6.3	17.6
1965	40.4[a]	6.6	16.4	6.6	16.4
1966	53.0	10.4	19.7	10.4	19.7
1967	61.7[a]	10.1	16.4	10.1	16.4
1968	66.0[a]	17.0	25.8	17.0	25.8
1969	67.3[a]	17.7	26.4	17.7	26.4
1970	76.3[b]	18.3	24.0	18.3	24.0
1971	87.5[b]	21.8	24.9	21.8	24.9
1972	112.4[b]	33.5	29.8	33.5	29.8
1973	146.4[b]	44.5	30.4	44.5	30.4

Source: Burger, E.J. "Regulation and Health: How Solid is Our Foundation?" *Environmental Law Reporter*, 5, September, 1975: 50179-50187, Copyright © 1975, Environmental Law Institute.

[a] Food and Drug Administration, Justification of Appropriation Estimates for Committee on Appropriations, Fiscal Year 1972, Department of Health, Education, and Welfare.
[b] Budget of the United States, various years.
[c] Budget of the United States, Special Analysis, various years.

The Food and Drug Administration has fared better—especially in recent years (table 7-2). Since 1970 between a quarter and a third of its total budget has been dedicated to research. Commissioner Edwards' testimony to Mr. Fountain indicated, however, it has been because of that agency's pressure and persuasion, not that of Congress [8].

Table 7-3

Atomic Energy Commission Budget Figures for the Entire Agency and Those for Research and Development within AEC, Fiscal Years 1970-73

Fiscal Year	Total Budget[a] ($'s Million)	R&D Budget ($'s Million)	(Percent of Total)	Health Research[b] ($'s Million)	(Percent of Total)
1970	2,220	1,346	60.6	102.5	4.5
1971	2,308	1,303	56.4	101.1	4.4
1972	2,293	1,298	56.6	104.5	4.6
1973	2,633	1,359	51.6	104.0	4.0

Source: Burger, E.J. "Regulation and Health: How Solid is Our Foundation?" *Environmental Law Reporter,* 5, September, 1975: 50179-50187, Copyright © 1975, Environmental Law Institute.

[a] Budget of the United States, various years.

[b] Budget of the United States, Special Analysis, various years.

A marked contrast is seen in the case of the former Atomic Energy Commission (table 7-3). The total budget of that agency was of the same order as that of EPA ($2.6 billion in fiscal year 1973). The expenditure in behalf of R&D—especially that aimed at an understanding of the biological effects of radiation—was impressively large. Thus, of a total R&D budget of 50 to 60 percent of the total agency's budget, nearly 10 percent of that R&D effort is dedicated to biology and medicine. The interpretation this author draws is that the Atomic Energy Commission (either with the acquiescence or encouragement of the Joint Committee on Atomic Energy) saw that it was to its advantage to make investments in behalf of information as insurance for good regulatory decisions. Indeed, while the field of radiological health and safety is still filled with public controversy, there exists a better scientific understanding of the biological effects of radiation and the research work has been generally more sophisticated than for nearly all if not all other physical and chemical substances that are specific environmental hazards to man. To emphasize this point one more time, an accounting of all of the federal research monies spent in behalf of an understanding of the human health effects of environmental agents reveals that almost half has been dedicated to ionizing and nonionizing radiation.

Research and science for regulation imply investments in futures. From the viewpoint of an administrator, this future is long in comparison to the time he is permitted by his constituency and by Congress to show tangible results. He is acutely aware of the admonition heard in some quarters that it is time to stop studying and to start regulating. Accordingly, and especially where he has no incentives for the maintenance of the visibility and economic health of the institutions and industries regulated, he is led inevitably toward a posture of playing down the importance of science and research in his regulatory business.

A consequence has been an appalling lack of solid information on which to base decisions and standards. In the field of environmental chemicals, both for chemical products and pollutants, judgments have been taken more in ignorance than on the basis of solid information. Two trends have occurred: Both legislators and regulatory agency policy makers have tended to raise the issue of human health as a surrogate for other desirable features of man's environment, often because implied threat to health is a more emotionally and politically salable item than is deterioration of buildings, visible smog, or altered vegetation. Second, and often because the threat to health issue has been stretched thinly to back a political decision, the scientific basis for the decisions is often extraordinarily weak. For example, considerations of removal of tetraethyl lead from gasoline have turned on two questions: One was the necessity to provide lead-free gasoline throughout the country for automobiles equipped with catalytic devices designed to remove hydrocarbons and nitrogen oxides. Lead is recognized as a poison for the noble metal catalysts in these devices and would destroy their action. The other question was the effect on human health of airborne lead and lead fall-out reaching the ground that emanated ultimately from the tetraethyl lead in automotive fuels. In order to make what it considered a persuasive argument for the removal of lead, the Environmental Protection Agency placed the health issue ahead of the catalytic converter poison issue in its advertisement to the public. As this is being written, this tactic appears to have been of questionable virtue since the need for catalytic converters is fading somewhat and the health issue by itself, may not be sufficiently scientifically persuasive to sustain the issue ultimately.

In the same way that there is little incentive for decent science behind regulatory decisions in the independent agencies, there is also little support for balanced decisions nor for the necessary resources to produce balanced decisions. Consideration of economic consequences of regulations require economists and economic analyses. Congress, until recently, has not encouraged a consideration of economic consequences of regulation by the independent, health-related regulatory agencies and some congressional committees have frankly discouraged these exercises.[a]

Similarly, there has been no incentive for the independent agencies to

---

[a] As discussed in chapter 2, the amendments to the Clean Air Act of 1970 explicitly struck out considerations of economic costs in deriving standards of emissions from various classes of vehicles and engines (mobile sources). The intent of the new act was to base standards purely on the amount of control presumed to be required, not that which could be offered as a result of existing technology nor with costs in mind [10]. On the other side, in interpreting the Federal Insecticide, Fungicide, and Rodenticide Act for the regulation of pesticides, Judge Bazelon in 1971 insisted that ". . . the statue leaves room to balance the benefits of a pesticide against its risks" [11].

consider systematically the relationship between their regulatory proposals and other government programs and priorities. Of course, one might argue, this latter is an inevitable and perhaps even desirable consequence of the independent administration of regulation. However, a striking effect has been a high degree of frustration within the Executive Office of the President. There has been dismay over the quality of the evidence and arguments used by the independent agencies to back their decisions and judgments and over the highly advocate character of their position. Most of all, perhaps, there has been mounting frustration over a lack of systematic balancing among alternative courses of action and over a lack of systematic and reasonably sophisticated analysis of the several consequences of each proposed regulatory action. The direct result was the tendency for the Executive Office or the White House to "lift" regulatory matters out of the independent agencies to a higher level for review.

This pattern has been most marked in the case of EPA regulations, especially those dealing with air pollution. The higher level review process became modestly institutionalized in 1971 with the instigation of a system known as the Quality of Life Review Process. When Senator Muskie and the Senate Interior Committee had introduced the amendments to the Clean Air Act in 1969, there had been relatively mild opposition from the administration to the provisions of the act—including the unusual move of mandated emission standards. The new law contained a large number of new regulatory authorities (listing of hazardous substances, fuel additive provisions, ambient air quality, aircraft emission standards, etc.) providing for various degrees of administrative discretion but unquestionably imposing a tight schedule of obligations on EPA. There was little time permitted for careful deliberation before offering each proposal in the *Federal Register*. More important, however, and for all of the reasons discussed above, there was little incentive found for that agency to perform the careful, broadly based prior analysis in each case, which the subject deserved. At the same time, there began to arise a series of grumblings from without the government and from the Department of Commerce over the prospective cost of meeting the environmental schedule. In July 1971 Secretary of Commerce Maurice Stans came forth with his famous "Wait a Minute" speech in which he admonished the country to exercise caution before dedicating itself entirely to the environmental issue [12]. This speech corresponded roughly in time with what might best be described a "battle of the briefs"—a virtual cross fire of memoranda and position papers from various agency heads to the president purporting to speak to the economic consequences of the clean air regulations [13, 14, 15, 16, 17]. The principal spokesmen for economic positions were Maurice Stans, Russell Train, chairman of the Council on Environmental Quality, William Ruckelshaus of EPA, and Herbert Stein, chairman of the Council of Economic Advisors. These memoranda and briefs inevitably disagreed and it was thought necessary to find an objective, credible arbiter. Some sense of the degree of frustration can be gleaned from the president's reaction to the memorandum from his chairman of the Council on Environmental Quality and his ensuing instruction transmitted by his staff secretary, Jon Huntsman:

While the President read with interest Mr. Whitaker's memorandum of July 1, 1971, containing Russell Train's memorandum of June 30, 1971, it was noted that he did not believe Mr. Train's analysis. It was requested that you obtain for the President's review an *honest* and unbiased report by someone other than an environmentalist [18].

More important, this activity served to heat up the issue of regulatory decision making and to highlight the narrowness of the interests brought to bear in EPA in their rule-making and standard-setting activities.

Unhappiness with this process had been building for some time. On June 16, 1971 the president directed members of his Domestic Council (essentially the members of his Cabinet), plus Mrs. Virginia Knauer, special assistant to the president for consumer affairs; Peter Peterson, then presidential assistant for international economic affairs; William Ruckelshaus; and Russell Train to consider whether or not an institutionalized method of review of regulatory decisions should not be instituted. The memorandum that introduced the subject began by noting that:

On a daily basis in your capacity as a Department or Agency head, each of you must make decisions that affect the balance of many inter-related Quality of Life Variables—particularly consumer and environmental interests, industrial requirements, and safety aspects—some decisions working to the disadvantage of others. The President has directed that a study be undertaken of this balance to determine whether a governmental vehicle (for example, a small, permanent group) should be established to review decisions affecting this balance [19].

Edward David, the president's science adviser, was named as chairman of a committee to ponder this question and was given roughly three weeks to deliver an answer.

The agencies asked to consider this question generally agreed with the desirability from the point of view of the national interest of broadening the agenda of review of regulatory actions. However, there was serious anxiety expressed over the legality of raising for intragovernment review and comment proposed but publically unannounced actions by an agency such as the Environmental Protection Agency. The separation and relatively independent character of that governmental body was consistent with congressional intent, and did not this Quality of Life Review Process promise to compromise that independence? There was fear, too, that the large volume of regulatory proposals would overwhelm a single office. Finally, there was anxiety that no matter how virtuous the intent, the quality of the analytic resources located centrally would be no better nor were these resources any more available or prevalent than they were within the agencies themselves.

What eventually emerged as a Quality of Life Review Process was an obligation on the part of the agencies to exercise judgment as to what constituted a sizable and important, forthcoming regulatory action and to return to the Office of Management and Budget a broadly based review of each of these important actions. In practicality, with only one exception, only the Environmental Protection Agency was asked to submit these reviews.

This question of the breadth of environmental health and consumer issues versus the narrowness of the interests of the agency responsible for them is fundamental in this discussion. Since the interested and influential constituency of the "independent" regulatory agencies is inevitably a narrow one, one could not reasonably have expected any other result. The constituency is not interested in balanced decisions. Unless a politically driven administrator is either exceedingly secure or simply unmindful of this fact, he can surely only be expected to reflect the views of his constituency. There is a traditional fear that government regulatory agencies tend to become "captured" by this clientele—by the very industries or institutions they are supposed to regulate. In part, of course, the fear is confirmed from time to time. The public interest is not well served when regulation is heavily influenced by the industries regulated. However, the trading of one narrowness of decision making for another does not necessarily further the public's interest. In a way, the health-related regulatory activities have been "captured"—if not by industry then by a different but vitally interested constituency that is well-meaning, dedicated, sometimes well-organized, but questionably informed. It seems to be a misnomer to think of a regulatory agency, separated from other parts of administrative government, as *independent*. In fact, in some important aspects, it may become wholly dependent or responsive to certain elements or institutions of public and private life and, thereby, skewed in its views. James Q. Wilson, in a seemingly heretical admonition, suggested that ". . . whether a (regulatory) Commission does or does not serve the ends of industry is much less important than whether it serves the correct ends" [20].

What is required is a device for broadening the constituency for regulation in behalf of health, to encourage a better-infomred, more explicit, and broader debate of the several issues involved in each decision, and to increase the quality and breadth of the analysis that accompanies decision making. The governmental processes badly need a mechanism that preserves the most desirable aspects of separation of promotion from protection, but that compensates for those adverse by-products of separation.

Lack of Support for Science and Scientists

The science linking the environment and health has not attracted sufficient numbers of the best of the scientific community in universities and government. There are outstanding exceptions but they are few in number. Rewards of academic progression have not flowed to these endeavors. In spite of the cries for relevance for science in the past few years and in spite of the fact that the evident opportunities have been plainly visible and articulated, this area of science has failed to galvanize and attract the very best of academic scientists in appropriate numbers.

What are the reasons for this relative lack of support? Clearly, part of this phenomenon is related to the fact that this scientific enterprise is perceived of as lying on the applied side of science and therefore somewhat less worthy of scholarly attention. Note, however, the circularity of this argument. The less sophisticated is the scientific contribution, the less sophisticated will be the scientific product. An especially difficult challenge is to be found in the case of chronic disease epidemiology with its long dedication necessary to reap useful results and the paucity opportunity to lay claim to academic rewards through publication.

The important and governing factor, however, in determining the size and shape of this scientific enterprise would seem to be the lack of a public constituency for good scientific information for decision making. The problem is not a new one but has been recognized and acknowledged at intervals for some time. A variety of published reports—some with presidential endorsement—have all called attention to environmental health problems and have acknowledged a striking lack of information for decisions [21, 22, 23, 24, 25].

In 1972 President Nixon sent a special message to the Congress along with a report on the health effects of environmental pollution. The need for research to provide adequate information was highlighted in this report and the seriousness of this void was acknowledged [26].

The federal government responded to the admonitions in some of the advisory committee documents with a series of administrative reorganizations—some benign and some clearly counterproductive. In 1968, however, a new National Institute of Environmental Health Sciences was established within the structure of the National Institutes of Health. An important part of the background of this institute was anxiety over the poor quality of the information used by the Food and Drug Administration in its decisions about foods, pesticides, drugs, cosmetics, and consumer products. It was hoped that the new institute would act as a bridge between the needs of the regulatory endeavor and the best of the basic scientists in government and universities. In fact, the National Institute of

Environmental Health Sciences has contributed in precisely the expected pattern. However, its level of financial support has never grown to the point where it could truly flower and fulfill its intended mission. It remains the smallest of the NIH institutes with a budget roughly one-twelfth that of the National Heart and Lung Institute and one-twentieth the size of the National Cancer Institute!

The fact is, there is little constituent support for science for regulation. As the director of NIH put it during the budget hearings before the Office of Management and Budget one year, "Congressmen and Senators don't get sick from environmental health sciences as such." It was pointed out in an earlier section that the constituency of the regulatory agenices had been narrowed in interest as a result of the rendering of the protective and the regulatory functions independent of the promotional ones. The active support of a regulatory agency tends to be as narrow as its focus and to include only those strongly interested in the *promotion* of regulation to the virtual exclusion of all else.

A major consequence of the absence of scientists from the constituency of regulation is a lack of critical concern for the quality of the scientific fabric upon which regulatory decisions are based. This lack of a critical and moderating influence from scientists in regulation, which has been so prominent in the case of the Food and Drug Administration and the Environmental Protection Agency, was held up as an admonition at one point by Charles Edwards when he was commissioner of the FDA:

It's a particularly difficult environment for the Food and Drug Administration because in a sense, we're in the middle. We are on the one hand, criticized for being "soft" on the industry and on the other, called repressive, the enemy of free enterprise: on every *major* decision, we are accused by some of acting too fast without sufficient evidence, and by others of acting too slowly and too timidly to prevent unnecessary harm. We're expected to deliver on the promises to complete safety made by others but when the time comes to take action we find ourselves standing alone. We have had very little support and understanding from the medical and scientific community [27].

There are a number of unfortunate consequences of noninterest by scientists in the character of regulation and in the science behind regulatory decisions. Obviously, there is the risk of missing opportunities to prevent disasters associated with undetected or poorly understood environmental exposures. Mercury poisoning in Minimata, Japan, exposures of uranium miners to radium daughter products, or public exposure through the ingestion of rice oil to dibenzylfurans contained in leaked polychlorinated biphenyls are recent examples. In each case, there occurred a lag between the exposure event and the perception of its significance. In some instances (uranium miners) this was measured in years. The consequences are excess morbidity or premature death.

The other major consequence of scientific ignorance in regulation is that of injudicious decisions. Regulatory decisions typically imply very large expenditures such as cost penalties to industry through the banning of products, through changes in patterns of transportation as a result of air pollution standards, by relieving society of certain products upon which its members have become dependent, or by "creating" new hazards in the course of relieving the old.[b] Since these are large, expensive, and far-reaching decisions, logic would dictate that they should deserve to be based on data of correspondingly high quality. Where these decisions are taken in the name of human health, they represent a portion of the national resource dedicated to health but imply that some other national desire has been to some extent foregone. To the extent that regulatory decisions are injudicious, they prohibit scare resources from meeting their expected goals in health.

There is, finally, a potentially serious political consequence of poor information for decisions. With repeated revelations of environmental and consumer decisions made on the basis of poor science, there can be expected an eventual falling away from the environmental and consumer movement of the present constituency—environmentalists and consumerists. There is a very strong case for gathering the scientific community more closely to the regulatory affairs of the government that are concerned with human health. The public's perception is that this area of government is rooted in science. To the extent that these roots are only superficial, there can be expected a certain let down—a disappointment in unfulfilled expectations. Economic and other considerations, public desires for information on how decisions are rendered, and a general trend toward more openness in government may all be expected to force increasing public examination and scrutiny of the quality of information used for regulation decisions. To the extent that poor science is increasingly revealed behind standards and environmental decisions there may be expected a further erosion of the public's forth in science and in scientists to play useful roles in behalf of the environment.

The value of sufficient and valid information for regulation has, in practice, characteristically been discounted. Hence, there has generally been an under investment in the derivation of information as through appropriate scientific investigation. Whatever the reason, the phenomenen of under investment in this area of science is a particularly dangerous one. The seriousness of this issue has led one economist to observe:

Thus the rational environmentalist must turn away from the "don't do anything for the first time" philosophy, and turn toward one which says, "it's better and even safer to spend some of our income to obtain information" [28].

[b] The trading of a hazard for a hazard occurred inadvertently with the restrictions imposed by state and local ordinances on phosphates and detergents. The flameproofing of children's clothing had been developed using a number of chemical materials whose effectiveness was found to be compromised if they were washed in soap or, indeed, in any other product than a phosphate-containing detergent.

Knowledge is power. Yet, the responsible parts of the federal government have been reluctant or unwilling to receive their appropriate share in this case.

References

1. Leone, R.C., Public Interest Advocacy and the Regulatory Process, *The Annals of the American Academy of Political and Social Science*, 400: 46-58, 1972.
2. McConell, G., *Private Power in American Democracy*, New York, Alfred A. Knopf, 1966.
3. Caldwell, L., Environmental Quality as an Administrative Problem, *The Annals of the American Academy of Political and Social Science*, 400: 103-115, 1972.
4. Burger, E.J., Science, Politics and Regulation, *Proceedings of the Federation of American Societies for Experimental Biology*, 32: 5-9, 1973.
5. National Commission on Product Safety, *Final Report*, Washington, D.C., June 1970.
6. U.S. Senate, *Consumer Safety Act of 1972*, Report of the Senate Committee on Commerce on S.3419, April 13, 1972.
7. Seidman, H., *Politics, Position, and Power: The Dynamics of Federal Organization*, New York, Oxford University Press, 1970.
8. U.S. House of Representatives, *Regulatory Policies of the Food and Drug Administration*, Subcommittee on Intergovernmental Relations of the Committee on Government Operations, June 9, 1970.
9. *Congressional Record*, H.4811, June 15, 1973.
10. *National Air Quality Standards Act of 1970*, Report of the Committee on Public Works, United States Senate, Report NO. 91-1196, Committee on Public Works, September 17, 1970.
11. Environmental Defense Fund vs. Ruckelshaus, U.S. Court of Appeals, District of Columbia Circuit, January 7, 1971, 439 F. 2d 584.
12. Stans, M.H., Wait a Minute, Address delivered before the National Petroleum Council, 25th Anniversary Meeting, Department of the Interior Auditorium, Washington, D.C., July 15, 1971.
13. Memorandum from Russell E. Train, chairman of the council on Environmental Quality, to the president, Environmental Quality and Economic Progress, June 30, 1971.
14. Memorandum from Maurice H. Stans, secretary of commerce, to the president, June 28, 1971.

15. Memorandum from Maurice H. Stans, secretary of commerce, to the president, Costs of Environmental Compliance, June 29, 1971.

16. Memorandum from Russell E. Train, chairman of the Council on Environmental Quality, to the president, June 30, 1971.

17. Memorandum from Paul W. McCracken, chairman of the Council of Economic Advisors, to the president, July 20, 1971.

18. Memorandum from Jon M. Huntsman, staff secretary to John D. Ehrlichman and John Whitaker, the White House, July 3, 1971.

19. Domestic Study Memorandum #15 from John Ehrlichman to members of the Domestic Council, June 16, 1971.

20. Wilson, J.Q., The Dead Hand of Regulation, *The Public Interest*, 25: 39-58, 1971.

21. *Report of the Committee on Environmental Health Problems,* Prepared for the surgeon general, Public Health Services, U.S. Department of Health, Education, and Welfare, U.S. Government Printing Office, Washington, D.C. 1962.

22. *A Strategy for a Livable Environment*, Report of a Task Force on Environmental Health and Related Problems, Prepared for the secretary, U.S. Department of Health, Education, and Welfare, U.S. Government Printing Office, Washington, D.C., 1967.

23. *Waste Management and Control*, Report of the Committee on Pollution to the Federal Council for Science & Technology, Publication No. 1400, National Academy of Sciences, National Research Council, Washington, D.C., 1966.

24. *Restoring the Quality of Our Environment,* Report of the Environmental Pollution Panel of the President's Science Advisory Committee, U.S. Government Printing Office, Washington, D.C., 1965.

25. *Report of the White House Task Force on Automotive Pollution*, The White House, Washington, D.C., 1971.

26. Environmental Pollution Effects on Health, Message from the president of the United States, February 1, 1972, Document No. 92-241, House of Representatives.

27. Edwards, C.C., FDA and the Medical Community, Presented at the Annual Meeting; Institute of Medicine, National Academy of Sciences, Washington, D.C., November 17, 1971.

28. Olson, M., Ignorance and Uncertainty, Background Papers for the Environmental Protection Agency Symposium on Risk-Benefit Analysis for Water Pollution Control, Washington, D.C., 1973.

8

Risk-Benefit Analysis: A Discussion of What Is Really Possible

People make choices about their lives and in their patterns of dealing with risks, or in many other cases, defer to surrogates—physicians and elected governments, for example—to make or guide these chocies for them. Risk taking is a characteristic to which one is more or less resigned (for the racing driver or the cigarette smoker, willingly and eagerly anticipated). At the same time, in some instances, risk taking is thought best avoided or at least reduced in scale to a minimum.

The assumption of risk in the individual case is typically done on the basis of some knowledge or experience and some "feeling" for the size of the risk. The National Safety Council has gone far toward educating the public about the hazard of riding in an automobile and of driving under the influence of alcohol. The surgeon general has repeatedly warned us (on every package) of the implications for health of smoking cigarettes.

For those classes of risks known as public or involuntary hazards, the collective point of view is almost always favored over an individual view. In large numbers of instances, including water and air pollution, nuclear power plants, additives in food, the issues presented are exceedingly complex. Increasingly, therefore, in order to add a measure of orderliness or systematic accounting to the process of decision making for regulation of drugs or pesticides, the tools known collectively as risk-benefit analysis have been invoked. The hypothesis offered is that systematic analysis will produce or guide a "better" decision than intuition alone (whether the intuition is individual or collective). Further, in the political advocacy process, on or other point of view may prevail from time to time not as a function of the inherent logic of the matter under consideration but by dint of the voting power of the constituent advocates. If balancing in the decision process is desirable, a mechanism for systematic sorting of various risks and various kinds of benefits for each possible decision route is undoubtedly necessary.

As pointed out several times earlier, decisions about chemical and physical environmental agents are complex. Risks are typically of several kinds because uses or patterns of commerce are numerous, because patterns of human exposure are complex, and because biological behavior is not described simply. Further, the combination of chance of human exposure and low exposure levels often make likelihood of human disease a matter of low yet finite probability. Benefits, too, are difficult to estimate in many cases. Benefits of a single product are usually plural in number. If a substance in question has been in commerce for several years or has unusual properties, certain dependencies may have developed that rival the health-at-any-cost view expressed in other quarters. Second- and higher order effects at times accrue from actions thought originally to have only simple or single consequences. Sulfuric acid mists from catalytic devices on automobile exhaust systems represent a current example. The biological methylation of mercury in ponds and streams, thought otherwise to be inert, is another. Finally, the distributional effects of decisions are often seen to be important. Benefits and risks often flow to different parties. Private benefits may be at the expense of public costs (or vice versa). Individual decisions may revise these distributions.

Accordingly, analytic tools termed in the collective, risk-benefit analysis, have been increasingly called upon to aid environmental decision making. Risk-benefit analysis has become a household phrase where the expectation is that deliberate and explicit review for decision making will improve the quality of decisions. Further, it is generally thought that the addition of quantitative methods (insofar as possible) will complement an otherwise intuitive process and sharpen both administrative and political debate.

Cost-benefit analysis in the simplest form represents a quantitative framework to assist decision makers in composing and in dealing with issues to be "traded" against each other. The idea of a framework encourages or even forces a decision maker to gather and array information. It makes information gaps immediately apparent. It may point to alternatives and to unexpected relationships where simple intuition may have failed. In brief, it tends to inform the decision process and the parties to the decision.

At the same time, a caution should be voiced. The application of quantitative methods and the translation of social values into quantitative or probabilistic terms may give the false illusion of certainty or definitiveness not always warranted by the original assumptions or facts. Many of the factors of cost-benefit analysis are subject to subjective estimation and virtually all such exercises rest on assumptions viewed differently by different parties. For these reasons, cost-benefit analysis should not be considered as an instrument for *making* decisions. Rather, its usefulness is limited to assisting decision makers and to informing the public debate.

What Are the Available Analytic Tools?

The past few years have seen a sizable increase in professional interest and contribution to the analytical methods designed for risk-benefit analysis. Most of the theoretical framework has come from quantitative economics. This has provided an increasingly high degree of sophistication to the theory and to some of the methods [1, 2].

In its simplest (and early) form, perhaps, risk-benefit analysis was thought of as the derivation of a ratio of a factor representing benefits divided by a corresponding figure for risks. A ratio greater than unity would indicate that the project or product under examination was of relative benefit and was worthy of proceeding with.

The evolution of the subject has led to a high degree of elaboration of the meaning and components of both risks and benefits. Further, the deriving of a simple ratio is seen to be of very limited use and has given way to a less rigid construction. Perhaps, most important, for the reasons discussed below, the quantitative language and methods useful to analysis of risks and benefits have come increasingly to be seen as a framework for assisting or guiding decisions rather than for making decisions.

Successful articulation of benefits depends, in the first instance, on a successful articulation of desired goals in each case. Economists have pointed out that the term, benefit, subtends in each case a number of components and that these accrue to different parties. Thus, a change in the level of an emitted chemical substance in the outflow of an industrial plant into a river may show up as a change in the ambient concentration of that chemical in the river. This may be found to bear a relation to the health of those who drink the water from the river (the ultimate criterion). However, in addition, there are intermediate and secondary benefits and there are tangible as well as intangible benefits.

A great deal of attention has been focused by economists on the distinction between benefits that satisfy economic efficiency and those concerned with distribution or equity. Efficiency is a traditional economic desire to insure the greatest benefit (or level of production) from a given level of input of resources. Decisions and actions that tend to expand the benefits (or in economic language, the production or consumption potential) for the society for a given expenditure of resources are deemed desirable and "efficient." Many decisions, however, lead to a shift of benefit from one group to another group. These "pecuniary private" effects expand the potential for one group and simultaneously contract it for others. The expenditures exacted from a polluting plant (and ultimately from its stockholders) to clean up its effluents may lead to an increase in the property values of the surrounding abutters—a shift in distribution of benefits.

In practice, many benefits are not capable of description in common, monetary terms. This is discussed in greater depth below. Health, for example, is translated into pecuniary terms only if one first "values" the presence of health or its loss. The process of assigning values to intangibles and the handling of incommersurable factors are exceedingly difficult and, in the view of some, should not be attempted.

As in the case of benefit, the concept of cost in the analysis of costs and benefits is a complex issue. Costs accrue to a variety of parties in typical regulatory decisions and are perceived or "valued" in a corresponding variety of ways. In the first instance, cost appears equitable with monetary price, and marketplace reflections in price in an idealized setting should reflect costs. Such a construction, however, implies a perfect market in which "marginal social costs" are equal to private marginal costs and, in turn, are reflected in prices.

Limitations of Cost-Benefit Analysis

There are severe limitations in the usefulness of cost-benefit analysis. The analytic methods and the quantitative models have, in many cases, been developed to a high degree of sophistication and elaboration. Limitations arise in the derivation of the coefficients and the values used in the numerical models. As one observer pointed out recently in a discussion of cost-benefit analysis and water pollution, cost-benefit analysis would be acceptable as a formula for making decisions but only if certain conditions were met:

1. If there were unanimous agreement as to the definitions and measurement of welfare
2. If the factors and trade-offs that comprised each choice could be described in terms of a single, common unit (such as dollars)
3. If all needed information was available and if there were perfect certainty about assumptions and consequences [3]

In fact, of course, these conditions are not generally achievable and there are limitations.

By far the most severe limitation is lack of sufficient information. In spite of the high degree of development of the quantitative methodologies, this limiting feature of lack of data stands out prominently. Evaluation of both risks and benefits is hampered by a paucity of data. This fact was commented on at length by the Panel on Chemicals & Health of the President's Science Advisory Committee:

In spite of the most rigorous and sophisticated of methodologies, an analysis is worth no more than the information used in the analysis. In practice, it appears to be lack of good data (in many cases of any data) which has inhibited the systematic performance of risk-benefit analysis [4].

This same point was made during a review of risk-benefit analysis held by the National Academy of Engineering in 1971[5]. More recently, it was again the subject of considerable comment during an EPA study of cost-benefit analysis for water pollution decisions [3] and during a National

Academy of Sciences review of decision making for chemical regulation [6].

In the case of regulation for ambient air quality, the biological effects of the materials emitted from industrial processes and from automobiles are very poorly known. The relationship between particular emissions and consequent ambient levels is inevitably a complex one involving meteorology, effects of topographic features and natural cycles, and background levels. These relationships are little understood and are typically represented in turn by theoretical models. Accordingly, when a policy maker raises a question about the marginal improvement in health that could be expected from a marginal exchange in regulation or in incentives, or in technology, the number of assumptions that replace solid information tend to cascade upon each other. This same picture is found in the field of water pollution or questions of food additives or industrial chemicals.

Although several have taken note of the severe limitations to meaningful cost-benefit analysis occasioned by the lack of basic information, few have delivered such a severe indictment as the economist, Mancur Olson:

. . . no one has yet even begun to do justice to the awesome ignorance and appalling uncertainties that probably are—and at any event should be—at the bottom of the uneasiness about the application of cost-benefit analysis to certain environmental and social problems [7].

Olson observed that the ignorance is not that of economics or other social sciences but rather is related to the limited understanding in the biological and physical sciences and ecology. In the face of such high degrees of uncertainty, Olson argues, the exercise of cost-benefit analysis is reduced to little more than a sophisticated form of common sense [8]. Again, it is this severe lack of basic information that, more than any other single factor, sets apart the theory from the practice of cost-benefit analysis.

One line of reasoning has urged that characteristics and relationships, however uncertain in absolute value, be expressed as probability rather than attempting to define absolute values. According to that scheme, probabilistic values will substitute appropriately for solid information precisely because they reflect uncertainty in their definition while at the same time providing quantitative terms that can be used in risk-benefit models [6]. However, the estimate of the probability in question can be no better than the fundamental information from which it was taken.

A second major limiting feature of cost-benefit analysis concerns the challenge of valuation. For example, of what worth or value is a decision to clean up a river or restrict the manufacture of a chemical or pesticide? Where health protection is the major motivation, this question of valuation becomes one of how much is it worth to avoid the possibility of risk.

Valuation is considered to be synonymous with society's willingness to pay. The value of risk aversion (especially of involuntary hazards) is generally considered to be underestimated by conventional measures. The sum of the direct and indirect costs of death are thought by some to underestimate what society is generally willing to pay in order to avoid ill health or death. The reasoning usually given turns on the anxiety that fear or ignorance provoke. Society, it is believed, will pay to relieve itself of this anxiety. It was observed during the course of the study of automotive emissions that ". . . people are more willing to hedge against the unknown . . . than against a risk of known consequences" [5].

A great deal of attention has been devoted to the questions of valuation of health and avoidance of death. Thomas Schelling considered the value of death (or the avoidance of death) from three points of view. One was society's interest in life and death. A second was the economic impact of the loss of livelihood associated with death. The third was the "consumer's" interest in reducing mortality per se and in reducing the anxiety associated with possibility of death. The third of these categories was seen as particularly difficult to deal with. Peoples' views toward risks (such as of death) may bear little relation to the real actuarial value of risks [9]. Although the probability of a death occurring may be very small, the magnitude of the event is large—generally tending to raise the level of anxiety (and willingness to pay). Similarly, the relative magnitude of an event (such as an earthquake or a nuclear accident) that causes a series of deaths tends to influence the perceived cost or "value" of the risk. Death in a disaster is more newsworthy than a "statistical" death [7].

There are generally two methods of determining how much people are willing to pay for the avoidance of risk. One is to observe their spontaneous risk-taking behavior and their willingness to make expenditures (as for insurance, safety programs, etc.) to avoid risk. The other method is to ask people what they would be willing to pay to avoid risk and relieve themselves of anxieties of risk.

C. Stan, among others, has observed patterns of risk taking and risk avoidance and patterns of willingness to pay to avert risks [10]. Observed risk taking or risk averting behavior may fail to reflect actuarial risks because of incomplete information available to the public about the nature of the risks or because of any combination of a number of special biases. People exhibit strikingly different behavior toward risks assumed voluntarily and those suffered involuntarily. "As one would expect, we are loathe to let others do unto us what we happily do to ourselves" [10]. Stan noted that the public's willingness to accept voluntary hazards can on occasion be one thousand times greater than for those experienced voluntarily. Smoking of cigarettes and refusal to use automobile seat belts are obvious examples. The larger and more visible the event (even though it may be unlikely in occurrence) the more it is to be avoided. The larger the number of persons exposed or at risk the lower is the public's threshold for spontaneous risk taking. Finally, risk taking appears to be related to the perception of benefits that would accrue with the assumption of the risk. The greater the perceived benefit, the larger is the acceptable risk. Thus, it is acceptable to permit into the market curative drugs for life-threatening disease processes even though they may carry sizable adverse biological side effects.

The public may be "questioned" about its risk-taking preferences and its willingness to pay by interview and survey. As well, the instrument of voting is commonly used for this purpose. However, referenda are generally complementary to cost-benefit analysis but are to some degree a substitute for cost-benefit analysis [11]. Voting has been considered as a method of compensating for the failure of suitable market for allocating, voting, and exchanging public goods. Voting would be a rationale accommodation if those voting possessed adequate information, if all individuals voted and if the costs were equally divided among the members. In practice, these assumptions are not met perfectly. Further, certain inevitable biases lead the voting process to underestimate benefits of various environmental improvements such as water quality [11].

The problem of incommensurables is one that constantly plagues risk-benefit analysis. The economist's propensity is to reduce all terms to the extent possible to monetary units. Such a process leads to a neat and describable problem that can be reduced to numerical terms. However, the derivation of pecuniary units for factors such as health and avoidance of death or for aesthetic consequences again rests on questions of valuation. One school of thought urges that one of the beneficial results of the process of reduction to monetary terms (however done) is to make explicit what a decision maker otherwise would consider implicitly [12]. "Our thesis is that since valuation of noncommensurables is unavoidable, it is better to confront the choice of values openly and explicitly rather than to allow values to be hidden" [12].

At the other extreme is the notion that monetary values should not be "forced upon nonpecuniary but important effects. Rather, they should be presented as such, leaving valuation to be done by as much of the workings of the political process as possible.

A third suggestion is to reduce the number of noncommensurable effects to the extent possible leaving a residue of other, nonpecuniary items. Again, to a certain extent, this means forcing the (monetary) valuation of items where assigning values is difficult and inevitably fraught with questionable assumptions. One form of compromise is to accompany the valuation process with a description of the underlying assumptions.

Ideally, as discussed above, the market valuation of components of a regulatory decision (costs and benefits) can be used to determine the marginal value of the decision. For example, the observed value in the market for labor and capital inputs for an emission control system can be used to determine (or represent) the dollar value of control costs.

However, there are market failures or imperfections—especially for public goods such as health and environmental integrity. Estimates made of values for public goods from observations of surrogates in private markets may be at variance from the truth. Public goods do not pass through private markets and perceptions may be faulty. However, approximations or "shadow prices" may be inferred from certain types of market experience that is complementary or related to public transactions [12].

There are, however, other and more difficult, noncommensurable economic effects. One of these concerns distribution of costs and benefits among sectors. Some regulatory decisions may have economic impacts but these may not be immediately commensurate with the costs and benefits. This distinction is sometimes described as real versus pecuniary effects. Real effects refer to real changes in the quantities of goods and services produced. Pecuniary effects, by contrast, might include costs of relocation of plant and workers occasioned by the closing of a plant as a result of an environmental decision. In many instances it is important that these two not be confused. Noncommensurate dollar impact measures should be presented separately from real economic impact factors as they are not directly additive. Alternatively, they may be converted to real effects by according to some recognized economic rules.

As well as distribution across regions and across sectors, distribution of economic impact is also recognized over time. The classical challenge here is that of treating with intergenerational transfers. According to traditional cost-benefit analysis, benefits and costs at different points in time are made commensurate by the use of some agreed-upon rate of social discounting. However, there has not been general agreement as to what the proper rate of discounting should be. That is, the issue of the extent to which present generations should pay for risk aversion in the future is unclear.

Any positive rate of discount will directly discriminate against choices that involve bad impacts on early generations but not on later ones. A very low discount rate offers the advantage of protecting future options. A low or zero discount rate will have the effect of transferring present resources into the future. On the other hand, such a scheme, by definition, imposes short-term costs and leaves near-term opportunities foregone. The pro-future proponents argue that discount rates commonly seen in the private market are inappropriate and that the market is inherently a short-sighted mechanism. Those on the other side of the argument maintain that overconcentration on future well-being inevitably leads to serious inefficiencies in the investment process. Further, the argument goes, each generation tends to be wealthier in assets and resources than the one before. If this is a real and continuing trend, it is unwise policy to transfer resources from a poorer to a relatively more affluent generation.

Finally, there is the point of view that maintains there is an effective threshold effect. That is, certain decisions made now (no matter what the discount rate) will lead to irreversible and irretrievable changes in health or the environment. The spectre of foreclosed future options has led some to urge a very cautious point of view [13].

The Theory and Practice of Risk-Benefit Analysis

All of the theoretical formulations and elegant refinements aside, there continues to be a fairly wide gulf between the theory and the practical applications of risk- or cost-benefit analysis. As suggested at the outset of this discussion, analytic techniques and numerical methods are properly used to *contribute* to the decision process, not to *make* choices. Numerical methods, while orderly in appearance, may give false confidence of rigor and validity precisely because they are quantitative. Henry Rowen has summarized major criticisms or limiting features of cost-benefit analysis:

1. Analysts concentrate on tangible, quantifiable factors and ignore or depreciate the importance of intangible, unquantifiable ones.
2. Hence, analysts tend to leave out of consideration certain "fragile" values such as those concerned with ecology or aesthetics.
3. Analysts focus on end results and ignore the processes by which political decisions are made.
4. Policy analysis tends to operate within the interests and values of the clients.
5. Policy analysis, in an effort to be objective, employs neutral and detached language in dealing with intensely moral issues.
6. An artificial separation is made between facts and values.
7. Distributional objectives tend to be overlooked in favor of efficient ones.

Rowen concludes that cost-benefit analysis ". . . in its conventional form . . ." is of very limited utility. He lays much of the blame for the limited usefulness to the "capture" of the science of cost-benefit analysis by economists.

"Economists' tendency to concentrate on static comparisons combined with their central concern with the logic of choice leads to a neglect of the role of creativity. The essence of the policy problem is not to manipulate the familiar variables but to find some new ones that will transform the problem'' [14].

In fact, of course, most governmental regulatory decisions and policies do arise from at least rough exercises designed to compare expected benefits with expected costs. The question raised here is to what extent can formal models or numerical methods be used and how should they be used in practice. In one of the more extensive attempts at cost-benefit analysis, the National Academy of Sciences in 1973 estimated the costs and benefits of the legally mandated automobile emission standards. This exercise was elaborate in its detail and numbers of explicit assumptions. Further, it provided a variety of "answers" according to various strategies (choice of nitrogen oxide standard, schedules for compliance, technological accommodation, multiple car strategy, etc.). A review in 1972 by the Office of Science and Technology made use of a much less elaborate exercise to compare costs and benefits of various automobile emission control strategies and various mandated automobile safety features [15]. Perhaps most common and most useful have been cost-benefit studies done in behalf of vehicular accidents and choices of safety features for vehicles [16, 17, 18]. The prominence of vehicular safety questions seems to arise simply because accidents and incidents can be enumerated and there are more data for this area than for most.

In recent years, there has been an increasing search for better methodologies but also a search for opportunities to exercise existing methods in behalf of real problems and policies. The review by the National Academy of Engineering in 1971 was an early attempt of this sort [5]. A great note of caution was sounded during that review in which analytic methods could have at best a limited, background role in guiding political decisions. In this sense, a distinction is sometimes made between decisions and outcomes. An analytic procedure may point toward one or more desirable decisions. However, in a broader political sense, these may have disastrous outcomes and may be highly unacceptable.

More recently, the Environmental Protection Agency has explored the tools of cost-benefit analysis for decisions and policies dealing with water pollution control [13] and environmental chemicals [6]. In both of these cases policy and decision makers were urged to limit the use of cost-benefit analysis to that of a framework for organizing information, for displaying trade-offs, and for pointing to uncertainties. Analytic methods find their usefulness as orderly devices for pointing directions and for explicitly arranging the information and choices.

Who Shall Do Valuation?

A truly unresolved question in cost-benefit analysis is who is properly charged or entrusted with the task of assigning social values to scientifi-cally determined facts? That is, having ascertained that DDT residues are to be found in the fatty tissues of some human beings, who should be re-sponsible for determining the degree of badness that finding represents? How should the worth of the dumping of asbestos-containing waste into Lake Superior be determined? How should the implied threat of tetraeth-yl lead in gasoline to the health of urban-dwelling children be ascertained? Should this be part of the responsibility of the scientists themselves? It has become the practice increasingly frequently to invoke these judg-ments from scientists called together in the forum of the National Acade-my of Sciences. Should it be done or done exclusively by those in the ex-ecutive branch regulatory agencies who perform the analytic cost-benefit exercises? Should valuation be determined by individual or legislature voting? Should it flow from a public process such as a public hearing or should it be the product of the deliberations of dedicated wise men clos-eted *in camera*? Alternatively, should the valuation process inevitably look to the wise men of the courts—at least in important decisions?

A few years ago, Alan Kneese, writing in *Resources*, described the "Faustian Bargain" society was about to strike with the nuclear scientists of the day. The "bargain" concerned the decision to depend increasingly upon nuclear fission for the generation of electric power in the United States.

It is my belief that benefit-cost analysis cannot answer the most important policy questions associated with the desirability of developing a large-scale, fission-backed economy. To expect it to do so is to ask it to bear a burden it cannot sus-tain. This is so because these questions are of a deep *ethical* character. Benefit-cost analyses certainly cannot solve such questions and may well obscure them. . . . If so unforgiving a technology as large-scale nuclear fission produc-tion is adopted, it will impose a burden of continuous monitoring and sophisticat-ed management of a dangerous material, essentially forever. . . . The society confronts a *moral* problem of a great profundity. . . . In a democratic society the only legitimate means for making such a choice is through the mechanisms of rep-resentative government.

For this reason, during the short interval ahead while dependence on fission ener-gy could still be kept within some bounds, I believe the Congress should make an open and explicit decision about this "Faustian Bargain" [19].

Valuation is, by definition, a matter of social choice. In the first in-stance one is justified in asking whether an individual consumer should not be permitted the luxury of making his own mistakes. The common an-swer given to such a question is yes he should but, in practicality, the lux-ury does not exist for the series of hazards to which he is exposed invol-untarily. An individual cannot pick and choose the water quality in his portion of the lake nearby nor can he elect the ambient characteristic of the air *he* breathes exclusively. Neither can he in many cases choose voluntarily the character of the processed and preserved foods he purchases. One limitation is simply the common character of the exposure. Another is the technical complexity of the issues in virtually any case, making informed individual judgments difficult. Related to this again is the almost inevitable great area of technical or scientific uncertainty that accompanies any judgment [8, 20].

Hence, surrogates have assumed the role for both technical analysis and value judgment in regulatory decisions. The "who is the proper surrogate for social evaluation" question, however, is not clearly resolved. In practice, the task of valuation has been handled by different surrogates for various classes of decisions.

In many (or most) instances, the executive branch regulatory agency has assumed both the roles of technical analysis and social judgment. The legal instruments that give those agencies their power and authority clearly indicated that at least some members of Congress intended the Food and Drug Administration and the Economic Development Administration and the Consumer Product Safety Administration and the Atomic Energy Commission to perform valuations. The Food, Drug and Cosmetic Act and the Clean Air Act, for example, clearly charge the agencies to protect the human health of the populace. Where an agency head is given discretion and latitude in declaring a material or product safe, he is by definition asked to make a social decision.

At times, in practice, an agency head may share this task with others. The commissioner of the Food and Drug Administration responded to the 1962 amendments to the Food and Drug law by asking the National Academy of Sciences to help in the judgments of efficacy for all of the prescription drug products on the market. Similarly, a more recent FDA commissioner has turned to the Federation of American Societies of Experimental Biology to help determine the efficacy of nonprescription or over-the-counter drugs. At other times, Congress has directed that other groups of experts or surrogates "assist" the executive branch in reaching social valuations. The recent assessment of the costs and values associated with the automobile emission standards was of this sort. In this case, the Congress ordered the EPA to enlist the assistance of the National Academy of Sciences and included a budgetary authorization to cover the costs [21]. The Senate Report that directed this study asked the National Academy of Sciences for an "independent evaluation of the health standards specified in order to meet the goals of the Clean Air Act" [21].

In practice, too, a certain amount of social judgment making has been referred to the judiciary. As discussed in an earlier section and because of the construction of the law, the entering of the courts into regulatory decisions generally occurs late in the process of decision making and takes the form of reviewing the decisions of others. Parties aggrieved by a regulatory agency's decision bring their grievances before the courts for resolution (and, hopefully, relief). Thus, the judicial opinion reversing EPA's decision on tetraethyl lead was of this sort [22] as was the series of judicial judgments on the practice of waste discharge by the Reserve Mining Company in Minnesota. This is characteristically a cumbersome and lengthy process. The factoring in of both technical expertise and social judgment is exceedingly difficult in this setting. Further, one might well question the representativeness or other qualification of a judicial surrogate over any other surrogate to strike "Faustian bargains."

As mentioned in an earlier section, there is a school of thought that urges the executive branch be responsible solely for technical analyses leaving social judgments to Congress as the representative body [23]. Congress has indeed assumed this role and has preempted the executive branch in three instances: One is the (Delaney) Anticancer Amendment to the Food, Drug and Cosmetic Act. A second is the congressionally mandated series of automotive emission standards. The third is the Water Pollution Control Act, which directs that there be zero pollutant discharges by 1980. In each case Congress has made the "judgment" concerning the value of preserved health and clean environment. There is little or no latitude permitted in interpretation and little or no discretion allowed in enforcement.

It seems to this writer that the "social" review process should be done explicitly, fully, and well and should be moved, as much as possible, "up front." Congress has properly delegated to certain executive branch agencies a series of regulatory tasks that are indeed quasi-legislative, quasi-judicial, and quasi-administrative. If these tasks are to be performed well, the agency charged with the initial decision should be given the authority and support to examine questions thoroughly from both a technical and a social point of view. The Environmental Protection Agency, for example, should engage in public hearings where these are appropriate before rendering its first judgment or proposal in the *Federal Register*. Thus, the regulatory agency should (with appropriate congressional oversight) perform a surrogate role. However, it should perform this role well. As one observer noted in discussing the decisions concerning the SST, in major policy issues, the political considerations will outweigh the technical ones [23]. The admonition offered here is to render social judgment as full and as accurate as possible.

In spite of the recognized limitations to the doing of risk-benefit analysis for regulatory decisions and policies, Congress has called for these analyses with increasing frequency in recent years. In some cases (such as the Clean Air Act) this has reflected a frustration of some parts of Congress with the narrowness of the law promoted by other parts of Congress. A call for risk-benefit analysis in these cases is a device not only for getting "another opinion" but more importantly for broadening the agenda of items to be considered. In this, Congress is certainly correct. Yet, suitable institutional mechanisms for deriving and articulating social judgments are still to be found.

References

1. Mishan, E.J., *Economics for Social Decisions: Elements of Cost-Benefit Analysis*, Praeger, New York, 1972.
2. Raiffa, H., *Decision Analysis: Introductory Lectures on Choices Under Uncertainty*, Addison-Wesley, Reading, Mass., 1968.
3. Environmental Protection Agency, Symposium on Cost-Benefit Analysis in Water Pollution Control, Washington, D.C., September 1973.
4. *Chemicals & Health*, Report of the Panel on Chemicals and Health of the President's Science Advisory Committee, Washington, D.C., September 1973.
5. National Academy of Engineering, *Perspectives on Benefit-Risk Decision-Making: Report of a Colloquium,* The Committee on Public Enquiry Policy, Washington, D.C., 1971.
6. National Academy of Sciences, *Principles of Decision-Making for Regulating Chemicals in the Environment,* Washington, D.C., 1975.
7. National Academy of Sciences, National Academy of Engineering, Air Quality and Automobile Emission Control, Washington, D.C., August 1974.
8. Olson, M., Ignorance and Uncertainty, Background paper for the Symposium on Cost-Benefit Analysis in Water Pollution Control, Environmental Protection Agency, Washington, D.C., September 1973.
9. Schelling, T.C., The Life You Save May Be Your Own, in Chase, S.B., *Problem of Public Expenditure Analysis, Studies of Government Finance*, The Brookings Institution, Washington, D.C., 1967.
10. Stan, C., Benefit-Cost Relationships in Socio-Technical Systems, Presented at the International Atomic Energy Agency Symposium on Environmental Aspects of Nuclear Power Stations, United Nations Headquarters, New York, August, 1970.
11. Portney, P.R., Voting, Cost-Benefit Analysis and Water Pollution Policy, Background paper for the Symposium on Cost-Benefit Analysis in Water Pollution Control, Environmental Protection Agency, Washington, D.C., September 1973.
12. Freeman, M., Hazard-Cost-Benefit Comparisons, in National Acad-

emy of Sciences, *Principles of Decision-Making for Regulating Chemicals in the Environment*, Washington, D.C., 1975.

13. Fisher, A.C., and Krutilla, J.V., Valuing Long-run Ecological Consequences and Irreversibilities, Background paper for the Symposium on Cost-Benefit Analysis in Water Pollution Control, Environmental Protection Agency, Washington, D.C., 1973.

14. Rowen, H., The Role of Cost-Benefit Analysis in Policy Making, Background paper for the Symposium on Cost-Benefit Analysis in Water Pollution Control, Environmental Protection Agency, Washington, D.C., September 1973.

15. U.S. Office of Science and Technology, *Cumulative Regulatory Effects of the Cost of Automobile Transportation*, Washingotn, D.C., January 1972.

16. Lave, L.B., and Weber, W.E., A Benefit-Cost Analysis of Auto Safety Features, *Applied Economics*, 2: 1-2, 1970.

17. Calibresi, G., *The Cost of Accidents,* Yale University Press, New Haven, 1970.

18. U.S. Department of Transportation, *Economic Consequences of Automobile Accident Injuries*, Automobile Insurance and Compensation Study, Two Volumes, Washington, D.C., April 1970.

19. Kneese, A., Benefit-Cost Analysis and Unscheduled Events in the Nuclear Fuel Cycle, *Resources*, No. 44, September 1973.

20. Carpenter, R.A., Legislative Approaches to Balancing Risks and Benefits in the Regulation of Chemicals, Unpublished manuscript, 1972.

21. U.S. Senate, Report 93-369, Committee on Public Works, 1973.

22. Ethyl Corporation v. Environmental Protection Agency, U.S. Court of Appeals, District of Columbia, January 28, 1975.

23. Roback, H., *Politics and Expertise in Policy Making, in Perspectives on Benefit-Risk Decision Making,* Report of a Colloquium Conducted by the Committee on Public Engineering Policy, National Academy of Engineering, Washington, D.C., April 26-27, 1971.

9

Public Information and Questions of Credibility

James S. Turner, lawyer and spokesman for consumer viewpoints, once remarked to the commissioner of the Food and Drug Administration during a meeting, "We agree with your decisions but we don't know how you arrived at them." The public's perceptions and appreciation of the regulatory decision process have become issues fully as important as the substance and content of these decisions. The public wishes (or demands) to know and to understand the processes by which decisions were reached and to have available the information and data used in arriving at a particular conclusion.

The traditional pattern of a Congress' (representing public desires) delegating food and drug and environmental decision making to a dedicated government agency in isolation is neither satisfying nor satisfactory. Public demands for information on regulatory decisions have been voiced for some time and with a rising intensity. More recently, these demands to inform the public better have been combined with demands for opportunities for public participation. Indeed, the line between an informed public and a participating public is inevitably a thin one. Further, the longer the demands for information are unmet, the more suspicious grows the public and the more aggressive are the importunings.

We have been passing through an era of intense public concern for the integrity of the general environment and for human safety in the face of chemical substances and radiation. Behind much of the expressed concern has been a measurable degree of suspicion and anxiety about both the elements and the course of the decision process done in the public's behalf by government. The public has now let it be known in many ways that it either does not understand how the governmental decision processes work or it does not trust those it comprehends.

What are the reasons for this increasing clamor for public accountability? There appear to be several factors that contribute to this outcome, all of which combine more or less in each case to foster public concern.

1. Part of the problem lies with the scientific or "factual" data upon which the decision or judgment rests. The scientific information is characteristically complex—not only in concept but in interpretation. This fact has on more than one occasion led scientists themselves to the point of view that the public would not understand the scientific data, that it would be of no benefit and perhaps do harm to place the scientific information in

the hands of the general public. Even if this point of view were valid (and I doubt its validity), it is viewed as a particular arrogance of scientists and regulators that is not to be tolerated by the public.

Not only are the scientific facts inevitably complex, but their interpretation by peers in the scientific community is often not straightforward. Further, different scientific spokesmen often disagree as to interpretation.

In addition, as is discussed below, the "frontier science" itself, which is often characteristic of this area, provokes confusion and uncertainty. *Frontier science* is the term chosen to describe experimental results and observations taken directly from the laboratory into regulatory decisions without the benefit of maturation and interpretation by other scientists. Since this pattern has become so common in regulatory activity, it has emerged as an important influence in molding public perception and understanding.

2. In the second place, as was discussed earlier, the decision process itself is often not a crisp, well-defined one. Ultimately, the aggregate of governmental actions that affect the public is a combination of several processes—usually occurring serially, and often involving two or even three branches of the government. The entire process may extend over a period of years and may include confirmations, contradictions, or extensions of initial administrative decisions along the way. Without giving the process considerable attention in each case, it is difficult at times for the public to discern which "decisions" are definitive and which are tentative and subject to further governmental review.

3. The processes of regulatory decision making have been commonly thought of as (and, in fact, to a great extent have been) carried out in secret and out of the public's view. Basic information—especially that obtained by the government from commercial firms subject to regulation—has until recent years not been available to the public. Further, as Turner contended, the particular analytical methods and judgmental factors, the weightings given to social considerations, etc., have traditionally not been explicitly offered to public view by those entrusted with the decisions.

4. Finally, and without question, questions of credibility and accountability of government regulation for human health are inevitably related to the problems of credibility of government in general.

All of these factors have combined with a heightened awareness of consumer and environmental concerns in general in recent years. There is strong reason to examine questions of public understanding of regulatory decision processes and of the resulting decisions. In brief, however well intentioned the decision makers may have been, major questions of credibility and accountability and of public understanding remain to be satisfied. All three of the principal parties to these questions bear a responsibility—the press, members of the scientific community, and the government.

How the System Is Supposed to Work

The Congress begins the process by passing a law that enables or requires an agency of the executive branch to take some action toward the protection of health. Typically, for each class of substances, the Food and Drug Administration or the Environmental Protection Agency is empowered to investigate or survey, to make regulations or set standards and, with the help of the Justice Department, to enforce them. In most cases, before coming to a definitive decision, the government agency publicizes its intentions in the form of proposals. These proposals are published in the *Federal Register* and are intended to invite or provoke public comment, which the administrator is supposed to take into account when he comes to a more definitive judgment. A period of weeks or months is permitted for receiving these comments before the administrator takes the next step.

A major problem arises, of course, from the fact that, in general, members of the public are not regular readers of the *Federal Register*. Hence, its contents go either unnoticed or are transmitted to the public via an intermediary—the press or the trade press. Further, those who return comments to the government agency are those who are aware of the procedure, who have apprised themselves of the details of the proposal, and, in general, who are organized to interact with the system.

Federal Register notices of "proposed rule making" are often complex and difficult to comprehend. Their language typically conforms to that of the legal instruments that provide for them. They often contain references to other documents and materials that must be understood in order to appreciate the intended impact of the proposal. To the uninitiated, the language is often confusing or misleading. As was spelled out in some detail in an earlier chapter, the unorthodox use of the terms cancellation and suspension in the law governing the regulation of pesticides is an example.

Finally, the formal notices of proposed rules and standards in the *Federal Register* are typically narrowly circumscribed. They deal strictly with a restriction in the use of a material or the establishment of a numerical standard. In the past, they have not, generally, provided a discussion of the basis for the standard in the first place. They have not offered an analysis of alternatives or the range of costs and benefits that one might expect from the avenue proposed compared with alternatives. They characteristically do not reflect a full discussion of all of the questions that arise in the public's mind in each case. The narrowness of point of view may arise because of constraints in the law. As noted in an earlier section, the 1970 amendments to the Clean Air Act effectively prohibit the administrator from considering questions of economic implications and technological competence when devising certain standards for ambient air quality. Alternatively, a narrow rather than a broad point of view may be chosen specifically in order to avoid raising issues that might otherwise remain dormant. The reasoning in this case is that to decrease the number of points available for public information and public discussion effectively reduces the areas of controversy. Finally, the discussion in the *Federal Register* may be limited simply because of a pressure of time.

In brief, the material in the *Federal Register* has not generally permitted a reader who is a member of the general public to follow the reasoning from first principles that lay behind the proposal nor to understand the proposal in the broad perspective that his own intuition would dictate. In Turner's language, it has generally been difficult for a reader of the *Federal Register* to know how the proposals were "arrived at."

In the sequence of the "administrative process," the administrator of the agency takes the solicited comments into account and makes a decision. The public comments, thus, are advisory. His decision is similarly published in the *Federal Register*. At that point and for a circumscribed period following, interested parties enjoy the opportunity of appealing the decision according to the process of "administrative review." The rules governing this process vary among regulated classes of materials. In general, in both the legislative history and in judicial decisions, the trend has been to broaden and make more liberal the access to administrative and judicial review. Past practice has, in many cases, been to restrict this access to parties who had special interests in the cases in question or who were injured by the administrator's decision. In the case of the Clean Air Act, the courts have granted review to those being regulated and to those others seeking to protect the public interest and the proper administration of the regulatory system. In the case of the pesticide law, parties who can "trigger suspension or cancellation are not only those adversely affected but also citizens' groups backed by "substantial evidence." The legislative history of this act made it clear that the agency was to seek broad, public views. Hence,in the 1972 amendments the special provisons for citizens' suits were deleted as unnecessary. "Standing" in cases of review and appeal logically reflects a desire on the one hand to encourage a broad portfolio of views and, on the other, a desire not to encumber the process by irresponsible, last-minute protestations.

The forms of review that can be elected in each case again vary among classes of materials according to the variety of enabling acts. Thus, in the case of pesticides, a party that petitions for a review may elect a scientific review panel or a public hearing. In certain circumstances as occurred for DDT, both may be elected. This, in theory at least, is an effort to "go public" with the decision process and to seek a broader base for the decisions. In the case of the scientific review panel, the aim in essence is to seek a second, informed opinion.

When the administrative processes or review have run their course, the administrator again renders a decision or "judgment." At that point, in most cases, the parties to the decision can seek a further course of review through the courts—a judicial review.

The time taken to run the course of all of these processes can be very long and the course is often exceedingly convoluted. The president's science adviser announced a series of governmental actions in behalf of the herbicide 2,4,5-T in October 1969. Over the next five years, there ensued several announced "decisions" by spokesmen for the executive branch, a report of a scientific advisory committee, and a public hearing. Each one of these delivered a judgment, pronouncement, or recommendation. In addition, two series of congressional hearings punctuated this sequence. In the case of DDT, the current set of government decisions began in 1967 in the Department of Agriculture. An initial series of decisions by the secretary of agriculture was followed closely by another. In 1970 there occurred another that in turn provoked a bout of litigation followed by judicial appeals. There was closely followed by a scientific advisory committee, a public hearing and, finally, an order issued by the administrator.

Further Complications

There are still further complicating features that conspire to make public understanding a special challenge. It is difficult, at times, for a public, which may observe the behavior of the regulatory process only casually, to discern the difference between decisions made by a chief administrator for executive branch agency and those made by Congress. In the case of the Sec. 409 (c) (3) (A) of the 1958 Food Additive Amendment of the Food, Drug and Cosmetic Act (Delaney amendment), and in the case of the automobile emissions standards of the 1970 amendments to the Clean Air Act, Congress in fact made the decisions as to standards and levels. The margin of discretion left to the administrative agency is very small. Its major tasks in such cases are administrative and judicial (enforcement) in character. A naive public may, in such cases, understand the announcements of governmental regulatory action to be the product of administrative analysis and administrative discretion when, in fact, they represent a congressional mandate. FDA decisions in 1973 on diethylstilbestrol (DES) used as a growth promoter in livestock are an example. DES had been demonstrated to be related to neoplastic disease (cancer). According to the law, its addition to livestock feed was permitted unless its presence were detected in the tissues of the slaughtered animals. Eventual refinement of analytic methods made clear the presence of DES residues in the muscle and other organs of beef even when DES was withdrawn from the feed for a period prior to slaughter. The FDA found itself with no choice but was obliged to follow the proscriptions of the law and ban the additon of DES to animal feed [1]. In spite of the signed mandate that obtained in this case, from the character of the public's reaction, it was clear that many perceived this decision as having been taken on the basis of administrative choice.

Certain other decisions are intrinsically complex both in background and in administration. The Environmental Protection Agency, in February 1972, elected to move for the reduction in use of tetraethyl lead in gasoline. This regulatory move, in fact, took the form of two decision processes, each possessing a slightly different rationale and representing two separate schedules. In January 1973 EPA announced that lead-free gasoline would by law be available for sale in every gasoline station that purveyed at least a certain minimum amount of fuel each year. Here, the rationale was to insure that automobiles equipped with exhaust catalytic devices (which would be poisoned by lead) would have an available source of lead-free gasoline [2]. In addition, in January 1973 EPA proposed the gradual decrease in this amount of allowable lead in the remaining gasoline. In this case, the decision was based on the reasoning that tetraethyl lead from gasoline ultimately represented a hazard to human health by adding to the body's lead burden of city-dwelling children already exposed to lead from other sources [3]. This regulatory question has proved to be exceptionally complicated in the public's eye because of the double action with somewhat similar arguments initially, because of a relatively uncertain scientific rationale behind the health arguments with some apparent disagreement among scientists, and because of some backing and filling on the part of the government after the initial proposals were made [2]. Two different schedules of action resulted from these two decisions. Yet on the surface, the somewhat similar reasoning behind the decisions makes them less easily separable in the public's view. The public is not always clear about which decision is being considered in the press accounts of governmental action [4].

Finally, the schedules chosen for implementation of an announced decision are, themselves, often so complex and subject to so much alteration that real public understanding is exceedingly difficult without an extraordinary effort at information. The automobile exhaust emissions standards are perhaps the best and most current examples. The 1970 amendments to the Clean Air Act were explicit and relatively inflexible on the subject of exhaust emission standards for light-duty vehicles (passenger automobiles). The law as passed ordered a reduction in emissions of hydrocarbons and carbon monoxide by at least 90 per cent by 1975 relative to the pattern of emissions in 1970. For nitrogen oxides, a 90 per cent reduction over 1971 levels was to be achieved by 1976. As a small concession, the law permitted the administrator of EPA to grant a one-year suspension in the time schedule for meeting these standards if requested by an automobile manufacturer and if certain findings and qualifications were met. The law named the National Academy of Sciences to assist the administrator in ascertaining the state of technology available to meet the standards.

By 1971 William Ruckelshaus, EPA administrator, had prescribed the testing procedures and the details of meeting the emission standards. Several manufacturers applied for the one-year suspension. The National Academy of Sciences reported that the technological capacity for meeting the mandated standards was very narrow if the original time schedule were kept and suggested that there were advantages to deferring the schedule. (The report went further, suggesting that staying with the original deadline might discourage research and exploratory development of alternate technological avenues.) Public hearings were held early in 1972. In spite of considerable advice to the contrary, EPA declined to grant a suspension. The manufacturers then sought judicial relief by taking their applications for postponement to court. The Court of Appeals refused to support EPA's decision but remanded the issue back to the government agency. (The court's opinion in this case pointed to the sharp differences in findings between the administrator of EPA and the report of the National Academy of Sciences concerning technological feasibility of meeting the standards.)

A second National Academy of Sciences report followed closely, in which new and, as yet, unconsidered technological options were discussed. The weight of the court's directive and the NAS's consideration of alternate technologies led EPA in April 1973 to grant a one-year suspension of the standards for hydrocarbons and carbon monoxide (postponing the targets to 1976). At the same time, the agency promulgated interim standards for these two pollutants. In announcing the decision, EPA elected to adopt a strategy of *gradual* introduction of the original technology, the catalytic converter.

Three large automobile manufacturers applied for a one-year suspension of the nitrogen oxides standard (originally set for 1976). This request was granted in July 1973 on the basis again of technological limitation to meet the standard. EPA also set an interim standard for nitrogen oxides at the same time.

In December 1973 the Senate acted to amend the Clean Air Act to delay the 90 per cent reduction of emission standards until 1977. That is, this would have the effect of a further year's grace for hydrocarbons and carbon monoxide. Further, a provision for an additional one-year suspension for nitrogen oxides was provided for allowing for a potential postponement in that case until 1978. In June 1974 the Energy Supply and Environmental Coordination Act was passed, which extended the nitrogen oxide standard until 1978, permitted the EPA to postpone the other emission standards until 1978, and continued the interim standards until those target dates.

In January 1975 the president forwarded to the Congress the Energy Independence Act of 1975. Title V of that act proposed a series of automotive emission standards less stringent than the statutory levels in the Clean Air Act and, further, proposed that these remain fixed for a period of five years (1977-1981). In March of that year, the administrator of EPA, independent of the president's proposal, offered a different set of standards. He proposed a schedule of increasingly stringent standards over a period of six years and culminating in the original statutory standards plus a new standard for sulfates.

Several factors (shortage of petroleum, economic recession, scientific uncertainty, second thoughts about technological capability, etc.) have conspired to alter and stretch out a schedule imposing an ultimate set of emission standards. This is all the more remarkable since stability and predictability seemed to have been written into the law at the outset. From this brief resume it can be seen that following an understanding the details of this picture is a sizable task. Conveying of this complex story and its transient character to the public for their understanding has been done poorly or not at all.

All of this points to an enormous task of adequately informing and educating a public on the details of regulatory matters. Reasonable and ordinary measures are not sufficient. The challenge is one that calls for extraordinary and aggressive methods and imaginative if unorthodox solutions. All three parties to this question, the press, government, and the scientific community, share in this responsibility. All three have a stake in it. All three contribute both to the substance and the tone of the present debates. Until recently, none has truly accepted its share of responsibility for public education and information in any forthright manner and to any significant extent.

The remainder of the discussion that follows considers the responsibilities of each of these three groups. The order of the discussion is not meant to imply any order of importance or priority.

Responsibilities of Scientists

One of the striking characteristics of the science for regulation, as was mentioned earlier, is its "frontier" aspect. Not uncommonly, experimental observations are rushed from the laboratory into public visibility and regulatory action in the name of protection of health. The rationale is typically of the sort that ". . .we can't afford not to share this information concerning implied hazard or apparent danger with the public. . . ." The initial government actions concerning 2,4,5-T announced in October 1969 were reflective of a series of unconfirmed pilot or screening experiments sponsored by the National Cancer Institute of NIH [5]. The next series of government actions months later were based upon a rough series of quickly assembled laboratory experiments [6]. The joint announcement by EPA, the Council on Environmental Quality, and the surgeon general in September 1971 about nitrilotriacetic acide (NTA) and cancer was the result principally of a single experiment that had not been designed to consider the carcinogenic properties of NTA [7]. The FDA's restrictions on further experimentation on a novel series of contraceptive drugs were based on a finding of mammary tumors in beagle dogs. Here, it was unclear (and still remains unclear) what the significance of these findings was, whether or not the benign tumors might be expected to be transformed into malignant ones, and what the implications were for humans. The ban in October 1969 on the unrestricted use of cyclamates reflected a finding of bladder tumors in mice. Again, observations from very few experiments were translated directly into regulatory action. Yet, it later became clear that there was great uncertainty over what substance may have actually provoked the bladder changes (cyclamates, other substances in the mixture that had been fed to the experimental animals, or metabolic derivatives of the test substances). Still another example, which was discussed earlier, was the setting of the standard for nitrogen oxides in automobile exhaust emissions on the basis of a single, preliminary set of observations in an epidemiological experiment never intended to be definitive. The observations were those of absence of children from school because of respiratory illness related to measured ambient levels of nitrogen oxides in the air in Chattanooga, Tennessee [8].

During the course of an examination of the subject of regulation for human health by the Office of Science and Technology, it became apparent that the phenomenon of an individual scientist's "going public" with unconfirmed results was an important and influential one in this arena. In a report on environmental health research in 1972, it was noted that,

Perhaps the most difficult problem for the public is caused by the premature release of unconfirmed findings or one-sided interpretation of findings, often by investigators seeking personal aggrandizement. While such releases will always go on, the frequency might be reduced by steps to assure prompt publication with proper refereeing, establishment of communication channels so that findings by 'bench scientists' inside or outside the Government promptly reach the regulatory authorities . . . . Responsible commentary by scientific peer groups would probably go a long way toward placing premature disclosures in proper perspective [9].

Given a general public fear of environmental chemical and physical influences on human health and given a press especially sensitive to the sensational, there is a ready-made responsive audience for experimental findings—even if unexplained and unconfirmed. In this setting, it has been far from unknown to find scientists who make available to the press the results of their work, however tentative, creating the impression as they do, of an implied threat to human health and well being. A case in point, perhaps, was the offering for public consumption the results of experiments in which doses of pesticidal chemicals were administered to fertile chicken eggs. During the course of congressional hearings on 2,4,5-T in 1970, Dr. Jacqueline Verrett, a scientist at the FDA brought into the congressional hearing room a flock of young chickens—some exhibiting deformities—to dramatize her experimental findings [10]. While there have arisen no challenges to the experimental observations, the meaningfulness of that particular test procedure and the interpretation of the results were later called into serious question by other scientists [11].

Examples of individual scientists' "rushing into headlines" have occurred all too frequently in relation to their area of environment and health. Unfortunately, many factors combine to encourage that pattern. Not the least, of course, is the scientist's own hunger for recognition. In part, he is frustrated by the slow and tedious process of publication and airing through orthodox channels (scientific meetings, their published proceedings, and scientific journals). In part, as has been explained, the press and the government "system" encourage the pattern and offer a favorable reception. In the face of widespread press coverage of a "new", sensational finding, a government regulator cannot easily ignore public pressure to "take some action."

There is a thin line between acting responsibly by bringing to light new information that may have important implication for human safety and not raising unreasonable fears. Scientists need an appropriate receptor for new and potentially important findings that can bring to bear the elements of scientific interpretation and critical analysis which normally characterizes the maturation of scientific findings. Orthodox channels are clearly too slow in many cases.

Notwithstanding, scientists have an obligation to act responsibly. The parading of tentative, unmatured, and unconfirmed experimental results before the public and the press cannot be viewed as responsible. Scientists should seek confirmation of their results and should place their findings before their peers for critical judgment and further interpretation. It is only in this way that the meaning of experimental results of interest to regulators can be understood.

In addition, scientists should bear some of the responsibility for interpreting the details of the scientific fabric to the public. Again, there exists no single, really suitable vehicle to accommodate this interpretive activity. Collaboration with the press and with science writers in some as yet to be explored forms is necessary. The point is that the scientists have an obligation, in this case, to go further than simply to offer raw, unexplained experimental results.

Responsibilities of the Press

The Fourth Estate has a sizeable stake in the regulatory affair. It is a powerful tool in the shaping of public information and public understanding of the nature of the scientific background for individual regulatory decisions. Because of the complexity of the technical information behind decisions and the convolutions of the administrative processes within which decisions are made and announced, the press becomes the major interpreter of government decisions to the public.

In practice, however, the press has been torn between its felt responsibilities to inform and to shape public understanding and the lure of the sensational or newsworthy. It has generally been the dramatic report of a new hazard that finds its way into the public press. The objective, balanced treatment of a finding is characteristically not newsworthy—especially when the net result is to relieve public fears and anxieties.

One of the National Institutes of Health, the National Institute of Environmental Health Services, elected in the early 1970s to engage a series of "scientific" reviews of materials of impending regulatory concern for which no systematic accounting of scientific information had been done. The philosophy in this case was to bring together in a conference spokesmen for the principal research projects— published or underway—in order to take the measure of the available scientific understanding. At the same time, members of the press— especially science writers—were invited to attend these sessions in order to acquaint them with the base of scientific knowledge in each case. Thus, the aims were to educate both scientists and the public about the science and its interpretation.

In December 1971 NIH held the first of this series of conferences in North Carolina—this one on PCBs [12].[a] Those who were then currently engaged in research on PCBs and several who were then undertaking reviews of the subject made presentations at this "open" conference. The details of the research were systematically laid out. Interpretation and criticism by scientific peers were provided. The net (and immediate) effect of that exercise was to take the newsworthiness out of the PCB issue

---

[a] Since then, NIH has held similar reviews on lead, automotive emissions, and other substances of public and governmental concern.

and to remove it from the category of the sensational. Where the lay press had been filled with stories about the excesses and hazards of PCBs during the weeks and months before, very little was actually reported in the press of that meeting. More important, relatively little more was reported on PCBs in any form in the lay press for several years. The wind of sensationalism had been taken out of the subject by instilling a discussion of the facts and by forcing the representatives of the press to pay attention.

The press has a special opportunity (if not obligation) in this case to educate as well as to inform. The public interest would be well served by a press that undertook the task of acquainting the public about a number of special issues of regulation for health. One is the dynamic nature of science and the changing character of scientific understanding. This would properly foster expectation of rather than surprise over occasional reevaluations of past decisions. What the government regulatory agency does when it evaluates and passes on a commercial product or environmental agent has often been thought of as leading to a sort of certification of *proof* of safety. Except when understood in the narrow sense of scientific proof (tentative demonstration of a scientific phenomenon) this idea of proof is a misnomer. Assurance of safety cannot be guaranteed by the process of scientific fact finding and interpretation. If experimentation and review have been exercised appropriately, if science has been squeezed for understanding and evaluation to the extent that it can be on any particular question, then it can be said that according to the present level of understanding, the probability of hazard is low. This assignment of low probability or risk is based on an area of uncertainty as well as on scientific understanding. It is not possible to ascertain definitively the extent of this uncertainty. Further, the scientific basis for regulatory decisions is inevitably tentative and liable to be overturned from time to ime by new scientific evidence.

The press has a responsibility to educate the public not only about this series of "special issues" that characterize regulation but about the scientific details (and their meaning) for each major individual regulatory action. The press should reflect the best scientific opinion available concerning how new findings fit into a background of established data and concepts. As well, the press should describe the limitations and cautions that may accompany scientific observations. The pattern of engaging science writers fully in the discussions at specially called scientific meetings is a good one and has proved its value [13]. The President's Science Advisory Committee urged that "bold and aggressive steps" should be taken to brief members of the press through special scientific meetings and background sessions. In turn, they admonished the press to take on the special tasks of public education of the scientific details of regulation [14].

Responsibilities of Government

The proper role of government agencies is as promoters of public understanding through candor and full disclosure. In fact, there can be no other way. The spirit of the Freedom of Information Act [15] and the Federal Advisory Committee Act [16] is clearly of this sort. The combination of a greatly increased level of suspicion of government in general and public demand for openness in regulatory decision making leads unequivocally to that conclusion.

However, even if openness and candor were not being "forced" on the system extrinsically, the narrower cause of providing for the broad public interest best through regulation would be better served by providing full and adequate public explanations. If regulatory decisions are to be made in a way that takes into account and "balances" the myriad of consequences and impactions in each case [14], the administrator of the government agency will find himself at odds with those in Congress and those among his identifiable constituency who favor regulation per se in a narrow sense. In brief, he will be obliged to go against the grant of his pro-environmental and pro-consumerist constituency at times. So that he can afford to set standards and make decisions that best serve the broad public interest, the public must be well informed and in possession of a comprehension of the choices available, the nature of the information available, and the reasons why he elects the particular choice he does in each case.

All of this argues strongly for one or more devices capable of full public explanation and disclosure. Public hearings are supposed to serve this purpose. The particular public hearing process used in the case of pesticides regulation before a proposal is offered in the *Federal Register* is the most forthright of such procedures. However, there remain severe limitations associated with public hearings. They are not good instruments for discussion of technical issues. They take on the strong flavor of adversary and quasi-judicial proceedings rather than settings for engaging in informed public discussion. Their rules are sometimes exclusionary or restrictive when it comes to some types of information on certain issues.

The open scientific meetings held by NIH designed to inform and educate the press as well as scientists are an effective step. The number of these has remained very small thus far. These sessions are expensive procedures and require a great deal of careful preparation to insure their effectiveness.

Some have advocated the issuance of a "white paper" on the occasion of each important regulatory decision [14]. As conceived, a white paper would provide for public consumption a full listing of the scientific findings and their best interpretation for each decision. It would consider each of the possible avenues of decision considered by the agency head along with the factors and expected consequences for each "option." Finally, it would offer the reasoning and analysis behind the particular choice and the series of judgments used in arriving at the final judgment.

Since this "white paper" recommendation was first offered, the Food and Drug Administration moved part way towards meeting it by giving fuller analyses and fuller information in their *Federal Register* notices. Wholesale adoption of the white paper suggestion, however, has not yet been forthcoming. To do so is seen as weakening the hand of the chief administrator and his staff in each case. To go public with full-blown analyses as to how decisions are reached and to declare candidly what kinds of information he has available (often exceedingly thin in quantity and quality) would weaken his further bargaining position and render him vulnerable to further criticisms. Full analyses and explanations of this sort might also tend to weaken the bargaining positions of some in Congress who hotly espouse certain narrow points of view (either pro- or antienvironment or health). This is in the spirit of he who controls the information controls the decision. Hence, there has been no ground swell of support from Congress for making full public disclosures of data and analyses. Yet, this is precisely in the spirit of the National Environmental Policy Act, which obliges the provision of broad analyses termed Environmental Impact Statements. The notion of a white paper has great virtue, would in fact strengthen the bond of the various parties to regulatory decisions, and, most of all, would go far toward serving the best and broadest of public interests.

References

1. U.S. Department of Health, Education, and Welfare, Food and Drug Administration, Diethylstibestrol Order Denying a Hearing and Withdrawing Approval of New Animal Drug Applications for Liquid and Dry Premixes, and Deferring a Ruling on Implants, August 2, 1972.
2. *Federal Register*, Regulation of Fuels and Fuel Additives, January 10, 1973, Volume 38, No. 6, pp. 1254-1256.
3. U.S. Environmental Protection Agency, *EPA's Position on the Health Effects of Airborne Lead*, Washington, D.C. November 29, 1972.
4. Environmental Protection Agency, Regulations Proposed for Lead and Phosphorous Additives in Gasoline, Press Release, February 23, 1973.

5. Innes, J.R.M., Ulland, B.M., Valerio, M.G., Petrocelli, L., Fishbein, L., Hart, E.R., Pallotta, A.J., Bates, R.R., and Peters, J., Bioassay of Pesticides and Industrial Chemicals for Tumorigenicity in Mice: A Preliminary Note, *J. National Cancer Institute*, 42: 1101-1114, 1969.

6. Steinfeld, J., Testimony on 2,4,5-T before the Subcommittee on Energy, Natural Resources, and the Environment, Committee on Commerce, U.S. Senate, June 18, 1970.

7. U.S. Department of Health, Education and Welfare, News Release, September 15, 1971.

8. U.S. Environmental Protection Agency, *Air Quality Criteria for Nitrogen Oxides*, Washington, D.C., January 1971.

9. Report of OST-CEQ Ad Hoc Committee on Environmental Health Research, Washington, D.C., June 1972.

10. Verrett, J., Testimony on 2,4,5-T before the Subcommittee on Energy, Natural Resources and the Environment, Committee on Commerce, U.S. Senate, April 15, 1970.

11. 2,4,5-T Advisory Committee, 1971, Report submitted May 7, 1971, to William D. Ruckelshaus, administrator, Environmental Protection Agency, Washington, D.C.

12. National Institute of Environmental Health Sciences, Meeting on Polychlorinated Biphenyls (PCBs), Rougemont, North Carolina, December 20-21, 1971. Proceedings published in *Environmental Health Perspectives*, Experimental Issue No. 1, April 1972, National Institute of Environmental Health Sciences, Research Triangle Park, North Carolina.

13. Burger, E.J., Jr., Public Information, Science and the Regulatory Process. *Environmental Health Perspectives*, 1(2):1-3, 1972.

14. *Chemicals and Health*, A Report of the Panel on Chemicals and Health of the President's Science Advisory Committee, Science and Technology Policy Office, National Science Foundation, September 1973.

15. P.L. 93-502, Freedom of Information Act, November 21, 1974.

16. Federal Advisory Committee Act, P.L. 92-463, October 6, 1972.

17. National Environmental Policy Act of 1969, P.L. 91-190, January 1, 1970.

10 Lessons to Be Learned from Experiences Abroad

There are certain common characteristics among industrialized nations in their dealing with chemicals through governmental regulation. Virtually all engage or impose some sort of regulatory activity aimed at protecting human health. Many countries have made their regulatory system more complex or more comprehensive and more aggressive in recent years. In many cases, the patterns and practices in other industrialized nations seem to have followed the lead of the United States. (Without question, the United States has sustained the most comprehensive and ambitious of environmental programs through regulation. It has been very common for specific regulatory actions in the United States in recent years to carry similar decisions in other nations in their wake.) It has been true, too, that stepped-up programs in the United States of gathering and assessing information for regulatory decisions have, by default, had the effect of setting the pace abroad. For example, much of the deliberations of the World Health Organization concerning criteria for air pollution control and much of the documentation have been patterned after the background documents and criteria adopted by the U.S. Environmental Protection Agency [1].

By the same token, the decision in the United States concerning polychlorinated biphenyls led quickly to a series of complementary decisions in other countries such as Japan and West Germany and a flurry of consultative activity within the Organization of Economic Cooperation and Development.

At the same time, other nations have by no means automatically or unequivocally followed the United States lead. In 1970, when the United States government discouraged (through pronouncement) the use of nitrilotriacetic acid (NTA) in household detergents, a number of countries including Canada, Sweden, and the United Kingdom made extensive investigations into the technical background of the United States decision. After completing their own reviews, the governments of Canada and Sweden, for example, elected to endorse the use of NTA.

Most if not all industrialized nations have felt the common impact of national concerns for abating environmental pollution and for treating with consumer issues—including personal and collective health. Industrial production has brought with it environmental pollution. Increasing affluence has permitted the luxury of concern and action. Public spirit has been aroused throughout the world where this combination has occurred. Increased public awareness has translated commonly into a questioning of governmental institutions for dealing with environmental challenges and has brought similar demands for *action* in all industrialized societies.

However, there are some striking differences and variations. Some of those differences relate to the size and style of government in each case. Some differences are due to variations in the importance which the populace attaches to environmental and environmental health issues.

Among the factors that stand out in relief when considering regulation of food additives, pesticides, and therapeutic drugs in the United Kingdom as well as many European nations is the modest size of the government organizations dealing with regulation. The U.S. Food and Drug Administration has a total of 6,000 employees of whom 40 per cent comprise the Bureau of Drugs. Approximately 600 of these are physicians and other professionals. By contrast, the drug regulatory enterprise in Great Britain, the Office of the Senior Principal Medical Officer for Drugs, is comprised of 11 professionals (physicians and pharmacists).

The pattern of regulatory behavior in many Western Europe nations typically includes a great deal of informality and voluntary cooperation or compliance, it is of small relative scale in comparison to our own, and, in many cases, it is done out of the public's view. As in the United States, the majority of the scientific and background information used by the government in reaching decisions is supplied by the petitioning industries. Resources for basic investigation and fundamental research are typically underwritten by arms of the government as in the United States. In addition, in some European countries, hybrid private-public research institutions have been established to undertake certain borderline or applied short-term studies.

The differences in scale are related in part to differences in style and mechanisms of regulating. In the United Kingdom, for example, there have traditionally been very few statutory provisions for regulation of drugs and environmental chemicals. Rather, the carrying out and enforcement of decisions reached by the governmental mechanisms rest on a great deal of voluntary compliance.

There are no statutory regulations governing pesticides in the United Kingdom. Since 1957 the government has maintained through a voluntary agreement with the chemical industry a scheme under which it informs itself about pesticides and influences their manufacture, sale, and use. The government solicits from pesticide manufacturers certain types of information relating to efficacy and safety of new pesticidal chemicals, and thereby prescribes what types of research it expects the industry to perform. The industry provides this information to the government for its review with the understanding that it will always remain confidential. The vehicle for review is an Advisory Committee on Pesticides and Other Toxic Chemicals. This committee, and its associated scientific subcommittees and specialist panels, reviews data on new chemicals and on problem cases. The advice from the committee is directed *in camera* to the minister of agriculture.

If a pesticide is approved, the committee makes public its recommendation in the form of specifications for use and details that are to be published on the container label. Pesticides undergo various stages of approval during the course of their development and review ("trial stage," "experimental clearance," "full clearance"). The goal of a manufacturer is to see the inclusion of his chemical on the approved list. (Note, in fact, that there exist two approved lists, one for safety and one for efficacy.)

The British government has little apparent leverage to use in regulating pesticides. It relies, first of all, on voluntary compliance. The inclusion of a pesticide on the "approved list" is one important step that the manufacturer must achieve in order for his product to be recognized by retailers and users. If other than recommended practices for "approved" pesticides are noted, the practice would be for the federal government to advise local (county) authorities who can then take judicial action against manufacturers or users by passing special bylaws.

There is no formal appeal mechanism to which a British manufacturer may apply if he feels aggrieved over the government's decisions about his products. Again, these questions are characteristically handled informally between the government and the private sector.

In the case of food additives in Great Britain, the only federal statutory provision is an enabling act, the Food and Drug Act. This law allows ministers to pass laws from time to time concerning food standards, food additives, and food contaminants. As in the case of pesticides, almost all business is done in an informal and voluntary manner. Food additive manufacturers and the government agree informally about what information the former should supply in order to receive approval. At some point, the submitted information is reviewed formally by a Food Additives and Contaminants Committee. This advisory committee provides its recommendations in an open and visible manner to the minister of agriculture, fisheries and foods. The advice is in the form of a series of reports on topics and also the inclusion (or noninclusion) of the proposed food additives on an approved list. Again, nonapproval places the food additives user or the retailers of the "contaminated" food in the position of being the subject of local actions and bylaws.

Interestingly, the British government does require that "need" be demonstrated before a new food additive is approved. The term *need* implies either economic or technologic necessity and also includes the idea of benefit over other additives already in use. In Great Britain the food processor (not the chemical additive manufacturer) is responsible for demonstrating both safety and need. There is no formal mechanism for appeal for cases in which approval is not granted.

Traditionally, there has been little regulatory authority over therapeutic drugs in the United Kingdom. The only statutes that have applied in the past were the Therapeutic Substances Act (governing vaccines), the Poisons List (a list of restrictions governing the retail dispensing of selected products), and the Poisons Rule.

In 1964 the Dunlop Committee recommended that independent scientific advice be sought by the government to review information concerning new drugs and that the government be responsible for approving new drugs. This led to the formation of an advisory committee (Committee on Safety of New Drugs) that supplies its advice to the minister for health. The committee's review is focused on three points in drug development, before clinical trials, before marketing, and surveillance of marketed drugs for adverse reactions. Thus, began a voluntary system for drugs similar to that for the other two classes mentioned above. Government approval was given in stages corresponding to the stages of committee review (approval for clinical trials, certificate for two years of preliminary introduction, and a license for marketing).

The British government in the past has taken special pains to avoid prescribing or dictating to the drug manufacturers what information it would like to receive (and what research they must do) in order to seek approval. Rather, it has invited the manufacturers to take the initiative in describing the necessary preapproval experimentation.

In 1968 a new law (the Medicines Act) was passed. Eventually this promised to put into statutory form many of the provisions and procedures characteristic of the voluntary system. By the fall of 1971 the British government was armed for the first time with specific statutory authority to seek preliminary information from industry and to regulate in the true sense the manufacture of drugs. The principal vehicle for decision making, the Advisory Committee on Safety of New Drugs, remained in place.

A common feature in government decision making and exercise of regulations in many Western European countries is an advisory committee. There is typically an advisory committee for each of the major regulatory areas (drugs, pesticides, food additives). Characteristically, these advisory boards or committees are composed not exclusively of scientists but represent a broad grouping of experts from outside the government (or a combination of outside and governmental experts). The advisory boards sit very close to the top, politically appointed ministers or administrators. (Alternatively, as in Sweden, they sit apart from the politically appointed heads but share some of his powers.) The advisors, chosen with some care and considerable prestige mostly from universities, usually hold that office without limit of time and, in practice, for many years. (This pattern assures some stability and wisdom but may tend to sacrifice an infusion of fresh ideas at times.)

The advice and recommendations offered the administrator are sometimes transmitted in confidence and sometimes in full public view. The degree of confidentiality varies from country to country and sometimes among the various regulatory categories within a country.

Most important, the advisory committees, in reality, become a highly important part of the decision process. The chief administrator shares some of his power with his advisors (in the same way that a corporation president shares his with a board of directors). In return, he gains a sizeable element of credibility and confidence for his decisions. An administrator or minister can visibly lean on his committee as well as on his staff for support and justification for a decision that otherwise might be much more difficult to reach. To some extent, it is said, this arrangement tends to make the regulatory decision-making process less sensitive to short-term political influences. However, the broad backgrounds of the appointees are said to go far toward representing a spectrum of points of views. From an administrator's point of view, on the other hand, some may see the partial sacrifice of autonomy in decision making as undesirable.

Government agencies provide the staff for the advisory committees. While these staffs are typically very small, they often serve two important functions. On the one hand, they provide the committee members with the background material and analyses for their deliberations. In some instances, as well, they advise the advisors as to the political implications of their proposals and draft recommendations.

This sytem of high level, broadly based advisory committees is a phenomenon unknown in the United States' experience although it has been advocated in recent studies [2].

In the Netherlands a pharmaceutical firm seeking registration of a new drug supplies the Ministry of Public Health and Environmental Hygiene with data supporting its petition. This information is considered by several groups within the ministry. An Advisory Commission on Pharmaceutical Compounds advises the ministry on which substances may be sold with or without a prescription.

In Sweden a great deal of the authority for exercising the policies of regulation rests with a series of administrative boards. By design, these boards are set apart from and are independent to a great extent of immediate political influence. In Sweden the deliberations are all publicly available and open for public viewing. The National Poison and Pesticides Board is responsible for advising on registration of pesticides. Manufacturers' data are assembled by a small staff and presented to the board when they are thought to be adequate. The board is composed of a full-time chairman plus 11 members and 11 alternates. This membership is composed of physicians, veterinarians, pharmacologists, technical director of one of the manufacturers, representatives of prominent research institutes and universities, and at times by members of the Swedish Parliament. This board, which meets monthly, reviews between 100 and 200 applications a year.

The major advisory body in Great Britain for pesticides is the Advisory Committee on Pesticides and Other Toxic Chemicals. The membership includes persons drawn from universities and hospitals, experts chosen from the government and from the Research Councils. Industry is deliberately not represented and an attempt is made to exclude persons who are consultants to industry. The committee meets seven times a year to provide advice to the minister of agriculture and to the minister of state for health and social security. The substance of the advice is not made public. However, where approvals of new pesticides have been recommended, these are published together with the recommended patterns of use. There appear to have been no instances where the committee's recommendations have not been accepted by the administrator.

The membership of the Food Additives and Contaminants Committee for food additives in the United Kingdom is selected one-third from universities, one-third from industry, and one-third from government and private laboratories. Most of its deliberations are published as recommendations.

The Committee on Safety of Drugs in the United Kingdom operates in similar fashion. As in the case of pesticides, information is supplied to the committee by the manufacturers in confidence. Recommendations are made by the committee to the government in secret. Visible evidence of the committee's work appears as approvals of the petitions for clinical trials as for marketing of a new drug. The committee is composed of pharmacologists, toxicologists, clinicians, anesthesiologists, and pharmacists. Consultants to industry are included on this committee. (The spirit of choosing these has been to select persons who consult to several rather than to just one industry and those who consult occasionally rather than consistently.)

In the Federal Republic of Germany, the decision-making authority for regulated chemicals resides within the governmental system but in a way that tends to approximate scientific judgement to these decisions. For pesticides, for example, applications for new products are reviewed by the Federal Biological Institute. The scientists within the institute who are engaged in investigation themselves are responsible for analyzing the data supplied by the manufacturer. Professionals, drawn from several areas of scientific and public health interest, comprise a committee that performs these reviews.

Sources and Performers of Research

As in the United States, manufacturers in Europe are generally responsible for providing to governments the data upon which regulatory decisions are made. The ultimate sources of the data and the institutional and financial arrangements underlying the research present some interesting patterns, however.

In Great Britain the operating departments of government (Health and Agriculture, for example) have essentially no monies budgeted for biological research aimed at questions of safety of products. The government resource that does aid this process is the aggregation known as the Research Councils. Of the five councils, the Medical Research Council is the major contributor in this area. The councils, while semi-independent, receive an annual allocation from Parliament. Budget planning is done on a five-year basis and a Council for Scientific Policy makes decisions about allocation of the total council budget among the five research councils. The Medical Research Council supports research in 78 research units (including a Toxicology Research Unit) located in various parts of the country—often in proximity to universities. Less prominent is a series of direct grants to universities.

The total direct research undertaken by the drug and chemical industries in Great Britain was approximately $5 million in 1971 and represents roughly half of that nation's total investment. A prominent tendency in recent years has been to place an increasing proportion of this research in the hands of private research institutions through contractual arrangements. On the one hand is a series of private for-profit organizations that have assumed an ever-increasing role in this field. This pattern, which really had its origin in the United States, has assumed a rapidly growing place of importance in both the United Kingdom and in the rest of Western Europe.

A third pattern that has become common in Western Europe has been that of joint government and industry cooperative arrangements. In the United Kingdom, there developed several years ago a series of 40 research associations whose general aim was to assist research and development for industry (especially small industry). Among these is the British Industrial Research Association (BIBRA) whose general task is applied research of a biological and toxicological nature especially in the area of food toxicology. BIBRA's origin in 1961 was encouraged by the British confectionery industry, which saw advantages to a joint government-industry resource to provide applied research and toxicological advice for food and food additives. Subscribing industries now comprise approximately 300 members including breweries, petroleum companies, soap and detergent manufacturers, pharmaceutical firms, chemical industries, and food processors. The total annual private subscription is matched one-and-one-half times by a corresponding contribution from the government. Subscribers may seek answers to problems of common concern to the membership. In addition, individual subscribers (as well as others) may bring special problems to BIBRA and pay for essentially privately contracted research from BIBRA.

A somewhat similar institutional arrangement has existed in the Netherlands since 1923 in the National Council for Applied Scientific Research (TNO). The TNO is comprised of 18 research institutes arranged along subject lines. The public philosophy, again, was the felt virture of assisting small industry by sharing and pooling the task of research and development. As in the case of the British research associations, the TNO is jointly funded by the government and industry.

References

1. World Health Organization, *Criteria for Air Quality Standards.*, Geneva, Switzerland, 1973.
2. *Chemicals and Health*, Report of the Panel on Chemicals and Health of the President's Science Advisory Committee, Science and Technology Policy Office, National Science Foundation, Washington, D.C., September 1973.

11 Epilogue

If this work has been at all successful it will have raised or provoked many more questions that it will have answered. At the very least, some issues considered by many as "settled" or agreed upon through conventional wisdom will have been lifted for reappraisal. A major purpose in assembling these materials has been to examine with the scrutiny of experience and some analysis a few of the driving forces and important issues in government regulation for health.

An Opportune Time to Take Stock of Government Regulation for Protection of Human Health

Consumer interests and environmental betterment are seen by some (including some economists and government policy makers) as luxury items—available to society only after a certain threshold level of industrial production and national prosperity have been achieved. At the time of this writing, price inflation of goods and services is a prominent issue, the purchasing power of wages and salaries has declined with economic recession, unemployment is more than noticeable and, in fact, is a politically felt issue, and the costs and availability of fuels for energy have suddenly become prominent issues. According to the philosophy of "environmental betterment only with sufficient affluence," there is now serious reason to question or at least retard the momentum of the past few years of environmental and consumer issues. Hence, governmental regulation done for these purposes is increasingly under attack and in jeopardy of being toned down or deferred.

Indeed, of course, some deferrals have already taken place if one refers to some of the earlier schedules and lists of public expectations. I am not so pessimistic to think that the country will reverse itself in its major goals of preserving and protecting health and in maintaining the integrity of the physical environment. (In fact, if anything, the nation can be expected to take more and more seriously the impact of certain aspects of social behavior and environmental insults on health than they have in the past.) However, it does appear to be opportune to take stock of the particular subject of regulation of involuntary hazards and its relationship to health. Clearly one of the underlying themes of the preceding pages has been one of urging increasing realism in public expectations and honesty in the governmental institutions designed to meet these expectations. If false expectations are encouraged for short-term political rewards that cannot be met in practice (or can be accommodated only at a societal price that ultimately would be seen as unacceptable) a profound disaffection can assuredly be predicted. A letdown and public falling away from environmental issues will surely follow an erosion of faith in the governmental response to felt public issues such as health and the environment.

Accordingly, some stock taking is highly desirable if not imperative. The United States has set the pace in governmental programs and investments in behalf of human health including through regulation. We have a rich legacy of experience. We will be a wealthier and a more confident nation if we were to look into that experience critically and considering in the bright light of forthright public accounting such questions as how much health does and can regulation purchase and how effective can regulatory activities be. This final section is a resumé of some of the more important issues raised by the discussions in the preceding chapters.

Regulation as a Continuum of Activities

Consider the matter of regulation for health as a continuum of activities. In the first instance is the matter of information. The working assumption here is that it is in all the parties' interest (and, hence, in the nation's best interest) that regulatory decision be well informed. It was pointed out above that, from time to time, some parties to regulatory actions consider it in their interest to keep other parties relatively uninformed. This notion of the power of knowledge is an old principle of political life and not by any means confined to regulation. The strong contention of this author is that, in practice, *no parties* to regulatory decision have had any monopoly on information since the general scarcity of good information has been so profound. Advocacy points of view (both pro and con) prevail not on factual grounds but by dint of opportunistic persuasion and emotional argument.

The second stage of the continuum of regulation is acting on information. Here it was pointed out that the state has answered the role of surrogate. Individuals reserve decisions to themselves concerning most aspects of their personal behavior including voluntary exposures to known hazards. They share these with physicians in matters of diagnosis and treatment of acute and chronic illness. It is in the realm of public or collective exposures to factors in the environment for which individuals were thought to have little choice (involuntary hazards) that we have deferred to governments to act in our behalf. Specifically, we have encouraged the establishment of "independent" regulatory bodies within but set slightly apart from the executive branch of the federal government. Congress has delegated and deferred to independent regulatory bodies with an increasingly rich mosaic of legal authorities. At times, of course, Congress has insisted on retrieving some of the direct exercise of this authority from the "independent" agencies. The outstanding examples are the Delaney anticancer amendment and the automobile emission standards. Thus, one might say that the Congress has insisted on a degree of collaboration with the executive in the judgements and exercise of the health-related regulatory activities.

One aspect that has emerged as an important element is the use of health as a substitute or proxy for other desired elements of or related to environmental quality. As noted in an earlier section, the prominent choice of human health as a goal of environmental improvement has been dictated at times by jurisdictional interest in Congress and often by the high political "sale" value of health over other issues such as aesthetic appearance, visibility of the atmosphere, physical integrity of buildings, etc. The tendency to "sell" environmental efforts and programs on the basis of a promise of protecting or improving human health (especially in the case of clean air) is particularly unfortunate. In practice this has often meant that health-related arguments were conjured up to fit an advocacy point of view. What evidence there was from past scientific investigations was not uncommonly stretched and bent in interpretation in order to accommodate a predetermined posture. More than once, as in the case of tetraethyl lead and gasoline, an uncertain (or even tenous) health-related argument was juxtaposed with a more definitive but less emotionally stirring technical argument in the background reasoning provided in the *Federal Register* to accompany a proposed standard or action. Time and economics will lead the nation to look more carefully and critically at the evidence for regulatory decisions. With increasing scrutiny will come some reversals and with reversals will come some degree of disaffection with the process of regulation as an honest and credible form of government. In brief, aggressive regulation even on the side of the angels of health and a clean environment will lose its supporters if it is found to be done less than honestly.

A key question in this discussion is whether the benefit of regulation exceeds its costs. The doing of regulation does impose costs. The question about net benefits over costs, in a sense, implies a grand experiment in which the test procedures have been in place but for which there has been no control for comparison. The hypothesis to be examined in the experiment is that the record of safe and effective products would have been as good as it is if there had not been an overlay of regulation. Would the pharmaceutical and pesticide industries, for example, have been at least as responsible as they are simply in order to better their competitive positions? George Stigler has stoutly maintained that competition is discouraged and displaced by coercion of regulation and that the resulting net benefit of such displacement is a negative one.[1a] However, in fact, we may never really know the answer.

From the point of view of benefits, which it is hoped regulation will visit upon society, there are in most cases probably tangible elements of protection. However, set in a background of all hazards from man's environment, we have allowed ourselves to be protected by the filter of regulation for only involuntary hazards and these are probably only the minor ones. This contrast between the morbid implications of cigarette smoking or alcohol use versus those of food additive exposure is probably not generally appreciated and leaves us with a paradox.

There are costs of regulation. The direct costs of administering the regulatory process are a minor part. We do deprive or delay the commercial offerings of a new product. However, there is no very convincing evidence as yet that the United States has specifically deprived itself of a proven useful and safe drug that was available somewhere else in the world. Further, the delay in getting new drugs or pesticides into the marketplace is experienced throughout the industry. Thus, products have a longer market life and are not as easily or as quickly displaced by new entrants.

There are increased costs caused by the obligations to perform more research and to supply the decision process with increasing amounts of information. Some have argued strenuously that the time delays and the monetary costs of obtaining this additional information are not "worth the trip." Sam Peltzman contends that the determination of efficacy of therapeutic drugs obliged by the 1962 amendments to the Food, Drug and Cosmetic Act is counterproductive. He insists that consumer (and physician) choices in the marketplace for drugs (as for any other product) will indicate efficacy and time and money taken to determine efficacy before marketing is wasteful. [2]. Against that line of argument one can most easily point to the conclusion of the few attempts to examine efficacy of therapeutic drugs that have been done with any rigor. The National Academy of Sciences, for example, in its Drug Efficacy Study, determined that, of all of the prescription drugs on the market, very few were accompanied by much evidence of any substance bearing on biological effectiveness. (That judgement was rendered, of course, after years of expression of patient and physician preferences!)

Regulation, by definition, abridges personal freedom and the scope of personal options. In one sense, it is designed to do just that but in the spir-

---

[a] Regulatory demands have discouraged competition in recent years in the sense of adding to burdens and forcing out of business a number of smaller companies in recent years. This has left chemical firms in an increasingly monopolistic position since it was only they who had sufficient resources to engage in increasingly lengthy development of products.

it of trading for that limitation a promise of some protection of health. One may question the wisdom of this pattern from a public policy point of view. Certain special groups, such as physicians, have complained in the past that what the FDA does, in fact, infringes on their therapeutic territory in the practice of medicine. More recently, a group of female witnesses in a congressional hearing on contraceptive agents took serious issue with their being left out of the decisions about whether contraceptive drugs were or were not safe. The general question here, of course, is whether it is sufficiently in the collective interest to live with surrogate regulation, which means giving up certain individual freedom to indulge or to take risk. The answer is that it probably is—at least if regulation can really deliver what it promises. However, the fulfillment of that promise implies informed regulatory decisions and such a pattern is commonly not the rule.

Murray Weidenbaum, in his recent commentary on government regulation [3], warned of the particularly insidious and potentially harmful aspects of government regulation and referred to a quotation of Justice Louis Brandeis:

Experience should teach us to be most on our guard to protect liberty when the Government's purposes are beneficial. Men born to freedom are naturally alert to repel invasion of their liberty by evil-minded rulers. The greatest dangers to liberty lurk in insidious enroachment by men of zeal, well-meaning but without understanding [4].

Thus, the patterns of government regulation in behalf of human health are seen to be under increasing criticism and attack—principally because of the perceived economic impact of regulation on the private sector. Carl Djerassi has repeatedly asserted that augmented demands for testing by regulatory agencies inevitably lengthen the period of development of new products and that for some products (such as new oral contraceptives) the penalty would be so great as to discourage further innovation [5,6]. By now, several analysts have documented the increase in development costs for therapeutic drugs [7, 8, 9] or for agricultural chemicals [10]. Most commonly in these analyses, these development costs are attributed to the increased demands for information by the regulatory processes. The usual argument is that the nation suffers a net penalty in accommodating these demands for information since they slow the process of innovation leading to new products [2] and represent unproductive expenditures [3].

The proper responses to these assertions are not simple and rest, themselves, on some assumptions. In the field of pharmaceutical products it is true that total numbers of new drugs developed and offered for sale have been falling in the United States. However, this trend began as early as 1955—seven years before the 1962 amendments to the Food, Drug and Cosmetic Act were passed and to which this phenomenon is commonly laid [11]. Further the rate of innovation for therapeutically important, new chemical entities appears to have remained essentially unchanged over at least 20 years [11]. At the same time a number of chemical manufacturing companies have complained they were obliged to expend an increasing portion of their research and development budget on "defensive" research. That is, the heightened demands of the regulatory process for information forced them to devote increasingly large sums to determine the side effects or the efficacy of their existing products as well as their new ones.

One proper response to these assertions is the asset value of better information about chemical products. Research and development aimed at uncovering knowledge about products is equally as valuable as R and D directed toward totally new substances. As an example, consider the knowledge recently gained through controlled clinical trials of the efficacy and side effects of oral antidiabetic drugs [12], and of a series of drugs aimed at reducing the likelihood of second heart attacks among those who had already suffered one heart attack by reducing blood lipid levels [13]. The drugs in both of these cases were on the market and were a recognized part of the therapeutic armamentarium of medicine. They were established enough to be considered as treatments of choice. Conventional wisdom would have frowned upon anything that might have delayed their development and entrance into use because of the valuable properties they seemed to possess. However, it was only after an investment of scientific energies aimed at documenting their clinical effectiveness that it was discovered in each case they did not produce the expected outcome in patients. Further, they were found unexpectedly to be associated with complications and may in fact provoke some net harm. The point in this description is the value of the information—at least as valuable as the research aimed at the original therapeutic innovation.

One way of viewing the regulatory process is in terms of the capital asset value of its end product—permission to market. What the Food and Drug Administration offers industry is a certain value added to its products in the form of a certification of safety and efficacy. The permission to market or "enter into interstate commerce" a new drug or food additive is, in effect, a valuable capital asset to the company. This provokes anew the question of who should pay for new developments and for the certification process. From time to time, arguments arise in favor of public (government) expenditures for testing of drugs and other chemicals where it is in the interest of large numbers of the public to have the products and for which extensive, long-term testing will be required.[b]

---

[b] In fact, the federal government does engage in some efforts of this sort as in the case of anticancer chemotherapeutic agents or certain cardiovascular drugs. Most of these elaborate

Alternatives to Regulation

An alternative proposal might go in the opposite direction. It has been suggested that in the absence of an FDA, there would probably have been less public confidence in outcomes and decisions. Accordingly, there may be virtue in a manufacturer's contribution to the administrative costs of regulation through user charges. The government has a variable policy toward user charges. In the health-regulation field, however, it has only sought to recover costs in the cases of testing of antibiotics and insulin.[c]

In summary, regulatory decisions deserve to be well informed. Indeed, this is a message common to much of this work. It is emphasized again because decisions in the past have been made against a background of extraordinary uncertainty.

The case for concern for the influence of environmental agents is a compelling one. The case is that of the opportunity to prevent ill health and mortality through recognition and avoidance of harmful environmental exposure. Yet, in order to be able to take advantage of this preventive opportunity one must be armed with sufficient, specific information in order to make wise and judicious decisions—as through regulation. Otherwise, through ignorance, one runs the very real risk of seriously erring in either direction—of missed opportunities on the one hand or large but unproductive expenditures on the other.

Many citizens believe that regulation for health is done with more understanding and knowledge than, in fact, it is. We have no real idea at times whether an environmental standard or a restriction on the use of a product or a particular policy will produce more good than harm because, in fact, there is little to no knowledge of either benefit or harm. It is impossible at times to say whether the country is at peril because of the delay in availability of a new therapeutic drug since, in fact, its true utility or its true spectrum side effects remain occult. Research and development fundamentally produce information. Its value should not be discounted. Knowledge, too, has a capital asset value—fully commensurate with innovative physical materials.

How to Improve the Government Regulatory Process

One issue that remains speculative concerns the best use of government in achieving environmental betterment. From time to time it is suggested that, if it is a cleaner environment or improved health that is desired, there

clinical trials are sponsored and directed by NIH. However, there is not a clear or explicit policy for the government's role in this area.

[c] In fact, the subject of user charges for the Food and Drug Administration was considered very seriously in 1971 as a result of some prodding by the Office of Management and Budget [14].

are other forms of government intervention that would be more efficient than the avenue of regulation. For example, the capacity of technology is clearly a limiting feature in reducing air pollutants from power plants and other fixed or stationary sources. Direct federal investment to aid the development of stack-gas cleaning equipment has been discouraged by government policies that defer to the private sector if there is a prospect of profit. For similar reasons, direct federal investment in R&D programs aimed at alternatives to the conventional gasoline engine for automobiles has remained very modest. Yet, in both cases, many have admitted that the private efforts at R&D have been much less than scientific opportunity would dictate.

If the route of regulation is to remain as a major government instrument in behalf of health, one is justified in asking whether the regulatory process should be approximated to or isolated from the political mainstream. What is the best posture from the point of view of the public's interest? Should regulation be a reflection of the heterogenity of national points of view in order to mirror the "public interest" better? Alternatively, should regulation be isolated precisely in order to "protect" it from politics? Do the combined functions of protection and promotion in single government agencies inevitably lead to the subversion of the protection task and capture by the agency's promotion clientele?

The question seems never to have been really answered. However, if perception is as important as fact, then the separation of these two functions probably has virtue. However, the answer does not stop there. There are some unforeseen if perverse consequences—negative by-products—of separating promotion from protection in the doing of regulation. One consequence is capture of the "independent" regulatory agency by those intent upon regulating to the exclusion of all else. As examined above, the constituency that favors protection through regulation generally is not much interested in decent information for regulatory judgments. In fact, as some examples have shown, at times the pro-regulation constituency actively discourages the gathering of information and frowns on suitable analysis for decision making.

Regulatory decisions should be *balanced*. If the public interest is really to be served, balancing must be honestly done among all of the major considerations and interests that are in fact confronted in any decision [15]. This forceful admonition, of course, implies that in practice, regulatory decisions are not balanced. Unfortunately, all too often the implication has been borne out in reality. Regulatory decisions for health have tended to be narrow decisions. Such a narrowness is an inevitable consequence of isolation of the regulatory agency where its own political rewards accrue for defending an advocacy point of view and for espousing the constricted views of regulating sometimes at any cost. At times, of course, this narrowness is enforced or reinforced by a particular congressional mandate as in the case of the health-only considerations in the Clean Air Act.

The frustrations at times are extreme in other parts of the governmental machinery provoked by narrowness in regulatory decisions. In practice, the political machinery steps in forcibly in reaction to these frustrations—sometimes because of a true desire to sway a particular decision and at times to aggrandize the political fortunes of a single party. There are by now examples that illustrate both phenomena. Senator Muskie reclaimed some of the delegated authority from the executive branch agencies and took it as his own. In each instance, the chief administrator of the regulatory agency was stripped of some power when he was divested of discretion in decision making. The narrowness of those parts of the Clean Air Act in which health was the only factor allowed to be considered proved too constraining. The president and his staff simply lifted decisions out of EPA for broader review via the "Quality of Life Review Process." Eventually, other members of Congress replaced consideration of broader elements such as cost-benefit analysis by engaging the National Academy of Sciences to perform a broad study of the Clean Air Act. By arming EPA with the money for that review, the regulatory agency was inevitably forced into the position of client for its results.[d]

Finally, we find ourselves in the situation of seeking public accounting and accountability of environmental decisions yet desiring not to destroy the very strengths of the governmental process. Theodore Lowi has argued strenuously that the administrative process—beginning with the regulatory activities—has drained governmental authority and power through delegation of authorities. Government, in his view, is reduced to a mere party to or ratifier of political bargains struck among contending interest groups where this drainage of power has taken place. In brief, he deplores participatory democracy as antithetical to strong, authoritarian, "juridical democracy" [16].

Lowi's prescription is one in which the Congress retains rather than delegates authority. If it does delegate, Congress, he insists, much accompany the delegation with strict and strong guidance. "A law made at the center of government focuses politics there and reduces interests elsewhere" [16].

Clearly, Lowi is dismayed by the disorderliness of government, by the dilution of forthright ability to decide and to plan occasioned, as he sees it, by the pluralistic inputs to decisions. In the particular case of regulation for health, Lowi's thesis has validity. Typically, the initial decisions

---

[d] A similar set of frustrations led Representative Jamie Whitten to attempt to add $200,000 in additional appropriation to the FDA budget to study carcinogens and the Delaney clause described above.

made by chief administrators of regulatory agencies are rendered academic and are overtaken by repeated assaults and reversals through both the subsequent administrative and the judical processes [17]. Yet, the proper solution is not to refuse to delegate authority to administrative regulatory agencies. The problem in a sense is not that too much power has been delegated but, at times, too little power and support have been granted or authority has been given only hesitantly or on a shared basis.

Public accountability is exceedingly important. The process of providing for public accounting should be strengthened and made much richer. Most important, it should be moved earlier in the decision process. Rather than awaiting the subsequent appeals to agency decisions to open up the process and force it into the public view, the administrator's original decisions should be explored and explained broadly and fully as he first proposes and promulgates them. To do this, he will of necessity be forced to consider the broad ramification of his decision options. He will be forced to explain his methods and the details of his analysis. He would be forced, initially, to explain why he rejected certain avenues. He will be forced to deal honestly with the scientific interpretation of technical facts and to admit uncertainty. Finally, if he follows such a course, he will need support from time to time in choosing decisions that are unpopular in some quarters. He will benefit in terms of credibility from a group of recognized authorities to whom he can defer. The European experience and use of broadly constituted advisory groups may have some virtue for our own procedures.

Both Lowi and Louis Jaffe, whom he quotes, I believe, err in their contention that Congress should give stricter guidance and standards along with delegations of authority.

Much of what the [regulatory] agencies do is the expectable consequence of their broad and ill-defined regulatory power. The fault, if there be, is at least as much in their statutory scheme as in the administration [18].

In the case of the health-related regulatory functions, problems arise precisely because too much guidance has been given or because discretion has been replaced by strict mandate and rigidity incompatible with the science involved.

Finally, we come full circle to the narrowness question. Truly balanced decisions and broad considerations are incompatible with narrow constituencies. As Seidman has suggested, when constituencies are narrowly based, it is ". . . the independent agency or the bureau which is most likely to be seized upon as the vehicle for safeguarding those interests" [19]. This theme of the pernicious and destructive implications of narrow constituencies for regulation in behalf of health has been central to the entire discussion. Reamalgamation of promotion and protection in single agencies is not desirable. However, compensation for the resulting narrowness of independent regulatory agencies is essential.

References

1. Stigler, G.J., *Can Regulatory Agencies Protect the Consumer?* American Enterprise Institute, Washington, D.C., 1971.
2. Peltzman, S., The Benefits and Costs of New Drug Regulations, Paper prepared for a Conference on the Regulation of the Introduction of New Pharmaceuticals, Center for Policy Study, The University of Chicago, Chicago, Illinois, December 1972.
3. Weidenbaum, M.C., *Government-mandated Price Increases. A Neglected Aspect of Inflation*, American Enterprise Institute, Washington, D.C. 1975.
4. Olmstead vs. United States, 1928.
5. Djerassi, C., Prognosis for the Development of New Chemical Birth-Control Agents, *Science*, 166: 468-473, 1969.
6. Djerassi C., Birth Control After 1984, *Science*, 168: 941-945, 1970.
7. Jadlow, J.M., The Economic Effects of the 1962 Drug Amendments, Ph.D. Thesis, University of Virginia, Charlottesville, Virginia, 1970.
8. Schnee, J.E., Research and Technological Change in the Ethical Pharmaceutical Industry, Ph.D. Thesis, University of Pennsylvania, Philadelphia, Pennsylvania, 1972.
9. Bloom, B., and Ullyat, G.E., eds., American Chemical Society, *Drug Discovery—Science and Development in a Changing Society*, Advances in Chemistry Series #108 American Chemical Society, Washington, D.C., 1971.
10. National Agricultural Chemicals Association, Pesticide Industry Profile Study, Washington, D.C., May 1971.
11. McVicker, W., New Drug Development Study, Industry Information Unit, U.S. Food and Drug Administration, Washington, D.C., 1971.
12. Universities Group Diabetes Program, A Study of the Effects of Hypoglycemic Agents on Vascular Complications in Diabetes Patients with Adult-Onset Diabetes, II Mortality Results, *Diabetes* 19 (suppl. 2): 747-783, 1970.
13. The Coronary Drug Project Research Group, Clofibrate and Niacin in Coronary Heart Disease, *J. American Medical Association*, 231 (4): January 27, 1975.

14. U.S. Food and Drug Administration, Funding Alternatives for the FDA, Washington, D.C., July 1971.

15. *Chemicals and Health*, Report of the Panel on Chemicals and Health of the President's Science Advisory Committee, Science and Technology Policy Office, National Science Foundation, Washington, D.C., 1973.

16. Lowi, T.J., *The End of Liberalism*, W.H. Norton and Company, New York, 1969.

17. National Academy of Sciences, *Principles of Decision Making for Regulatory Channels in the Environment*, Washington, D.C., March 1975.

18. Jaffe, L., The Effective Limits of the Administrative Process: A Reevaluation, *Harvard Law Review*, May 1954.

19. Seidman, H., *Politics, Position, and Power: The Dynamics of Federal Organization,* New York, Oxford University Press, 1970.

Appendixes: Case Studies

Appendix A
Polychlorinated Biphenyls

Introduction: Nature of the Decision

The process of federal government deliberation and decision on poly-chlorinated biphenyls (PCBs) was relatively circumscribed and straight-forward. The government actually possessed little in the way of legal reg-ulatory authority. Hence, the "decisions" leaned heavily upon persua-sion and on pararegulatory moves. Nevertheless, the government's decisions in this case did lead to the intended and recommended actions (reduction and restriction in certain uses of PCBs) and a tightening of the procedures governing the manufacture, importation, and continued use of these chemicals.

Most important, perhaps, was the fact that the decisions and actions assumed by the government (and by parts of the private sector) were tak-en deliberately and on the basis of unusually good analysis and informa-tion. The PCB decisions, in brief, were unusually well informed decisions when compared to others of this type and the analyses used to arrive at the decisions were probably fuller and of a higher quality than is the case of most regulatory actions.

The several agencies of the federal government concerned with the PCB question contributed to the deliberations and to the analyses. At the same time, an outside group of scientific experts was engaged by the Of-fice of Science and Technology to consider PCBs from a broad perspec-tive as a case study of a hazardous substance existing in the environment in trace quantities. The government's major deliberative body for its deci-sions was an interagency PCB Task Force—run jointly by the Office of Science and Technology (OST) and the Council on Environmental Qual-ity (CEQ). The case study of the outside advisers to OST was timely and useful to the government's own analyses.

Background: Chronology

The term polychlorinated biphenyls refers to a family of chlorinated or-ganic compounds developed for commercial use in the late 1920s. Their usefulness was attributed especially to their high degree of physical and chemical stability—even at high temperatures—and because of some unusual electrical properties (high degree of dielectric capacity). (Interestingly it was this high thermal stability that made PCBs so useful technologically that also presented an environmental hazard). Hence, PCBs found particular utility as heat transfer fluids (because they did not break down or burn), hydraulic fluids, insulating materials in transformers and capacitors, and in a miscellaneous category of "plasticizer" uses (paints, plasticizers, carbon-less carbon paper).

There was only one manufacturer in the United States, the Monsanto Company, which produced the basic material for all of the users. Production roughly doubled between 1960 and 1970 and the United States production was estimated to be roughly one-half the total world production.

The demonstrated usefulness of PCBs, especially in its electrical applications and as heat transfer and hydraulic fluids, led parts of the industrial and commercial worlds to become dependent upon them and to design certain types of equipment to use PCBs specifically. This was particularly true for certain heat exchangers and for enclosed, power transformers.

Beginning particularly around 1966, public and professional anxieties began to be raised over possible environmental and health hazards associated with PCBs. These generally were of two sorts:

1. *The discovery of fat-soluble, organic compounds including chlorinated hydrocarbons and DDT in trace quantities in a widely distributed pattern in the environment—often distant from apparent sources.*

PCBs were among the materials found but were often confused in an analytic sense with other substances. PCBs were first distinguished from the "unknown interfering compounds" found in nature in 1966 by S. Jensen [1] and the next year by G. Widmark [2]. On the basis of this latter report, the Food and Drug Administration was moved to develop analytic methods to distinguish between PCBs and chlorinated organic pesticides encountered in monitoring for regulation.

In February 1969 Dr. Robert Risebrough gathered attention by warning, in an article in the *San Francisco Chronicle*, of dangers of PCBs in the eco-system. Over the next six to seven months, the FDA increased its surveillance of foodstuffs for evidence of PCB residues. Notable positive findings were in fish. Monitoring of foodstuffs, raw agricultural products, fish, and feeds for PCBs was augmented throughout 1970. PCBs were found in fish and marine animals in high concentrations close to plants that manufactured the chemical.

2. *Accidental spills or leakages of large quantities of polychlorinated biphenyls with consequent contamination of foodstuffs and animal feeds.*

In 1968 PCBs, used as a heat-exchange fluid in a pasteurizer, leaked into rice oil being manufactured for home cooking use in a plant in Japan. More than 1,000 persons were affected by the contaminated rice oil, many of whom exhibited persistent skin lesions as well as systemic disease (Yusho disease). In July 1971 leakage of heat exchange fluid caused contamination of pasteurized fish meal used as a feed ration for chickens and catfish.

In addition to these two major areas of concern, PCBs began to be reported with increasing frequency in poultry and eggs, and in packaging material for food.

PCBs appeared with increasing frequency in 1970 and 1971 in the professional scientific literature dealing with wildlife and the environment [3, 4]. In September 1970 the National Swedish Environment Protection Board held a conference on PCBs [5]. One of the sessions of this conference highlighted the "environmental problem." This conference, perhaps for the first time, brought together the extent of understanding of the manufacture, use, extent of environmental contamination, analytic methods, and biological effects for PCBs [5].

In August 1971 an Environmental Quality Workshop was convened in Durham, New Hampshire by the National Academy of Sciences to consider Marine Environmental Quality and Ocean Pollutants [6]. PCB contamination was highlighted.

In addition, provoked by both the accidental spills and by the widespread finding of trace quantities of PCBs in the environment, there emerged in the lay press a series of stories and articles dealing with PCB contamination. Most of them occurred in late 1971 and reflected especially the contamination of foodstuffs [7, 8, 9, 10, 11, 12, 13].

The FDA, aware that PCBs were to be found as a contaminant in the environment, and alert to the occasionally reported cases of accidental spillages, elected to engage in watchful surveillance of food. It did this in part in cooperation with the Department of Agriculture. As a result of the findings of PCBs specifically in fish and milk, the FDA established, between December 1969 and February 1970, "Action Levels" for PCBs in milk, poultry, and fish. Action levels are temporary thresholds for regulatory decision pending the establishment of a more permanent regulatory policy and procedure. In August 1970 the FDA established a similar action level for eggs. During 1970 and 1971 the FDA used these guideline values in various seizures of foods found contaminated with PCBs.

The number of reported contaminations of foods, recreational fish packaging materials, and animal feeds increased toward the latter half of 1971. Accompanying the announcements in the public press (and, undoubtedly reflective of them), there also occurred toward the end of 1971 a series of inquiries from congressmen and other elected officials over PCB contamination of food and the environment. On August 16, 1971 Senator McGovern addressed a letter to the commissioner of the FDA reflecting this concern. In September Governor Milliken of Michigan sent a telegram to Elliot Richardson, secretary of HEW, in which he announced a restriction of commercial salmon fishing because of the finding of PCBs in fish.

By August 1971 the FDA (and to some extent, USDA) found itself rapidly propelled into a position where it would be "required" by public pressure and advocacy to take a stronger and more forthright position against PCBs. The scientific issues were still not clear and there were glaring gaps in information. What really were the biological effects of the complex known as PCBs? How did the various PCBs vary in human toxicity and which members of the PCB family were found as contaminants? Was observed toxicity due to PCBs proper or to contaminants produced during their manufacture? How widespread was the contamination and how good was the monitoring system in picking up accidental spills? Furthermore, it was clear that the twin issues of widespread environmental contamination by trace quantities of PCBs and the selective, higher level contamination of foods and feed had to be joined at some point in government decision making.

On August 5, 1971 the FDA, on its own initiative, called a meeting of spokesmen from each of several government agencies and federal research laboratories to review the state of scientific understanding of PCBs. The text for the meeting was the reported series of accidental spills and leakages. [14]. Shortly following that meeting, the Department of Agriculture and the commissioner of the FDA asked the Office of the President's Science Adviser to provide assistance and act as a focus for the government's actions and decisions concerning PCBs. This request was made because: (1) the issue cut across several federal agencies and also involved outside scientists; (2) the issue was rapidly becoming uncomfortable for the FDA to handle alone; and (3) the Office of Science and Technology already had under way a scientific review of polychlorinated biphenyls and had quietly begun to gather information several months back.

In April 1970, spokesmen for the Monsanto Company agreed to meet with the staff of the President's Science Adviser in OST to discuss a number of issues concerning PCBs, including a series of animal toxicology studies which Monsanto had undertaken. During this meeting, Monsanto was asked for information concerning the amounts of PCB it manufactured and distributed. The company, being the sole producer in the United States, was reluctant to make public this information although reported that it might be able to provide the data on a confidential, nonpublic basis to the government.

In October 1970 a review was begun in the Office of Science and Technology of the general subject of hazardous substances existing in the environment in trace quantities. This review, known ultimately as the Panel on Hazardous Trace Substances, had as its major goal the identification of the needs for information by the government in making judgments about trace hazardous substances. The panel was composed principally of non-government experts in the fields of ecology, chemistry, biology, environmental and occupational medicine, and geology. Three case studies were begun from which it was hoped to draw generalizable experience. The particular subjects for the case studies were chosen because they were thought to be of importance, because regulatory or other governmental action had not yet been taken but could be expected at some time in the reasonably near future and because it was thought that there existed sufficient information from which to draw conclusions. The choices were cadmium, arsenic and PCBs. Thus, as the government began to develop its own position on PCBs in 1971, the OST-initiated study was already under way. What followed, in part, was for the government to borrow the experience developed by the OST panel and even for the two exercises to be joined to some extent. Notwithstanding, a separate and identifiable PCB report was published by the members of the Panel on Hazardous Trace Substances [15].

On September 1, 1971 the FDA held a meeting with USDA, EPA, the Council of Environmental Quality, and the Office of Science and Technology to explore options for further action concerning PCBs. The FDA and the USDA requested that the Office of Science and Technology take a lead role in handling this matter. OST acceded to this request and agreed to collaborate with the CEQ in this task. This became known as the Interdepartmental Task Force on PCBs. The task force was announced on September 5 in a joint FDA-USDA press conference [16].

On September 15, 1971 the OST Panel on Hazardous Trace Substances and the governmental task force met jointly with representatives of the Monsanto Company. The principal agenda item of this meeting was a request for information concerning the amounts of PCBs produced, patterns of distribution and usage, and estimates of losses into the environment [17]. Again, the manufacturer expressed its willingness to supply information of this sort to the government but with the understanding that these data would not be portrayed publicly except in their full and detailed fashion. In addition, the Monsanto Company expressed some concern over the seemingly disconnected character of the government's activities up to that time and the difficulties involved in findng responsible spokesmen for each of the agencies involved. Monsanto made a strong plea (in the form of a condition for their supplying information) that they be permitted to deal with a single spokesman for the government.

The Office of Science and Technology, on the advice of the counsellor to the president, did reach agreement with Monsanto on the terms of receiving the information [18]. These were shortly rendered moot by a request by the Environmental Defense Fund for the same information. This information ultimately served as important background for the government's decisions and was leaned on heavily by both the OST panel and the task force.

The OST panel combined the production figures and the data on distribution and use with knowledge of the physical properties of PCBs to develop a composite picture of the rates and routes of environmental transport and disposition. The data were reflected in a series of coefficients for a model of transport of PCBs. While this was necessarily a crude description, it served as a very useful instrument for placing PCBs in perspective. It replaced what otherwise would have been a totally qualitative—even intuitive exercise. It pointed up important gaps in knowledge. Finally, some verification was afforded by the results of physical measurement and monitoring. This attempt at environmental modelling was a major contribution by the panel to decision making.

The OST panel report was also appropriately critical in its review of biological effects and analytic methods for PCBs. It considered what was known of the mechanisms of observed biological effects, relationships between variations in chemical structure and biological activity, and it attempted to compare the effects of controlled laboratory experiments with observations made on animal populations in nature.

The Interdepartmental Task Force reflected much of this information in its report. It explored additional territory as well—reflective of the fact that it was a governmental report that focused on a number of specific, pragmatic, government or public problems. Thus, as well as serving as a review of the scientific aspects of PCBs, the task force explicitly reviewed a number of broad aspects of the PCB question. Most important, perhaps, was the exploration of the benefits or utility of PCBs and of the industrial and commercial dependencies built up over the years. This explicit review of benefits of PCBs, which is often not done for regulatory decisions, was of vital importance for decision making for PCBs. The National Bureau of Standards engaged in a review and analysis of the benefits and even the "essentiality" of each of the several uses of PCBs. In this, the NBS received advice from the National Industrial Pollution Control Council especially for electrical uses of PCBs. In each of the cases examined, the question of a possible and satisfactory replacement for PCBs was raised. This review became the basis for the ultimate decision to preserve electrical uses of PCBs (for which there were true dependencies and no satisfactory substitutes) and to restrict other uses [19].

The Government Task Force report included a systematic summary of monitoring experience for PCBs in food. It had been this matter of PCBs in food as much as any other which had raised PCBs to public notice. Hence, it was thought highly desirable to lay out systematically the apparent extent of food contamination and to consider what the patterns of contamination would suggest for public policy and government action.

The task force report explicitly reviewed all of the pertinent federal regulatory laws for their applicability to PCBs. This was, therefore, an exploration of the power of the government to control and limit the manufacture, distribution, use and disposal of PCBs. This review pointed out (which was already known) that existing regulatory authorities were capable of responding to specific incidents of contamination of foodstuffs once they were recognized. However, it acknowledged that the government's legal armamentarium was generally ". . . inadequate to prevent more PCBs from entering the environment" [19].

In addition to the above, the Interdepartmental Task Force review considered the chemical and physical properties of PCBs, the occurrence, transfer, and cycling of PCBs in the environment and the known biological effects—especially on man.

During the time the government review of PCBs was being pursued, the height of public concern over these chemicals continued to rise somewhat. For this reason, the commissioner of the FDA felt compelled to hold a press conference to "try to help establish a perspective on PCBs" roughly a month after the task force began its work [20]. This was an appropriately reasoned statement that attempted to allay fears and discourage demands for a sudden, outright ban on PCBs (even if the government had been capable of invoking one). The statement deferred to the ongoing process of review and deliberation as the basis for considered decision and action.

There was, finally, a third review of PCBs undertaken within the federal walls. One of the National Institutes of Health, the National Institute of Environmental Health Sciences, had sometime before elected to engage a series of "scientific" reviews of materials of impending regulatory concern and for which no systematic accounting of scientific information had been done. The philosophy in this case was to bring together in a conference spokesmen for the principal research projects—published or under way—in order to take the measure of the available scientific understanding. At the same time, members of the press—especially scientific writers—were invited to attend these sessions in order to enjoy the products of this review process. Thus, the aims were to educate both scientists and the public about the science and its interpretation.

In December 1971 the National Institute of Environmental Health Sciences held the first of this series of conferences in North Carolina—this one on PCBs [21].[a] Many of the same spokesmen who were engaged in the other reviews made presentations at the "open" conference. One of

[a] Since then, NIH has held similar reviews on lead, automotive emissions, and other substances of current public and governmental concern.

the major accomplishments of this meeting was to impart an understanding to the press and science writers as to what the character of the scientific evidence was and what was the scientists' own interpretation of experimental findings. The net (and immediate) effect of that exercise was to take the newsworthiness out of the PCB issue and to remove it from the category of the sensational. Very little was actually reported in the press of that meeting. More important, relatively little more was reported on PCBs in any form in the lay press.

The principal "control" actions for PCBs were the result of persuasion by the federal government rather than by direct regulatory exercise. The government possessed no real regulatory authority to control the manufacture, distribution, or use of PCBs. However, the persuasive influence of the several government inquiries—especially the PCB Interdepartmental Task Force—was undoubted. Thus, the major action was taken "voluntarily" by the Monsanto Company, the sole United States manufacturer.

Beginning in 1970, the Monsanto Company had begun to reduce the sales of PCBs—especially for nonelectrical uses. Domestic sales for PCBs for nonelectrical uses had risen from 12 thousand tons in 1968 to 16 thousand tons in 1970. By 1971 this figure was reduced to approximately 4 thousand tons [22]. In addition, the Monsanto Company quietly assumed for itself the role of distributor as well as manufacturer in order to exercise some control over end use of PCBs. In this way, the manufacturer was able to "discontinue sales of PCBs for use in paints, plasticizers, sealants, adhesives and other 'open-system' uses."

Thus, during 1971 and 1972 the Monsanto Company also restricted (or attempted to restrict) sales of PCBs to installations in which food or animal feed was processed.

The principal recommendation of the PCB Task Force was the discontinuance of all uses of PCBs except in electrical capacitors and transformers. These latter were judged to be both essential uses and represented "closed systems" [23]. To the extent that it could exercise this type of restriction of distribution, the Monsanto Company again undertook "voluntarily" to control end use through its control of manufacture and sale of PCBs.

Objectives

The Interdepartmental Task Force report on PCBs was issued publicly in May 1972 and was accompanied by a statement of governmental "thinking" and governmental "action." Perhaps the major conclusion reached in the report, which became an objective in government decisions, was that of *limited* restriction of PCBs. PCBs were seen as having certain essential uses in electrical transformers and capacitors and it was judged in the country's best interest not to be totally denied of PCBs. This was a direct reflection of the analysis performed by the National Bureau of Standards of the utility and essentiality of PCBs that pointed to the possibility of an increase in fires and explosions from encased or enclosed transformers if PCBs could no longer be used—representing the possibility of trading a hazard for another hazard. In addition, it derived from the attempts to map out the patterns of environmental dispersal of PCBs that had been lost from human use. Electrical applications were seen as "closed" applications and were not thought to be contributory to environmental distribution.

Other uses of PCBs were reviewed as either not essential, potentially or actually contributory to the environmental "load," or were found to have suitable substitutes. This, then, pointed to an elimination of essentially all other uses—heat exchange fluids, hydraulic fluids, and the miscellaneous category of "plasticizer" uses. This objective of limited restriction became the basis for governmental persuasion of the Monsanto Company to restrict its distribution and sales of PCBs—in fact, the principal governmental action.

Highlighting of the fact that true regulatory control by the government was limited became the text for a plea for passage of a then-pending bill in Congress to close this gap. A second objective, then, became the enactment of the Toxic Substances Control Act, which would permit the government to exercise useful control of industrial chemicals at their source.

The regulatory tools the government did possess in this case permitted enforcement action after PCBs were found in foods for human consumption and in animal feeds. Here, the FDA and the USDA restated their thresholds for action (which had been evolving over the previous four years) and announced the strengthening of their monitoring and analytic efforts. The other avenue of governmental control was that over industrial effluents and ambient water quality. Here, the Environmental Protection Agency stepped up its effort to assess the foreign chemical content of waters downstream from plants manufacturing PCBs and the Justice Department was close behind with enforcement teeth.

Information

The PCB "decisions" were perhaps among the best informed of governmental actions of this type in recent years. There was, it turned out, a certain body of scientific and technical knowledge about PCBs and a modest documentation of past experience. In addition, this information was better assembled and analyzed than was usually the case. Perhaps time was an important factor since time was permitted for deliberate and reasonably careful study and reflection before decisions were announced. Third, there was more opportunity for public airing and scientific interpretation before decision making than is usually the case. A Swedish scientific meeting on PCBs had been held in 1970 [5]. The Office of Science and Technology had begun its review and analysis of PCBs by December 1970 and the results of its analysis were made available as they emerged. The government's own scientists reviewed and interpreted the base of technical knowledge over roughly six months beginning in September 1971. In December 1971 a third forum of scientists were brought together by NIH to review much of the same material. Thus, this process of interpretation and maturation of data by scientific peers—while characteristic of the traditional scientific process but unusual in regulatory decision making—was played out in this case.

The processes of review in this case explicitly sought information for a broadly based decision. Thus, there was a dedicated attempt, for example, to determine the benefits or utility of PCBs and of the costs that could be expected if their uses were restricted or denied. This information was later found to have been highly influential and important in formulating the government's position.

One other element of information that proved to be important was the analysis of environmental distribution and dispersal. This analysis, itself, was something of an experiment. It was reasoned early on by the participants in the OST review that it should be possible, starting with some elementary information on total amounts of PCBs produced and patterns of distribution in commerce and disposal, and armed with certain elementary understanding of physical and chemical properties, to build a model predictive of PCB distribution in the environment. This, in fact, was done and the coefficients used in the model were partially tested or "validated" against the physical measurements of PCBs in the environment that had been reported in the literature. This exercise and the information from it became the basis, for example, of the judgment that PCBs used in electrical capacitors disposed of in the earth by burying in landfills would not be expected to migrate very far through the soil and would not represent a significant source of environmental pollution.

Implementation

The principal "decisions" deriving from this exercise were to restrict PCBs to "closed-system" electrical uses. There soon emerged a few additional issues that reflected either loose ends or areas that deserve some additional study.

The principal reason for denying the use of PCBs as heat-exchange fluids was to avoid accidental spills and leakages of PCBs into foodstuffs (where heat was used to "pasteurize" the food material). However, there were often PCB heat exchanger applications. One of these, for example, involved the use of heat on off-shore oil rigs to maintain a low viscosity of the oil. PCBs had been chosen here because of the characteristics of high thermal stability and low probability of fire and explosion and many of the heat exchange devices had been designed specifically around the use of PCBs. Denial of the use of PCBs in this case raised the spectre of an increase in the number of fires in off-shore oil rigs or the continued use of PCBs from imported sources.

This general question of worldwide (as opposed to United States) production and use of PCBs became a matter of immediate concern. There was an early visit of a spokesman from the Swedish government to the Office of Science and Technology. The Tariff Commission and the Customs Bureau were pressed to search for signs of imported PCBs [24]. Perhaps, most useful was the fact that the Organization for Economic Co-operation and Development (OECD) was persuaded to take up the question of industrial production and commercial use of PCBs in the industrialized parts of the world. PCBs, in fact, became the major example for intergovernmental "consultation" in a mechanism the OECD had established for this purpose. The United States position and the information behind it became major elements in the OECD position paper [25] and in the deliberations at the OECD in November 1972.

Trace amounts of PCBs in packaging materials became a matter of particular concern. In part, this was due to uncertainty over their origin. There was some evidence that trace quantities of PCBs were magnified in the process of recycling of paper. To the extent that this was true, the government and national policies aimed at recycling were seen to be in possible jeopardy. One of the principal motives for exploring this particular issue, apart from the economics of paper and cardboard production, was the contamination of food wrapped with PCB-containing paper. There followed, therefore, a series of investigations by the Food and Drug Administration into the process and rate of migration of PCBs from packaging materials into foodstuffs the packages contained. In December 1972 the FDA provided in the form of an Environmental Import Statement (perhaps the only one of its kind from that agency) on its proposed rule making for PCBs [26]. Among other things, this document summarized the FDA investigations and positions regarding PCBs and packaging.

Conclusions, Observations, and Recommendations

The government "decisions" on PCBs constituted an unusual regulatory exercise compared to much of the experience of the past few years. In the first place, the government's position was generally well prepared. Related to that was the fact that time was taken for deliberate study and deliberate action, even in the face of public outcries for immediate action. Third, the "decisions" were taken without much tangible legal authority for governmental control. They represented rather persuasion and voluntary action. It is worthwhile, perhaps, to examine some of the factors that contributed to any successes that can be claimed.

1. The PCB decisions represented, perhaps, a somewhat more manageable challenge than many. Only a single United States manufacturer was involved. Further, the majority of commercial and industrial uses and the major users were known.

2. There was some information that proved useful in decision making. Quantitative figures showing production were provided—albeit only after a delay—that were essential in determining the scale of the problem and its change with time. Similarly, the corresponding figures for commercial distribution were essential in ascertaining the patterns of human use and dispersion. To complement these data, there were at least some results of physical measurement and monitoring of PCBs in the environment or indexes of dispersal.

In terms of hazards, there was a legacy of at least some documentation of previous human exposure and some laboratory data. However, many questions remained. Perhaps, most important, was the luxury of critical review (in fact, several critical reviews) of this information. Further, these reviews engaged some very good scientific talent—both inside and outside the government and in a way that permitted the decision makers to be very well informed of their advice.

In terms of benefits, a specific analysis was commissioned of the utility and essentiality of PCBs. (It is interesting to note that while this was done well, the National Bureau of Standards entered into this exercise very reluctantly—seeing in it the perils of the battery additive episode of some years before).

Finally, there was performed the unusual but highly useful attempt at modeling the patterns of rates and routes of distribution of PCBs in the environment. This was done for the most part as an experiment—to determine whether such an exercise could be performed. It did, in fact, provide some useful and immediate insight.

3. There was a single spokesman for the government. The agencies involved early determined that the PCB question cut across several departments. This, by itself, was probably not persuasive and the joint request from FDA and the USDA to OST to "take on" the PCB question arose also from a desire on their part to push on to someone else a tough or "hot" decision. It should be noted, too, the OST had already begun a review of PCBs.

The fact that there was a single spokesman proved important in arriving at an orderly decision. The Monsanto Company insisted on dealing only with a single spokesman after months of unconnected and frustrating interchanges with a variety of government agents. The fact that there was a single spokesman also undoubtedly made it easier to amass and analyze in an orderly fashion the variety of information from several sources. The fact that it was an executive office spokesman was probably important in soliciting certain other studies in parallel (such as the National Bureau of Standards' study of benefits) and the review of the government-wide legal option for regulatory action.

4. Although already mentioned, the scientific information (especially that related to biological effects) underwent the benefit of several reviews. This had two salutary effects. It did insure scientific interpretation by peers and it developed a constituency among scientists for the decisions ultimately taken.

5. The decisions were deliberately broadly based. While this may appear elementary, this facet is generally not characteristic of regulatory decisions concerned with human health. Both benefits and hazards were explicitly explored. Economic consequences were considered. Each of several avenues of possible action was examined in turn. Again, a single spokesman for the government and one placed above the operating agencies was probably a necessary feature in this broad examination.

6. The decision process was a relatively open one. The fact that there was an Interdepartmental Task Force was public knowledge from the outset. The Task Force published its full report. Similarly, the reports of the OST Panel on Hazardous Trace Substances and the report of the NIH meetings on PCBs were published. Further, science writers and other members of the press were specifically invited to participate in the NIH meeting.[b]

7. Time was permitted for deliberate decision making. At one point, in fact, the commissioner of the Food and Drug Administration held a press conference in which he specifically announced that he would not proceed with an outright ban on PCBs and deferred to the study process that was then underway [23]. This, of course, contradicts the classical argument that insists governments *must* make regulatory decisions immediately without the luxury of time for good decisions.

References

1. Jensen, S., A New Chemical Hazard, *New Scientist*, 32: 612, 1966.

[b] Note that the question of freedom of information was a matter of some concern during the deliberations of the Interagency Task Force in the Office of Science and Technology [18].

2. Widmark, G., Possible Interference by Chlorinated Biphenyls, *J. Assoc. Offic. Anal. Chem.*, 50: 1069, 1967.

3. Peakall, D.B., and Lincer, J.C., Polychlorinated Biphenyls. Another Long-life Widespread Chemical in the Environment, *Bioscience*, 20: 958-964, 1970.

4. Pichirallo, J., PCB's: Leaks of Toxic Substance Raises Issues of Effects, Regulation, *Science*, 173: 899-902, 1971.

5. PCB Conference, National Swedish Environment Protection Board, Research Secretariat, Wenner-Gren Center, Stockholm, Sweden, September 29, 1970.

6. Marine Environmental Quality, A Special Study held under the auspices of the National Scientific Committee on Oceanography of the National Academy of Sciences Ocean Affairs Board, Durham, New Hampshire, August 9-13, 1971.

7. Monsanto Limits Food Plants' Use of Chemical PCB, *The Washington Post*, September 30, 1971.

8. Some Dried Foods Found Tainted by Perilous Chemical, *The Washington Post*, September 28, 1971.

9. Tainted Turkeys, *The Washington Post*, September 24, 1971.

10. Turkeys, Salmon Tainted by PCB's, *The Evening Star,* September 23, 1971.

11. A Contaminant Is Found in Cardboard, *The New York Times*, September 28, 1971.

12. If You Think DDT's a Problem Meet PCB, *The New York Times,* September 30, 1971.

13. FDA Studying Chance of Contamination in Containers for Food, *The Wall Street Journal*, September 28, 1971.

14. Transcript of Proceedings of the Interagency Meeting on Polychlorinated Biphenyls (PCB's), Food and Drug Administration, Department of Health, Education, and Welfare, Washington, D.C., August 5, 1971.

15. Polychlorinated Biphenyls—Environmental Impact, A Review by the Panel on Hazardous Trace Substances, March 1972, *Environmental Research*, 5: 249-362, 1972.

16. Press release on Interdepartmental PCB Task Force, Food and Drug Administration, Department of Health, Education, & Welfare, September 5, 1971.

17. Letter from Edward J. Burger, Jr., M.D. of OST to Mr. John Mason, The Monsanto Company, October 15, 1971.

18. Memorandum from John Dean, counsellor to the president, to Ed-

ward J. Burger, Office of Science and Technology, concerning the Freedom of Information Act, October 4, 1971.

19. Polychlorinated Biphenyls and the Environment, Interdepartmental Task Force on PCB's, Washington, D.C., May 1972, National Technical Information Service, U.S. Department of Commerce, Springfield, Virginia, No. COM-72-10419.

20. Statement by Charles C. Edwards, M.D., PCB Press Briefing, Food and Drug Administration, September 29, 1971.

21. National Institute of Environmental Health Sciences Meeting on Polychlorinated Biphenyls (PCB's), Rougemount, North Carolina, December 20-21, 1971, Proceedings published in *Environmental Health Perspectives*, Experimental Issue No. 1, April 1972, National Institute of Environmental Health Sciences, Research Triangle Park, North Carolina.

22. Monsanto Industrial Chemicals Company, Press Release, Monsanto Releases PCB Production Figures to Department of Commerce, St. Louis, Missouri, November 30, 1971.

23. Press Release accompanying the release of the PCB Interdepartmental Task Force Report on PCB's, Washington, D.C., May 12 1972.

24. Letter from Alvin Alm, Council on Environmental Quality, to Mr. Vernon Acree, commissioner, Bureau of Customs, June 22, 1972.

25. Organization for Economic Cooperation and Development, Environmental Directorate, Sector Group on Unintended Occurrence of Chemicals in the Environment, Polychlorinated Biphenyls—Proposals for Concerted Action, October 13, 1972.

26. Food and Drug Administration, Final Environmental Impact Statement, Rule Making on Polychlorinated Biphenyls, Department of Health, Education, and Welfare, December 18, 1972.

Appendix B
DDT

In April 1969 the Food and Drug Administration took steps to seize 25,000 pounds of coho salmon from Lake Michigan, which had been found to contain excess residues of DDT. This discovery of these levels of DDT was set against a background of publication seven years earlier of Rachel Carson's book *Silent Spring*, and a growing awareness and public concern for the integrity of the physical environment. The FDA's announcement was followed in close succession by the establishment by Robert Finch, secretary of health, education and welfare, of a Commission on Pesticides and their Relationship to Environmental Health. The report of this commission, which was chaired by Dr. Emil Mrak, was issued in December 1969 [1]. The commission devoted much of its attention to DDT in particular and included an extensive, critical review of what was known about biological effects on human and nonhuman species, economics of usage, benefits, and contamination.

DDT had been introduced into use in the mid-1940s. It found substantial and well-recognized use during World War II as a valuable instrument to control malaria and other insect vector-borne diseases. It eventually became credited with the saving of millions of lives. During the 1950s, a number of domestic programs of control and "eradication" of various insects were begun. Applications of various insecticidal chemicals were employed including those of DDT. There were raised from time to time warnings from environmentally concerned persons who feared negative by-products of widespread dispersion of chemical substances.

One year after the publication of *Silent Spring*, a report of the President's Science Advisory Committee on Pesticides recommended that ". . . accretion of residues in the environment be controlled by orderly reduction in the use of persistent pesticides. . . . Elimination of the use of persistent toxic pesticides should be the goal" [2].

In 1965 another panel of the President's Science Advisory Committee on Environmental Pollution pointed to the rapid growth in the manufacture and use of organic chemical pesticides since World War II such as chlorinated hydrocarbons and phosphate esters. The panel also noted the accumulation of residues of pesticides such as DDT in both the physical environment and in human tissues found at autopsy. The aggregate accumulation was large (20 tons of DDT estimated to have been resident in bodies of people). However, on the average, the individual accumulation was small and no adverse health effects associated with these accumulations had been recognized [3]. The figures indicating United States manufacture and domestic usage of DDT did show a rapid rise from 1944 onward until the early 1960s. Much of the material manufactured in the United States was eventually sent abroad, however.

In 1966 a lawyer and a small group of scientists entered into litigation in an effort to stop the use of DDT by a local mosquito control commission in Long Island. Although the case was dismissed by the court, the action was successful in blocking the use of DDT by the commission. In October of the following year, the Environmental Defense Fund was incorporated with the objective of applying legal action to aid the protection of the environment. Material elimination of DDT was chosen as a prime objective. DDT was the most widely used pesticide. There was thought to be more information about DDT than there was for other pesticides. (The Mrak Commission in its review discovered that useful and valid scientific and economic information were exceedingly scarce for eventually all pesticides.) The potential leverage of action against DDT for other pesticides seemed sizeable.

Accordingly, within a week of incorporation, the Environmental Defense Fund took legal action against DDT and Dieldrin in Michigan. This action was to become important in making Michigan the first state to ban DDT. In late 1968 the EDF brought litigation against DDT in Wisconsin. After an exhaustive review and inquiry, DDT was outlawed in that state. Hence, with a legacy of success in three localities, the EDF joined with the National Audobon Society, the Sierra Club, and the West Michigan Environmental Action Council to file a legal petition with the secretary of agriculture of the U.S. Department of Agriculture in October 1969. The petition requested that the secretary issue notices of cancellation for all pesticide products containing DDT and that he suspend the registrations during the course of the cancellation proceedings. (Suspension was the more definitive of the two alternative actions and would have amounted to an immediate cessation. Cancellation is delayed in its effect until all deliberations and appeals are completed.) In addition, the EDF, in another petition requested that the Department of Health, Education and Welfare repeal tolerances of DDT in foods.

The Department of Agriculture, within a month of the petition, issued notices of cancellation for four uses of DDT:

1. On shade trees

2. On tobacco

3. In and around the house except for public health purposes

4. In aquatic environments, marshes, wetlands, and adjacent areas [4].

Six registrants requested "administrative" review of this decision but their requests were eventually withdrawn.

In addition, the secretary of agriculture announced that he was considering the cancellation of other uses of DDT unless it could be shown that ". . . certain uses are essential in the protection of human health and welfare and only those uses for which there are no effective and safe substitutes for the intended use will be continued." The USDA made no mention of the request for suspension of the registrations.

In December 1969 the EDF petitioned the District Circuit Court of Appeals to review the failure of the USDA to fully comply with the previous requests. The court replied in May of the next year that, indeed, the EDF did have standing and could therefore, challenge the secretary of agriculture. Further, the issue of suspension was considered reviewable and the court remanded the issue to the secretary of agriculture. Similarly, the petition to the secretary of HEW, which had been denied by the secretary, was similarly remanded to that agency.

The USDA denied the petition for suspension without giving reasons. The EDF again took the issue to the appellate court. For the second time the court remanded the case to the agency and ordered reconsideration without reasons. The USDA again denied the petition but included a "statement of reasons" as well as some additional cancellations. These cancellation notices covered registrations for use on a number of vegetable, fruit, and grain crops, for certain areas in forestry and livestock and for nursery and lawn uses. Although a number of registrants filed objections, all withdrew except for the Crop King Company of Yakima, Washington, which requested an advisory committee review.

In considering the suspension issue, the secretary of agriculture spoke of certain benefits of DDT. He asserted that the reduction in use of DDT should occur in an orderly fashion so as not to ". . . depirve mankind of uses which are essential to the public health and welfare." He urged continued study.

EDF accordingly for the third time, petitioned for review through the Court of Appeals. The court, on January 7, 1971, remanded the case again to the government—this time to the newly formed Environmental Protection Agency.

There were several important implications of this brief history and of the judgments of the Appellate Court. One was the matter of "standing" or recognized ability of petitioning groups of interested citizens to question administrative decisions and to provoke reviews of administration actions. In Judge Bazelon's opinion in January 1971, he was explicit about this matter of standing:

Not only the legislative history but also the statutory scheme itself points to the conclusion that the FIFRA [Federal Insecticide, Fungicide, and Rodenticide Act] requires the Secretary to issue notices and thereby initiate the administrative process whenever there is a substantial question about the safety of a registered pesticide. For when Congress creates a procedure that gives the public a role in deciding important questions of public policy, that procedure may not lightly be side-stepped by administrators [5].

At least as important was the principle of balancing. Judge Bazelon, in this instance, referred strongly to the necessity to consider a broad set of issues in deciding whether or not to cancel a pesticide registration. He insisted that issues such as these did not turn on scientific assessment of hazard alone but rather on a ". . . balance of the benefits of a pesticide against its uses" [5].

Third, Judge Bazelon in his opinion spoke forcibly of the necessity that the several important issues in the balancing process be explored in the ". . . full light of a public hearing and not resolved behind the closed doors of the Secretary" [5].

Finally, he referred to the increasing role of the courts as instruments of protection of citizens who sought relief from unexplained and arbitrary actions. Yet, he offered a special plea for stronger, more fully developed, and more forthrightly explained administrative decisions in order to "diminish the importance of judicial review" [5].

Eight days later on January 15, 1971, the administration of EPA issued notices of cancellation for all remaining registered uses of DDT. More than 50 registrants appealed by filing objections and by requesting a public hearing. Two registrants requested a review via a specially appointed advisory committee. In March Administrator Ruckelshaus responded to the court's order that he reconsider the petition to suspend the DDT registrations. He argued that suspension was unnecessary since cancellation proceedings were under way. He also provided a background paper containing some general principles relating to cancellation and suspension. This, in turn, led the Environmental Defense Fund to return to the D.C. Court of Appeals for a further time to argue in behalf of suspension. The court remanded the case again to EPA and set a target date of November 1, 1971, for EPA's reply on the suspension issue. (It was assumed that the advisory committee findings would be reflected in this reply.)

The DDT Advisory Committee was appointed on April 30, 1971, from a list of names provided by the National Academy of Sciences. The charge to this committee was to ". . . consider all relevant scientific evidence concerning DDT, and to prepare a report on recommendations as to the scientific issues raised by the use of DDT." The committee offered its report on September 9 of that year. In essence, it concluded that the worldwide environmental pool of DDT was significant, was widely distributed, and had not markedly decreased in spite of a declining usage. The committee acknowledged associations between DDT residues and effects on wildlife. Its principal recommendation was to ". . . reduce the use of DDT in the U.S. at an accelerated rate of the past few years with the goal of virtual elimination of any significant addition to the environment'' [6].

On November 1, 1971 the administrator issued a statement in which he stated his determination not to suspend DDT products. He considered the various hazards of DDT. However, he concluded, as had the advisory committee, that there was ''. . . no appreciable difference in hazard to the public whether the registration of DDT is immediately suspended or whether it is cancelled in the near future, if warranted, because of the existing burden of DDT already in the environment.''

The EDF once again sought to petition the Environmental Protection Agency on the suspension issue. The court denied this petition. By this time the public hearing process was under way and the court deferred to that review for its judgment.

The public hearing on DDT began on August 17, 1971. The hearing continued over a period of exactly six months and produced a transcript of 9,000 pages of testimony. The hearing examiner, Edmund M. Sweeny, was a coal mine accident investigator on loan from the Department of the Interior.

There were 123 witnesses who testified. These were divided roughly into four major groups:

1. Twenty-nine ''group petitioners'' (manufacturers appealing the decision)
2. The Plant Protection Division of the Department of Agriculture, which appealed as a petitioner
3. Secretary Hardin who intervened on the part of the farm community
4. Environmental Protection Agency, which acted both as an adjudicator (judicial officer) and as a prosecutor (administrator of EPA and the General Counsel)

The public hearing in this case was notable in many respects:

1. The provision and discussion of information (including scientific information) was done only with difficulty in this forum. The results of the DDT Scientific Advisory Committee review became available near the beginning of the public hearing process. However, the hearing examiner declined to permit these results to be inserted in any way into the hearing record.

2. There emerged a picture of great scientific uncertainty or lack of information on many fronts. The human body burden of DDT residues was repeatedly acknowledged. However, the interpretation of these findings was by no means clear. Similarly, the reports of tumors in experimental animals exposed to DDT were clearly difficult to interpret for human experience. There was evidence of increasing resistance among

target species to DDT. There was evidence of unexpected and undesirable impacts on nontarget species (such as eggshell thinning).

3. There was a surprising lack of data to document or determine benefits of DDT use, although there was a great deal of advocacy and assumption in this regard. As one observer of the hearing process noted:

Information gaps as to the benefits of DDT use are historic in origin. Prior to 1971 the USDA administered FIFRA, with a somewhat promotional air. At that time the burden of proving the efficacy of a pesticide was either very lightly assumed by the prospective registrant or it was assumed by the USDA itself. Thus, very little scientific research was done to quantify the benefits of a particular pesticide use [7].

4. The adversary or adjudicatory process of the public hearing included some peculiar relationships—some of which probably tended to inhibit rather than foster better understanding and analysis of the issues. The Environmental Protection Agency as an institution was divided between those whose job it was to provide staff support to the hearing examiner, those whose job it was to argue the pro-environmentalist position, and those who were responsible for aiding the administrator in reaching a judgment when the hearing was completed. Thus, for example, the deputy assistant administrator for pesticide programs (Dr. William Upholt) was a party to the agency's case in favor of cancellations. His immediate supervisor, the assistant administrator for categorical programs (David Dominick), was not. Dominick aided the administrator in his adjudication of the case.

5. The hearing examiner was often seen in the role of lecturing to those present and, therefore, of imposing his own views on the hearing process.

In April 1972 the hearing examiner issued his "decisions and recommendations." He proposed that all cancellation matters be withdrawn and that, with a very few exceptions, the registrations in question remain in force. He contended that the case had not been sufficiently established that prevailing uses of DDT cause an "unreasonable adverse effect" on man or the environment. Further, he ruled as a conclusion of law that DDT was not a carcinogen nor a mutagen for man. He acknowledged the essentiality of DDT in all of the uses upheld by the USDA and concluded they did not constitute a hazard to "fresh water fish, estuarine organisms, wild birds, or other wildlife." There were 27 findings of fact and 19 conclusions of law.

Industry (the "group petitioners") filed a brief in support of the recommended decision. The respondents (EPA and EDF) filed objections:

1. The Examiner's decision contains such serious errors of law, fact and methodology that, except in very limited respects, it is valueless as an aid to the Administrator;

2. The Examiner's rulings, concerning the admissibility of evidence at the hearing were, in a number of particulars, erroneous and highly prejudicial to the proponents of cancellation. Moreover, his conduct of the hearing generally reflected an irrational attitude which necessarily detracts from the value of his decision.

The administrator of EPA heard several hours of oral argument. His final step was to make his own "finding of fact" and to offer his conclusions and decisions on the basis of the public hearing. He did this on June 16, 1972. In this announcement he ordered the cancellation of essentially all domestic uses of DDT as of December 21, 1972. This action was taken on the basis of his interpretation of the evidence presented in the public hearing including the following principal points:

1. DDT is widespread in distribution in the environment, is persistent, and can be transported through the environment—all of which constitute a risk to the environment.
2. DDT accumulates and is concentrated in various biological organisms in the environment.
3. There is a causal relationship between DDT residues in tissues and toxic effects in some forms of wildlife.
4. DDT is found in the tissues of members of the general population. While the acute human toxicity of DDT is low, there is presumptive evidence of association between DDT exposure and cancer in man.
5. For the major uses of DDT in the United States (especially for cotton), correspondingly inexpensive substitutes are available. In some instances these are already in use and may prove more economical. DDT is not necessary for the production or processing of crops with three minor exceptions where registered uses would be retained.

There followed a judicial appeal of this decision in which the decision was allowed to stand.

Conclusions

1. The DDT issue was largely "driven" by the courts. The moves made by the executive branch were responsive to proddings brought by way of the courts.
2. The process was exceedingly lengthy and, at times, convoluted. There were no crisp, definable decision points until the very end. Every "decision" was subject and subjected to further review and objection.
3. The process, which began in a traditionally "closed" pattern, became increasingly open both for public viewing and public participation. This was a very cumbersome, lengthy, and expensive process. It may

not even have insured the scientific "correctness" of the decision. However, it did go far toward insuring public appreciation of the details of the decision.

4. During the process, especially with the aid of the courts, the pattern and proper breadth of EPA's decision process for pesticides were defined. To a large extend, during this time, the courts took to themselves some of the administrator's discretion in decision making. However, they admonished him to strengthen the administrative process in order to reduce the need for later judicial appeal.

5. There was a great deal of advocacy shown by all parties to the decision—including a number of the "independent" scientists.

References

1. U.S. Department of Health, Education and Welfare, Report of the Secretary's Commission on Pesticides and their Relationship to Environmental Health, Washington, D.C., December 1969.

2. *Use of Pesticides*, A Report of the President's Science Advisory Committee, The White House, Washington, D.C., May 15, 1963.

3. *Restoring the Quality of Our Environment*, Report of the Environmental Pollution Panel of the President's Science Advisory Committee. The White House, Washington, D.C., November 1965.

4. 34 *Federal Register*, 15627.

5. Environmental Defense Fund v. Ruckelshaus, U.S. Court of Appeals, District of Columbia Circuit, January 7, 1971, 439F. 2d 584.

6. Report of the DDT Advisory Committee to William D. Ruckelshaus, administrator, Environmental Protection Agency, September 9, 1971.

7. MacIntyre, A.A., A Case Study. An Outsider's View of the DDT Decision, Paper prepared for the Environmental Studies Board, Commission on Material Resources, National Academy of Sciences, Washington, D.C., 1975.

Appendix C
Tetraethyl Lead

The biological effects of lead probably have been as much studied and are better understood than most other environmental pollutants. Yet, the decisions to regulate tetraethyl lead as a fuel additive were (and still are) subjected to an extraordinary amount of debate and caused an extreme degree of controversy. As someone observed during the course of the debates over lead as an additive to gasoline, "lead poisoning is an age-old problem with new dimensions."

Lead is a normal constituent in the earth's crust and is widely distributed. It is a factor in man's immediate environment to a small but consistent extent in the food he eats and in the water he drinks. Cigarette smokers experience a bit more of it. Human activities that use lead, however, accomplish certain concentrations or redistributions of lead. The largest industrial consumer of lead is the storage battery industry. The second largest is the petroleum industry. The total industrial use of lead, 1.3 million tons in 1972, doubled over 30 years.

Man has been using lead for 6,000 years. Hippocrates (370 B.C.) described symptoms probably representing those of lead poisoning among persons working with lead. Lead poisoning as an industrial hazard has been recognized and studied for at least the past 180 years.

A vexing, well-established, and essentially preventable lead poisoning problem is that coming from lead-containing paint. Lead-based paints have been extensively used in the past and remain as the interior covering in very large numbers of older dwelling units—especially in cities. The population at risk is essentially composed of infants and small children who tend to ingest paint chips. It is estimated that as many as 225,000 children in the United States may have absorbed excessive amounts of lead and have elevated blood lead levels [1]. In 1969 in New York City alone, 4,500 children were believed to have unsuspected, serious lead poisoning [2]. The problem is frustrating especially since, while its solution is technically straightforward, the monetary cost of its accomplishment has always been too high to accommodate.

Finally, it is important to note that, in biological terms, lead is a cumulative poison. Lead is stored in the body (especially in bone) and is excreted only very slowly. Thus, persons exposed chronically to lead can build up body burdens—accumulations of lead—that, if sufficiently elevated, can lead to true lead poisoning with symptoms and impairment.

In particular, urban-dwelling infants and children who already may have a measurable body burden of lead from other sources are the population subject to particular risk to lead from automotive fuels. Tetraethyl

211

lead was first introduced in 1922 as an addition to gasoline to reduce the knock or "ping" in gasoline engines. The discovery that tetraethyl lead was effective in improving the efficiency of the burning in engine cylinders was more or less accidental and was based, at the time, on the improper theory that a dark-colored dye would absorb heat in the engine. The mechanism of antiknock characteristics of tetraethyl lead still remain elusive. However, tetraethyl lead (or tetramethyl lead) in combination with other chemical additives improves the efficiency of gasoline and effectively adds to its octane a number of the petroleum-derived materials used in gasoline. Through the years, both the design of gasoline engines and the composition of gasolines changed. These changes were essentially aimed at greater efficiency and increased power. Fuels of premium quality are now obtained from lower quality hydrocarbons by adding tetraethyl lead or by blending higher quality hydrocarbons without the use of lead. Although most improvements in the quality of fuels came from a combination of refining and blending processes, tetraethyl lead remained a useful constituent of gasoline. The amount of leaded fluid used in automotive gasolines has ranged from 0.75 to 3 ml per gallon. The legal maximum was raised with the concurrence of the U.S. Public Health Service in 1959 to 4 ml per gallon [3].

The significance to human health of the lead emissions from gasoline engines has been a matter of some scientific and public discussion for several years. In 1960, in his Harben Lectures, Dr. Robert A. Kehoe reviewed what was known of the metabolism of lead and of the significance of population exposure to low-level lead-containing emissions [4]. His observations and conclusions (which exonerated tetraethyl lead as a community hazard) were technically sound. Yet, they were contentious in some quarters since Dr. Kehoe's laboratory was funded by the very fortune that had derived from developments of the gasoline engine. In 1965 a geochemist, Dr. Clair C. Patterson, published an article strongly contesting the then-prevalent view that tetraethyl lead in gasoline did not represent a community health hazard [5].

In 1965 [6] the U.S. Public Health Service held a symposium on the health hazards of environmental lead. In 1967 an advisory panel to the Department of Commerce urged that there be no further increases in the quantity of lead emitted to the atmosphere and that ". . . steps should be taken to reduce current levels" [7]. In furtherance of that goal, the advisory panel recommended that the federal government establish standards for the lead content in gasoline. Lead from automobile exhaust emissions was recognized overwhelmingly as the major contributor to atmospheric lead levels [8]. However, the implications for human health of the emission of lead from gasoline engine exhaust were by no means clear and remained hotly contested.

In the late 1960s, a second issue arose that was eventually to be joined to the concern for human health in the governmental actions toward tetra-ethyl lead. The automobile was recognized as a major contributor of certain other airborne pollutants—especially to urban atmospheres. In the case of some cities (such as Los Angeles), the automobile was the preeminent pollutor. It was recognized that abatement of this pollution (other than through a restriction in driving habits or numbers of automobiles or through drastic changes in automotive power sources) would have to rely on the use of certain technological developments. Among these, the catalytic exhaust converter appeared most promising, if not essential [9]. It was early apparent that because lead was a poison to most of the potential catalysts, the presence of lead in gasoline was essentially incompatible next to the reliable functioning of an exhaust catalytic converter.

The basis for federal action with regard to lead in gasoline was strengthened by two related events. One was the enactment of the amendments to the Clean Air Act in 1970 [10] and the birth of the Environmental Protection Agency late that same year. Section 211 of the Clean Air Act authorized the administrator (eventually of EPA) to regulate fuels and fuel additives. For the first time, manufacturers were required to register with the government all fuels and fuel additives sold in interstate commerce. In addition, the administrator could restrict or prohibit the sale of certain fuels or fuel additives where he determined that their ". . . emission products will endanger human health or injure any emission device" [10]. Clearly, both the issues of human health and technological reliability were reflected in the legislative history.

The Clean Air Act (and especially the catalyst converter issue) gave new impetus to the idea of providing lead-free gasoline. One academic scientist who had been long concerned with the problem of atmospheric lead and human health remarked at that point that the scientific community "breathed a sign of relief." By this, he meant that the health issue alone was scientifically insufficient to make the case for removing lead from gasoline. The addition of the catalyst issue, however, greatly supported the case. The implications of possible dependence on the catalytic converter included the necessity of providing for the widespread availability of unleaded gasoline throughout the country. This in turn raised questions of conversion of refineries, cost of distributing lead-free gasoline, and cost in terms of extra petroleum products of compensating for the octane value of the removed lead [11].

In January 1971 the Environmental Protection Agency published an "advanced notice of proposed rule making" in the *Federal Register* [12]. This notice was designed to inform the public that EPA was considering available and relevant information of various sorts (scientific, medical, economic, technical) concerning the use of lead-containing fuel additives in gasoline. The ultimate intention of EPA was to introduce controls or prohibitions on the use of lead in fuels. At the same time, EPA engaged some specific analyses designed to shed insight on a number of derivative questions such as alternative technological solutions to the abatement of automotive emissions [13].

In early 1972 a committee of the National Academy of Sciences published a report on lead in the atmosphere [14]. The major emphasis of this report was on the implications of airborne lead for human health. The major findings of this review were:

1. The atmosphere over large cities contains 20 times the concentration of lead found in air over sparsely populated areas of the country.
2. The consumption of lead alkyl fuel additives is increasing substantially every year while the available data suggest that the concentration of lead in air, even over the largest cities is increasing only very slowly if at all.
3. Lead pigment paints are clearly the principal environmental sources for young children living in urban ghettos. Five to 10 percent of preschool children residing in deteriorating urban housing consume sufficient lead to have increased lead absorption judged by blood lead concentrations, and approximately 1 percent have symptoms compatible with clinical lead poisoning.
4. There have been no cases of characteristic lead poisoning due to lead as a community air pollutant.
5. Airborne lead could conceivably add to the lead burden of urban-dwelling children through the oral or the respiratory route [14].

In February 1972 EPA published in the *Federal Register* two sets of regulations for lead and phosphorus in gasoline:

1. There was to be generally available lead- and phosphorus-free gasoline by July 1, 1974.
2. The percentage of lead in the remaining gasoline was to be steadily reduced in stages between January 1, 1974, and July 1, 1977.

A period of 90 days was provided during which comments were invited.

This notice was accompanied by a series of background papers from EPA dealing with health and economic questions, implications for the petroleum industry, relationship to environmental control, etc. [16, 17]. The rationale for these regulations was to insure that lead-free gasoline compatible with catalytic devices would be available in time to meet EPA's 1975 automotive emission standards and to protect public health. (Interestingly, in order to make these proposals more saleable, the order of these reasons was reversed in the press release that accompanied their announcement [18].)

The period of comment was extended well beyond the original estimate of 90 days. Public hearings were held in Washington, D.C., Dallas, Texas, and Los Angeles, California. In June 1972 EPA published an additional notice in the *Federal Register* soliciting additional comments on its February proposals [19].

In September 1972 EPA published a reevaluation of its position on the health effects of airborne lead [20]. One of the arguments used by EPA in its proposed lead regulation was that airborne lead levels exceeding 2 mg/M^3 averaged over a period of two or three months were associated with ". . . a sufficient risk of adverse physiologic effects to constitute endangerment of public health." Accordingly, EPA aimed at achieving urban atmospheres with no greater than 2 mg/M^3 by reducing lead emissions from automobiles by 60 to 65 percent. EPA now wished to revise this proposal in the light of what it considered as new information.

The "new" information included some evidence that blood lead levels (especially in children) previously thought to be "safe" were in fact too high. Second, EPA leaned more heavily upon the hypothesis that dust found in cities and that contained measurable amounts of lead was *the* significant route of lead exposure for urban dwellers (especially infants and children). EPA's arguments were based principally upon:

1. The observation of higher blood lead levels and body burdens in urban inhabitants than in nonurban inhabitants
2. Knowledge of the fact that motor vehicle emissions contributed the majority of urban atmospheric lead and the assumption that urban lead dustfall was a function of lead levels in the atmosphere.
3. EPA's contention that the proportion of persons (especially children) having an already elevated lead body burden was higher than previously thought. This conclusion was based on measurements and survey, which were made after the time of the National Academy of Sciences review [14]. EPA concluded from these surveys that approximately 3 to 5 percent of adult males residing in urban areas had abnormally elevated blood lead levels. Similarly, EPA estimated that 25 percent of children tested had elevated blood lead levels. The problem with at least the latter of these estimates was that the sample surveyed was purposely selected from among probably exposed populations.

The NAS review judged that absorption of airborne lead via the respiratory tract was not a significant addition to body burdens of lead. The academy review considered (but did not document) the possibility that ingestion of lead-containing dust might contribute to the total body burden of some children. EPA by late 1972 considered its "new" evidence was strong enough to make the case for lead in urban dust (both airborne and in dust-fall) as forming the total body burden for some children and, hence, represent a measurable hazard in its own right [21].

EPA recommended that its previous recommendation calling for a 60-

to 65-percent reduction in the use of lead in gasoline to achieve a 2 mg/M³ ambient air level in urban atmospheres was "inadequate to protect human health." The agency, therefore, moved to place the health issue far out in front of the technological issue in arguing the case for lead regulations.

The reaction from some other federal agencies to these new proposals was quick and violent. HEW perhaps was the most candid in its objections ("The [draft] report does not provide sufficient evidence to support the conclusion that existing concentrations of 'lead in air' have adverse health effects") [22]. Equally forthright and critical was a letter from Merlin DuVal, assistant secretary for health in HEW to William Ruckelshaus, administrator of EPA. The letter was damning as it strongly hinted that EPA was trying to find ways to portray a health "case" for ordering the removal of lead from gasoline. Because it is such a good reflection of the tenor of this debate, the letter is reproduced in figure C-1.

Ironically, one of the strongest objectors in HEW to EPA's reasoning was Dr. Lloyd Tepper. Dr. Tepper was the associate commissioner for science in the FDA. He had come to that position from several years spent in research on lead at the University of Cincinnati. Before leaving the University of Cincinnati, Dr. Tepper had begun a survey of lead levels in the atmosphere and in the blood of urban dwellers in severn urban communities [23]. This study (which later became known as the "Seven City Study") followed a similar previous survey of three cities begun in 1961 [24]. The Seven City Survey was commissioned by HEW in 1969 when it was considering a legal limit of the amount of tetraethyl lead in gasoline. This study was designed in part to determine whether atmospheric lead levels had changed significantly with time and if blood lead levels were related to lead levels in the ambient atmosphere. The interpretation these investigators gave to the Seven City Survey was that a significant relationship between air lead exposure and blood lead level could not be demonstrated. There followed considerable controversy on this subject.

The Office of Science and Technology expressed objections to the EPA portion. However, when EPA appeared to adopt an advocate position and was accused by some to interpret the scientific information in behalf of that position, the Office of the Science Adviser was moved to adopt a different but equally strong advocate position. The primary issue taken up in this case was not regulation of lead per se but the appropriateness of the automotive emission standards—especially for nitrogen oxides. A part of the staff of the Office of Science and Technology was attempting very hard to develop a strategy to relax the standards and, for this reason, argued that the lead arguments were not appropriate. Actually, the Office of Science and Technology was a house sharply divided. Those who were arguing for a change in the automotive emission standards were seen by others on the staff as using EPA-like tactics to devel-

Honorable William D. Ruckelshaus
Administrator
Environmental Protection Agency
Washington, D.C. 20450

Dear Mr. Ruckelshaus:

In response to a request from Dr. Stanley Greenfield, members of my staff and I met on Wednesday, November 8, with Drs. Greenfield, Vaun Newill and Ken Bridbord. At that time, we were informed that EPA had recently decided that lead should no longer be used as an additive in gasoline.

The decision having been made on grounds other than those having to do with hazard to the public health, your staff now wished to explore with us the question of whether or not hazard to the public health could be invoked as a reason for accelerating the implementation date of the primary decision. It was our view that there is no firm evidence, at this time, that lead poisoning in humans could be traced per se to the presence of lead in gasoline; indeed, if there were, this would have constituted justification for the elimination of lead as an additive in the first instance.

At the same time, there is at least some evidence to suggest that the total body burden of lead, even if not of demonstrable clinical significance, is increased in environments and circumstances harboring higher levels of combusted, lead-containing fuels. Thus, there is a likely decrease in physiological reserve against the appearance of lead poisoning that may result were lead not to be used as an additive. This, however, is as far as HEW could go on that subject at this time.

There is one additional point. If lead is not used as an additive to gasoline, it would be important to assure the public that (a) the profile of the products of combustion of non-leaded gasoline does not, itself, constitute a new danger to the public health; and (b) a substitute for lead which we may know less about, will not be needed.

Sincerely yours,

Merlin K. DuVal, M.D.
Assistant Secretary for Health

Figure C-1. Letter Reflecting Criticism of EPA Proposal for Lead Regulation.

op advocate arguments to strengthen their position. They were, some thought, right for the wrong reason [25, 26, 27, 28].

On January 10, 1973 EPA published a portion of its recommendations and decisions for regulatory action. In doing so, it divided the two issues that previously had been closely coupled. Final regulations to provide for lead-free gasoline were promulgated [29]. Separate regulations based upon the health effects of airborne lead and providing for the phased reduction in lead were reproposed at the same time [30]. More comment was invited and a committee of EPA scientists was assembled to review the comments. Their report eventually became the published basis for the final regulatory decisions later that year [31].

In October 1973 the Natural Resources Defense Council brought suit against EPA in which it challenged the adequacy of the proposed regulations. A part of the problem in this case was the considerable delay that EPA had demonstrated in reaching its conclusions. This precipitated a court order directing EPA to reach a final decision within 30 days [32].

On November 28, 1973 EPA published its final decision in the *Federal Register* [33]. In effect, the administrator of EPA promulgated the phased withdrawal of lead from automotive gasoline based on the implications for human health. The report that accompanied this notice acknowledged the contribution of lead paint to lead body burdens of children, but argued that they were not necessarily overwhelming (in contrast to previous estimates), that urban dustfall, although only a hypothesis, should be considered seriously, and that in any case reduction of all sources of lead, however small, should be accomplished [31].

Several parties took issue with this promulgated regulation and sought judicial relief. The judicial proceedings begun in September 1974 produced a judgment in January 1975. By a 2 to 1 decision, the U.S. Court of Appeals of the District of Columbia reversed EPA's position on two counts:

1. The law had been misinterpreted.
2. The scientific evidence used by EPA to demonstrate a health hazard of lead was not adequate to make the case [33].

References

1. Oberle, M.W., *Science,* 165:991; 1969.
2. National Conference on Lead Poisoning in Children, March 25-26, 1969, The Rockefeller University, New York.
3. U.S. Department of Health, Education and Welfare, Public Health Aspects of Increasing Tetraethyl Lead Content in Motor Fuel, U.S. Public Health Service Publication No. 712, Washington, D.C., 1959.
4. Kehoe, R.A., The Metabolism of Lead in Man in Health and Disease. The Harben Lectures, 1960, *J. Royal Institute of Public Health and Hygiene*, 1961.
5. Patterson, C.C., Contaminated and Material Lead Environments of Man, *Arc. Environmental Health*, 11:344-360; 1965.
6. U.S. Department of Health, Education and Welfare, Symposium on Environmental Lead Contamination, Division of Air Pollution, Washington, D.C., December 1965, P.H.S. Publication No. 1440, 1966.

7. U.S. Department of Commerce, *The Automobile and Air Pollution: A Program for Progress*, Report of the Panel on Electrically Powered Vehicles to the Commerce Technical Advisory Board, Washington, D.C., October 1967.

8. Schroeder, H.A., and Lipton, I.H., The Human Body Burden of Lead, *Arch. Environmental Health*, 17:965-978, 1968.

9. American Chemical Society, *Cleaning Our Environment. The Chemical Basis for Action*, A Report by the Subcommittee on Environmental Improvement, Committee on Chemistry and Public Affairs, Washington, D.C., 1969.

10. The Clean Air Act as amended, 85 Stat. 1690 (1970).

11. U.S. Department of Commerce, *Implications of Lead Removal from Automotive Fuels*, Interim Report of Commerce Technical Advisory Board Panel on Automotive Fuels and Air Pollution, Washington, D.C. June 1970.

12. 36, F.R. 1086.

13. The Aerospace Corporation, *An Assessment of the Effects of Lead Additives in Gasoline on Emission Control Systems Which Might Be Used to Meet the 1975-1976 Motor Vehicle Emission Standards*, Fuel Report, Los Angeles, California, November 1971.

14. National Academy of Sciences, Airborne Lead in Perspective, Committee on the Biological Effects of Air Pollutants, Washington, D.C., 1972.

15. *Federal Register*, Notice of Proposed Rule Making Regulation of Fuels and Fuel Additives, Vol. 37, No. 36, February 23, 1972, pp. 3882-3884.

16. U.S. Environmental Protection Agency, *Health Hazards of Lead*, Washington, D.C., 1972.

17. U.S. Environmental Protection Agency, Background Information EPA's Proposed Regulations Affecting the Use of Lead and Phosphorus Additives in Gasoline, Washington, D.C., 1972.

18. U.S. Environmental Protection Agency, *Environmental News*, Regulations Proposed for Lead and Phosphorus Additives in Gasoline, Washington, D.C., February 23, 1972.

19. *Federal Register*, Vol. 37, No. 115, June 14, 1972, pp. 11786-11787.

20. U.S. Environmental Protection Agency, *Update of EPA's Position in Health Effects of Lead. The Agency's Health Position for Controlling Lead Emissions from Motor Vehicle Exhaust,* Washington, D.C., September 22, 1972.

21. U.S. Environmental Protection Agency, Preliminary Draft Document, Washington, D.C., September 22, 1972.

22. Comments from the Department of Health, Education and Welfare on EPA's proposed lead position to the Office of Management and Budget, November 1972.

23. Tepper, L., A Survey of Air and Population Lead Levels in Selected American Communities ("Seven City Study"), Washington, D.C., 1969.

24. U.S. Department of Health, Education and Welfare, *Survey of Lead in the Atmosphere of Three Urban Communities*, Public Health Service Publication No. 999-AP-12, Washington, D.C., 1961.

25. Memorandum from Lawrence A. Goldmuntz Office of Science and Technology, to Joel Rosenblatt, Office of Management and Budget, October 27, 1972.

26. Memorandum from Edward E. David, Jr., director, Office of Science and Technology, to Donald E. Crabill, Office of Management and Budget, November 1, 1972.

27. Memorandum from Edward E. David, Jr., director, Office of Science and Technology, to William A. Morrill, assistant director, Office of Management and Budget, November 2, 1972.

28. Memorandum from Edward J. Burger, M.D., to Edward E. David, Jr., director, Office of Science and Technology, November 17, 1972.

29. *Federal Register*, Vol. 38, No. 6, January 10, 1973, pp. 1254-1256.

30. *Federal Register*, Vol. 38, No. 6, January 10, 1973, pp. 1258-1261.

31. U.S. Environmental Protection Agency, *EPA's Position on the Health Implications of Airborne Lead*, Washington, D.C., November 28, 1973.

32. Natural Resources Defense Council v. Environmental Protection Agency, October 29, 1973.

33. Ethyl Corporation v. Environmental Protection Agency, U.S. Court of Appeals, January 28, 1975.

Appendix D
2, 4, 5-T

In 1941 a group of scientists convinced the secretary of war, Henry Stimson, of the potential dangers from biological warfare. Stimson requested advice on this subject from the National Academy of Sciences and, because of this advice, a research agency, known as the War Research Service was established. This became the site of work on a series of growth regulators as herbicides. Among the chemicals included for study were the phenoxy compounds 2, 4-D and 2, 4, 5-T.

2, 4, 5-T was first registered with the Department of Agriculture in March 1948 by the Amchem Products Company, Ambler, Pennsylvania. (Note that the term 2, 4, 5-T refers to the principle 2, 4, 5-trichlorophenoxyacetic acid, as well as a number of ester and salt derivatives.)

2, 4, 5-T became increasingly important as an herbicide for brush and weed control for both land and waterway management in the United States to such an extent that a fair degree of economic dependence resulted. Use on rangeland and pastureland, control of brush in rights of way, and control of aquatic weeds are important categories of domestic use. In addition, beginning in 1962, 2, 4, 5-T found use as a defoliant in military operations in Southeast Asia. This latter used increased rapidly and made large demands on the suppliers of 2, 4, 5-T—to the extent that material available for domestic use was more limited than it had been previously. 2, 4, 5-T production per year was as follows:

1960: 7,900,000 lbs.
1965: 13,500,000 lbs.
1966: 18,100,000 lbs.
1967: 27,200,000 lbs.
1968: 42,500,000 lbs.

Table D-1 gives an idea of the proportions applied for various domestic uses in 1964 [1].

Toxicological studies on 2, 4-D were first reported in 1944. However, there were no published reports of toxicological investigations of 2, 4, 5-T until the 1950s. In 1953 V.A. Drill and T. Hiratzka [2] reported a series of studies of acute and subacute toxicity of 2, 4, 5-T on dogs. The material used was commercially available 2, 4, 5-T (presumably the acid) and was administered in capsules mixed in dog food. Dosage schedules included single acute doses of 50 to 400 mg/kg and daily doses of 2 to 20 mg/kg, 5 days per week for up to 13 weeks. Observations and measurements included the determination of the number of days until death, changes in body weight, general observations of abnormal physical signs, gross pa-

Table D-1
Domestic Use of 2, 4, 5-T: Percent of Total Quantity Applied

Use Category	Proportion of Total Quantity Applied (Percent)
Farm use	
Hay, pasture, rangeland	7
Other farm use	12
Total farm use	19
Nonfarm use	
Federal government agencies	7
Lawn and turf treatment	7
Rights of way	49
Private nonfarm forests	10
Aquatic treatment	2
Other uses	6
Total nonfarm use	81
All uses	100

thology of organs, and selected histology. The number of animals used was small (as few as 1 per dose and as many as 4 per dose). In brief, the findings of this study suggested that a single, fatal dose for dogs lay somewhere between 100 and 400 mg/kg—indicating a low level of acute toxicity.

The Dow Chemical Company, a manufacturer of 2, 4, 5-T, undertook a series of acute toxicity studies of 2, 4, 5-T beginning around 1950. The results of these studies were to serve as the basis for a petition for registration and for a tolerance for the herbicide for uses on food crop. The series included a variety of species of animals and a number of the various salts and esters of 2, 4, 5-T and several of the various formulations. The studies were never published. However, a summary of some of this work was published by V.K. Rowe and T.A. Hymas in 1954 [3].

A second source of toxicological investigations was the Department of Defense, which undertook in some of its own laboratories a short series of acute toxicity tests on a mixture of 50 percent butyl ester of 2, 4-D, 20 percent isobutyl ester of 2, 4, 5-T, and 30 percent n-butyl ester of 2, 4, 5-T known as Purple. These investigations were never published but were summarized in 1967 [4].

There were a few accounts in the 1950s and 1960s of testing for acute toxicity of 2, 4, 5-T on domestic animals [3, 5]. The number of animals used in these studies were typically very small (single animals in some cases).

It was somewhat widely assumed that the metabolism and toxicity of 2, 4, 5-T would resemble those of other phenoxy herbicides. Although this is probably a reasonable assumption it has never been systematically examined. Human experience was gathered from incidents of excessive occupational exposure, suicidal efforts, intended oral feeding, and parental administration as an experimental form of treatment for coccidioidomycosis. From descriptions such as these it was inferred that around 50 to 100 mg/kg of 2, 4-D was acutely toxic to humans. However, the information is scanty and there are some inconsistencies.

In 1964 the National Cancer Institute embarked on a screening study of a number of pesticides to determine their potential for producing tumors, genetic alteration, or birth defects in experimental animals. The study, undertaken on contract by the Bionetics Laboratories, included a number of phenoxy compounds in both the carcinogenesis and the teratogenesis experiments. The sample of 2, 4, 5-T (which had been obtained from a commercial lot from one of the manufacturers) demonstrated teratogenic effects in the experimental animals at a rate higher than was expected when compared to control animals. These results, first demonstrated after parenteral administration, were confirmed in a second series of experiments in which the test material was administered orally and over a wider range of doses. The results were then submitted to some additional statistical analysis designed essentially to distinguish between inter- and intralitter differences. The immediate inferences drawn from these experiments were that 2, 4, 5-T appeared to provoke a higher than expected level of fetal abnormality in rats and mice in dosages used. Further, there appeared to be a suggestion of a dose-response relationship over the range of doses used.

The Bionetics experiments were designed as first approximation screening studies, not as definitive tests. (Because of the large number of compounds tested and the massive logistics of these experiments, the duration of the studies was roughly four years and the cost was $2.6 million.) Although the Bionetics studies were not meant to be definitive, for a number of reasons they became treated as such and their interpretation became a matter of controversy:

1. A number of criticisms of a scientific nature were registered over the design of the study.

2. It became apparent that the commercial material, termed 2, 4, 5-T contained some impurities at least one of which was highly toxic and was thought potentially responsible for the experimental results reported. This raised the issue of the concentration of this impurity, a family of chlorinated dioxins, in various lots of 2, 4, 5-T, including the one from which the Bionetics experimental sample was drawn. It emerged that commercial lots of 2, 4, 5-T had contained variable amounts of dioxins over the years (up to 32 ppm), that the Bionetics sample had contained about 27 ppm, and that production after the Bionetics study had begun contained less than 1 ppm.

3. The mechanism of chemical teratogenesis, which had not been clearly elucidated up to this time, was brought into focus. It was this subject more than any other that became most important in interpreting the results of teratogenic studies in animals to human experience. It emerged that the current theory (based on emperical observations) treated teratogenesis as an acute toxic phenomenon, (acute toxicity to the developing fetus at a time of unusual vulnerability to chemical damage). Observations suggested that there was a steep dose-response relationship for fetal-toxic events, the top of which was somewhat ($\times 10$) below a maternal toxic dose. Since the dose-response relationship could be described by a curve with a steep slope, a no-effect dose could be found at the bottom. A major factor in explaining interspecies differences was the residence time of the toxic material in the maternal blood stream and, hence, experimental animals could be "calibrated" to their human counterparts by making corresponding measurements of excretion rates.

4. Related to this last point is the interpretation of certain other biological tests for teratogenesis. Doses of test materials had been administered to developing chicken embryos and these were followed to birth and beyond. 2, 4, 5-T was examined in this way. These tests were thought to be very sensitive. However, since chickens are nonplacental animals, the interpretation of these results remains in some doubt.

The Bionetics experiments were completed in stages but most were finished late in 1968. The 2, 4, 5-T teratogenicity results that stood out were submitted to the National Institute of Environmental Health Sciences for the further statistical review reported above. This review was completed for discussion in late 1969.

Although completed in 1968, it is clear that the disposition of the results of the Bionetics studies remained in question for some time and, hence, their publication in any form was long delayed—in fact for a period of more than 18 months.

Between October 1968 and October 1969, a series of informal meetings was held between representatives of the National Cancer Institute, the Bionetics Laboratories and other government agencies interested in 2, 4, 5-T for one reason or another (DOD, USDA, FDA). These meetings were called at the initiative of the NCI or of the Bionetics Laboratories and were aimed at acquainting the agencies with these unexpected experimental results. There seemed to be no official recognition of the results of these experiments during this period. Scientifically, a possible next step would have been to have mounted some additional experimental studies to confirm or extend the outstanding Bionetics results. This involved an additional commitment of funds that were not immediately available. The pesticides tested were already marketed products for which government registrations or certifications had been obtained. It turned out that there was no simple way of bringing this new information, gathered outside the regulatory process, into a process of review of the existing registrations.

Over a period of approximately 18 months of latency, the results of the Bionetics study "leaked" out into more and more hands. Congressional interest in these results mounted to the point of threatening to publish the results in the *Congressional Record*. In the face of this threat, the National Cancer Institute provided summary data on the carcinogenesis experiments in published form in the *Journal of the National Cancer Institute* [6]. The teratogenesis experiments remained unpublished.

Starting on June 26, 1969 there appeared in the Vietnamese press a series of articles describing the occurrence of birth defects in children born in those parts of Vietnam where defoliants had been used. The implication was offered that these abnormalities had increased in frequency in the recent past and that they were related to the defoliants. No documentation was offered.

In addition, there was one other reported incident that heightened public attention. The U.S. Forest Service of the Department of Agriculture had made a series of applications of various herbicides (including 2, 4, 5-T) to its lands in the Torito National Forest near Globe, Arizona starting in 1965. In late 1969 the National Health Federation wrote to Clifford Hardin, then secretary of agriculture, and expressed a number of criticisms of this federal program. Their criticisms reflected a number of implied hazards to human health and plant and animal life in the surrounding area [7]. This in turn provoked an investigation by a task force of scientists who were dispatched to the area [8].

It was against this background of increasing publicity and rumor about the Bionetics 2, 4, 5-T results and their relation to defoliant operations in Vietnam that the science adviser called a meeting in October 1969 of several government agencies to review this subject. The immediate event that triggered this meeting was a telephone call to the science adviser from a university scientist who said he felt obliged to make a public declaration of the scientific information on 2, 4, 5-T, which was closely held by the federal government. The result of this meeting was an announcement on October 29, 1969 of a number of steps various government agencies intended to take in restricting the use of 2, 4, 5-T.

One of these actions would limit defoliation operations in Vietnam to nonpopulated areas. Another promised to cancel the 2, 4, 5-T registrations for foodcrop uses on January 1, 1970, unless the Food and Drug Administration could assemble sufficient information by that time to establish a negligible tolerance. The types of information thought wanting at that time were some data on residues and a clarification of the teratogenesis issue. Incidentally, the review of the registration of 2, 4, 5-T had had its origins in a general process of revision of the list of materials registered in a zero-residue category. This older review was pending when the birth defect issue arose. The January 1, 1970 deadline had been previously set as an end point of the prior review [9].

In addition to the announcement of concerted government actions, Dr. Lee DuBridge, as science adviser, assembled a panel of experts under the umbrella of the President's Science Advisory Committee chaired by Dr. Colin MacLeod to review the several aspects of 2, 4, 5-T. During the course of this review, it was discovered that an impurity in 2,4, 5-T was of potential importance. The impurity, a polychlorinated dioxin, was apparently very toxic and had been identified in batches of 2, 4, 5-T as early as 1957. It arose partly as an impurity of the chlorphenol starting materials and partly as a result of the ambient temperatures and pressures of certain of the reactions in the manufacturing process. It had provoked severe skin irritations among workers in 2, 4, 5-T plants in Germany and in the United States. The discovery of this industrial hazard had led one United States manufacturer to curtail his process until he was able to reduce the dioxin content to no more than 1.0 ppm in the 2, 4, 5-T product. Prior to that time (1967) the dioxin content had varied up to 30 ppm. (The 2, 4, 5-T sample used in the Bionetics study contained about 27 ppm of dioxin.) There had been a small amount of animal experimental toxicology done on dioxin that had indicated the LD_{50} (dose expected to produce 50 percent mortality) was as low as 0.6/g/Kg. Hence, it became important to ascertain whether the apparent teratogenic agent was the principle 2, 4, 5-T or a potent impurity. The report of the MacLeod Panel was published and released in early 1971 [10].

Within weeks after the DuBridge announcement, some additional animal experiments were begun in three laboratories simultaneously, the Dow Chemical Company, the FDA, and the National Institute of Environmental Health Services. The aims of these experiments were:

1. To confirm and refine the results obtained from the Bionetics study.
2. To separate the effects of the 2, 4, 5-T principle from those of the dioxin impurity.

The results of these experiments (although not conclusive) tended to confirm the previous results of the Bionetics studies and to indicate that both 2, 4 5-T and its dioxin impurity were capable of provoking birth defects in experimental animals.

The data supplied by the petitioner to back up his request for a negligible tolerance for 2, 4, 5-T were not found to be adequate and he withdrew his petition on December 29, 1969. The registration in effect (on the basis of the previous no-residue basis) was, however, not cancelled. This later became a matter of some public concern. The factors that went into this decision probably included the following:

1. Uncertain validity of the Bionetics results and uncertainty about their extrapolation to man
2. Uncertainty over the relative importance (in terms of toxicity and teratogenesis) of 2, 4, 5-T and the dioxin impurity
3. The relatively short time necessary to reap the results of the animal experiments designed to give answers to 1 and 2 above
4. Relative inflexibility of the options available under the Federal Insecticide, Fungicide and Rodenticide Act for curtailing the use of pesticides. In brief, there was no provision that would have permitted a temporary reduction in the use of a pesticide during the time of review of pertinent information.

In April 1970 the Subcommittee on Energy, Natural Resources and Environment of the Senate Commerce Committee held hearings on 2, 4, 5-T. During this hearing, the surgeon general announced a series of actions being taken by HEW, Department of Interior, and USDA on 2, 4, 5-T. The Department of Agriculture suspended the registration of liquid formulations of 2, 4, 5-T for uses around the home and of all formulations for use on lakes, ponds, and ditch banks. In addition, registrations were cancelled for uses for nonliquid formulations around the home and for all formulations for use on food crops intended for public consumption. It was estimated that these restrictions applied to about 20 percent of all of the 2, 4, 5-T used domestically.

All of the registrants (manufacturers) of 2, 4, 5-T were advised of these actions and two of them, the Dow Chemical Company and Hercules Incorporated, exercised their rights under the Federal Insecticide, Fungicide and Rodenticide Act to appeal the cancellations and suspensions and to refer the decisions to an advisory committee. The Environmental Protection Agency (to which new agency most of the former FDA and USDA pesticide activities had by then been transferred) established a Scientific Advisory Committee using a list of names supplied by the National Academy of Sciences. The central issue adopted by this committee for consideration was whether this herbicide did in fact constitute an imminent health hazard, especially with respect to human reproduction.

In May 1971 the advisory committee submitted its report in which it concluded that, ". . . as presently produced and as applied according to regulations in force prior to April 1970, 2, 4, 5-T represents no hazard to human reproduction" [11]. The recommendations of this advisory committee were:

1. That registration for use of 2, 4, 5-trichlorophenoxyacetic acid and its esters be restored to the status existing prior to April 1970, with the following exceptions.

2. That certain specific limitations and qualifications be added to the previously existing registration, as follows:

   a. A permissible residue of not more than 0.1 ppm of 2, 4, 5-T on the edible parts of food products and in potable water for human consumption be accepted. It is recognized that very few foods tested to date have contained this level of residue, but it is probable that some of the reports of no residue in the past were due to limited sensitivity of the analytical method. In view of recent and future advanced in methodology, which tend to make zero residues of anything increasing unlikely, a more realistic policy would be the setting of safe tolerance limits at this time.

   b. A limit of 0.5 ppm of contamination with 2, 3, 7, 8-tetrachlorodibenzo-p dioxin be set for existing inventories of 2, 4, 5-T except as specified in item c. below, and a limit of 0.1 ppm of contamination with this dioxin be established in all future production of 2, 4, 5-T. Surveillance should be maintained by requiring that a manufacturer submit a reference sample and a certified analysis of each future production lot to be the Environmental Protection Agency.

   c. All formulations to be used around the home and in recreational areas as of present date should be limited to 0.1 ppm of the dioxin, TCDD, and also should bear a conspicuous warning, e. g., "This compound may be dangerous to pregnant women and animals and its use must be such as to reduce the possibility of exposure to an absolute minimum."

3. That existing deficiencies in information relative to possible accumulation in the soil and possible magnification in the food chain of the dioxin TCDD be rectified by specific research directed to this end, with these questions to be subjected to scientific review within three years of the present data and yearly thereafter until these questions are resolved.

4. That additional post-registration monitoring for adverse effects of agricultural chemicals be established, to include both surveillance for such effects in man and domestic and wild animals, as well as consideration of the applicability of new methodology that may be evolved for specialized testing, e.g., for carcinogensis, mutagenesis or teratogenesis.

The administrator of EPA made the report of his advisory committee publically available. In August 1971 he announced that the advisory committee had exceeded its charge in examining benefits of 2, 4, 5-T and that he would not accept the advice of the committee. The series of cancellations and suspensions on 2, 4, 5-T, on record in April 1970, would remain in effect. Further, he noted that the administrative proceedings on 2, 4, 5-T would remain in effect and that a public hearing would be held. On November 4, 1971 the Dow Chemical Company asserted that the EPA decisions were not legal to which the administrator disagreed.

Conclusions

1. Very little information was available to describe the biological and human health effects of 2, 4, 5-T. 2, 4, 5-T was registered at a time when both science and the public were less sophisticated about the unwanted side effects of chemicals such as herbicides. There was less scientific understanding of disease processes and of biological effects that might accrue from human exposure to pesticides. The government, which registered the herbicide, did not pose the questions of the petitioning manufacturer and, partly for this reason, the manufacturer did not supply any insight.

2. With the passage of 20 to 25 years, scientific understanding altered to the point where additional scientific hypotheses became viable areas for investigation. Further, public expectations and curiosity were elevated in that period to the point where a great deal more scrutiny was exercised over the details of government decisions in this area.

3. There is no easy mechanism for deriving additional background research on products already registered and on the market. The classical philosophy governing the governmental processes in this area is that industry will supply the information to the government upon which the latter makes its regulatory decisions. (This is commonly translated as industry will prove its products safe before being permitted to enter them into interstate commerce.) This means that it is industry's responsibility to undertake background research, not the government's. Further, generally it is true that once a product is registered, it is certified once and for all. Industry has no incentive to question its efficacy and side effects further. The Bionetics studies on pesticides is an unorthodox one of the government's own investment in seeking information on products.

4. Information gathered outside of the registration process for pesticides is accommodated only with difficulty in the regulatory decision process. In the case of 2, 4, 5-T, the administrators of tolerances and registrations for pesticides were not able to use easily the results of the Bionetics study. The awkwardness of responding to the overtures made by the National Cancer Institute is illustrative.

5. Neither the beneficial uses of 2, 4, 5-T (at home or abroad) nor the risks occasioned by its use were sufficiently well documented to allow for a sound decision. Decision making in the face of great areas of uncertainty were apparent. This permitted a great deal of emotion-laden opinion and anecdotal information to creep into proceedings from both sides.

6. The use of 2, 4, 5-T in military operations colored the picture. Although its utility in warfare was not documented, a persuasive case has been made for its importance in saving human lives in the Far Eastern

conflict. It was inferred that restrictions on its use domestically would lead to a political climate in which its use abroad would be further restricted. (This was reflected by an announcement in December 1970 by the secretary of defense who said that practices of herbicide use in military operations would conform to the restrictions called for domestically.) On the other side, the fact that 2, 4, 5-T was an instrument of warfare undoubtedly raised more interest in this substance than would have occurred for a product used only within the United States.

7. Delay (or apparent delay) in publication of the results of scientific investigations heightens public attention, leads to an increasing degree of public attention that may eventually distort or ignore the scientific background when it finally becomes known.

8. The regulatory mechanism does not accommodate shades of gray. Science can be expected to raise additional questions as well as answers. This dynamic process of scientific understanding comes into conflict with the relatively inflexible regulatory mechanisms. There should be provision for the temporary restriction on the use of a pesticide on the occasion of unexpected information pending the collection of more definitive information.

9. One of the areas of uncertainty concerns the probability of human exposure. The judgments about 2, 4, 5-T have been based on some knowledge of its inherent biological effects. However, the degree to which its residues are likely to be found on food plants or other materials to which humans are exposed is not at all well known. Analytic techniques have been remarkably improved in recent years. Physical measurements and sampling, however, based on any consistent, statistically valid techniques, have not really been put into effect for pesticide residues.

References

1. A Report of the Panel on Herbicides of the President's Science Advisory Committee, Report on 2, 4, 5-T, March 1971.
2. Drill, V.A., and Hiratzka, T., *AMA Archives of Industrial Hygiene and Occupational Medicine*, 7:61, 1963.
3. Rowe, V.K., and Hymas, T.A., *Amer. J. Vet. Res.*, 15:622, 1954.
4. House, W.B., Goodson, L.H., Gadberry, H.M., and Dockter, K.W., Assessment of Ecological Effects of Extensive or Repeated Use of Herbicides, Midwest Research Institute, Project No. 3103-B. December 1967.
5. Palmer, J.S., and Radeleff, R.D., *Ann. N.Y. Acad. Sci.*, 3:729, 1964.

6. Innes, J.R.M., Ulland, B.M., Valerio, M.G., Petrucelli, L., Fishbein, L., Hart, E.R., Pallotta, A.J., Bates, R.R., Falk, H.L., Gast, J.J., Klein, M., Mitchell, I., and Peters, J.J., *National Cancer Institute*, 42:1101, 1969.

7. Letters from Charles I. Crecelius, president, American Health Federation to Clifford Hardin, secretary of agriculture, October 27, 1969.

8. U.S. Department of Agriculture, Agricultural Research Service, Investigations Report, Globe, Arizona, March 30, 1970.

9. Press Release, Office of Science and Technology, Washington, D.C., October 29, 1969.

10. *Report on 2, 4, 5-T*, A Report of the Panel on Herbicides of the President's Science Advisory Committee, Office of Science and Technology, Executive Office of the President, Washington, D.C., March 1971.

11. Report of the Advisory Committee on 2, 4, 5-T to the administrator of the Environmental Protection Agency, Washington, D.C., May 7, 1971.

Appendix E
Diethylstilbestrol

Diethylstilbestrol (DES) is a synthetic estrogen-like compound that was developed in 1938 and that was found to exhibit many of the properties of natural estrogens. DES was inexpensive and could be administered orally as a therapeutic agent and found important medical uses in several areas:

1. Treatment of certain forms of "functional" uterine bleeding.
2. Treatment of certain conditions in which natural estrogens were deficient.
3. Postpartum treatment for certain side effects and discomfort.
4. Palliative therapy for certain forms of cancers in both males and females.

In addition, DES in moderate doses was found to have possible or probable effectiveness for treatment of threatened spontaneous abortion and for treatment of osteoporosis.

Estrogens, including DES, were recognized as responsible for tumors in experimental animals since the 1940s. High doses were consistently used in these experiments and the recognized human therapeutic uses always involved much lower doses. (The doses used in treatment of metastatic cancer of the breast and cancer of the prostate were, in fact, larger but the relief afforded was considered worthwhile.)

In April 1971 reports first appeared of an association between adenocarcinoma of the vagina (a rare tumor in young women) and history of previous administration of DES in high doses to their mothers as treatment for threatened or feared spontaneous abortion. This practice began in the late 1940s. Dr. Arthur Herbst published these findings in April 1971 in the *New England Journal of Medicine* [1]. In addition, Dr. Herbst's statistical data were submitted to the FDA for confirmatory evaluation of the statistical material. Eight cases were reported by Dr. Herbst of whom seven had a history of maternal exposure to DES. In August 1971 five additional cases were reported by another epidemiologist [2]. By November the original sample of adenocarcinoma of the vagina had been expanded to 62 cases by Dr. Herbst.

In testimony before the House Subcommittee on Intergovernmental Relations in November 1971, the FDA commissioner asserted that:

1. DES was a useful therapeutic tool in the treatment of a number of medical problems and there was no evidence that it caused cancer when used in dosages recommended for estrogen replacement therapy.

2. New evidence indicated an association between DES in high doses and cancer of the vagina of offspring of those treated.

3. The FDA was proceeding to enforce the labeling of DES to all related compounds to reflect the new and unexpected epidemiological findings.

4. The FDA was moving to publicize in other ways the apparent association between DES exposure and vaginal cancer [3].

A related issue was the use of DES (in relatively high doses) as a post-coital contraceptive. This use was placed under clinical investigation in the form of an Investigational New Drug (IND). The original intent, in this case, was to provide for an efficacious method of preventing or averting pregnancy especially in those cases where conception was totally undesirable (as in cases of rape). However, simultaneous with the investigations and controlled trials of DES as a postcoital therapy, the drug was reported to have been heavily used outside the trial circumstances for postcoital contraception—especially by college students.

At third issue concerned the use of DES in animal feeds and by way of implants in cattle and sheep. DES, in these cases, was used to promote or accelerate the weight gain in meat animals.

In 1954 diethylstilbestrol was discovered to increase the rate of growth of steer and to render more efficient the conversion of animal feed to meat. It was estimated that DES would insure a 15 percent increase in the rate of weight gain in steer and would augment the rate of feed conversion by 11 percent. In lambs the apparent benefits were even greater—25 percent increases in rate of weight gain and feed conversion.

The economic advantages were so great as to encourage the use of DES in virtually 100 percent of all feedlot-fed cattle. DES was given either as an additive to the animal feed or was administered by way of an under-skin implant. In this latter form, the chemical would slowly and gradually be released into the animal's bloodstream.

In the years following the initial trials, the dosages used were increased in order to derive even larger advantages for the livestock industry. Residues were avoided by insuring a suitably long period of withdrawal of the material from the animals before the time of slaughter. The Delaney amendment to the Food, Drug and Cosmetic Act permitted the use of a substance in animal feeds recognized to be carcinogenic in man if no residues were detectable in the resulting meat and carcass at the time of slaughter.

In October 1971 the Department of Agriculture notified the FDA that DES residues were detected in samples taken from the livers of a series of animals that had been singled out for obsevation. In the face of those unexpected findings, the FDA expressed confidence that the problem could be resolved by lengthening the time between withdrawal of the feed additive and slaughter. This mandatory duration, it was proposed, was to be increased from two to seven days. The commissioner of the FDA expressed the view publically that, by extending the period of withdrawal of medicated feeds, further residues of DES would not be detected.

In March 1972 the FDA proposed in the *Federal Register* the withdrawal of liquid forms of DES.

In July 1972 the FDA was informed of new data from the Department of Agriculture that indicated the continued presence of residues of DES. These data resulted from both the use of a more sensitive analytic techniques (including radioactively-tagged DES) and more extensive sampling.

Accordingly, the FDA found itself with no further maneuvering room. It was obliged to order an end to the manufacture and use of DES as a growth promoter in animal feeds. Existing inventories were permitted to be used up over the next four months. The use of DES in implanted form was not affected by these orders.

In making this finding and in announcing the order to ban the feed use of DES, the FDA maintained that human health appeared not to be in jeopardy. The issue, rather, was one of conforming to a relatively rigid law that would brook no exception to its zero-level of allowable residue [4].

References

1. Herbst, A., *New England Journal of Medicine*. April 22, 1971.
2. Greenwald P., et al., *New England Journal of Medicine*, August 12, 1971.
3. U.S. House of Representatives, Statement by Charles C. Edwards, commissioner of food and drugs, Department of Health, Education and Welfare, before the Subcommittee on Intergovernmental Relations of the Committee on Government Operations, November 11, 1971.
4. U.S. Department of Health, Education and Welfare, Order denying a bearing and withdrawing approval of new annual drug applications for liquid and dry premixes, and deferring a ruling on implants, Docket Nos. FDC-D-452, 494; NADA Nos. 11-2952, 9525, et al.), August 2, 1972.

Index

About the Author

Dr. Edward J. Burger, Jr., is a physician-scientist who received his Doctor of Medicine at McGill University and a Doctorate in physiology at Harvard. He was a Guggenheim Fellow at Harvard and later a member of the faculty in the Harvard School of Public Health. At Harvard Dr. Burger was engaged in research and teaching in the area of the physiological basis for the effects of the environment on human health. Simultaneously, he was an Associate in the John Fitzgerald School of Government in the realm of Science and Public Policy. In 1969, he accepted an appointment in the Office of Science and Technology in the Executive Office of the President. As staff to the Science Adviser to the President, Dr. Burger had as one of his principal areas of concern the affairs of Government which seek through regulation to afford protection from environmental hazards. Dr. Burger has written and spoken widely on scientific as well as public policy issues. As well as serving the President's Science Adviser, he holds an appointment as Assistant Clinical Professor of Medicine at Georgetown University in Washington.

Related Lexington Books

Berkanovic, Emil, Marcus, Alfred C., Reeder, Leo G., and Schwartz, Susan. *Perceptions of Medical Care; The Impact of Prepayment.* 160pp, 1974

Berry, Ralph E., Field, Mark G., Karefa-Smart, John, Koch-Weisier, Dieter, and Thompson, Mark S. *Evaluating the Impact of Health Research: The U.S.-Yugoslav Cooperative Research Effort.* 208pp, 1974

Friedman, Kenneth M. *Public Policy and the Smoking-Health Controversy: A Comprehensive Study.* 240pp, 1975

Murphy, Thomas P. *Science, Geopolitics and Federal Spending.* 594pp, 1971

Scioli, Jr., Frank P., Cook, Thomas J. *Methodologies for Analyzing Public Policies.* 176pp, 1975